MUD, SWEAT, AND TEARS

MUD, SWEAT, AND TEARS

THE AUTOBIOGRAPHY

Bear Grylls

WILLIAM MORROW

An Imprint of HarperCollins*Publishers*

All images courtesy of the author (BG) unless otherwise stated.
NL = Neil Laughton. Section one, page 8: Mick and BG at base camp courtesy NL.
Section two, page 1: BG and NL at Everest summit courtesy NL; BG at end of
Everest ascent courtesy Mick Crosthwaite. Page 2: crevasse crossing courtesy NL.
Page 3: team at base camp courtesy NL; paraglider mission courtesy Frankie Benka
Photography. Section three, page 1: rigged inflatable boat courtesy Kinloch; high-altitude
balloon courtesy Peter Russell Photography. Pages 2–5: all images courtesy Discovery.
Page 6: Dave Pearce and Dan Etheridge/Pete Lee both courtesy Simon Reay; Paul Ritz,
BG, and Simon Reay courtesy Paul Ritz.

First published in Great Britain in 2011 by Channel 4 Books,
an imprint of Transworld Publishers.

HarperCollins books may be purchased for educational, business, or
sales promotional use. For information please write: Special Markets Department,
HarperCollins Publishers, 10 East 53rd Street, New York, NY 10022.

FIRST U.S. EDITION

Library of Congress Cataloging-in-Publication Data has been applied for.

ISBN 978-0-06-212419-7

12 13 14 15 16 DIX/RRD 10 9 8 7 6 5 4 3 2 1

To my mother. Thank you.

CONTENTS

PROLOGUE

The air temperature is minus twenty degrees. I wiggle my fingers but they're still freezing cold. Old frostnip injuries never let you forget. I blame Everest for that.

"You set, buddy?" cameraman Simon asks me, smiling. His rig is all prepped and ready.

I smile back. I am unusually nervous.

Something doesn't quite feel right.

But I don't listen to the inner voice.

It is time to go to work.

⚜

The crew tell me that the crisp northern Canadian Rockies look spectacular this morning. I don't really notice.

It is time to get into my secret space. A rare part of me that is focused, clear, brave, precise. It is the part of me I know the best but visit the least.

I only like to use it sparingly. Like now.

Beneath me is three hundred feet of steep snow and ice. Steep but manageable.

I have done this sort of fast descent many, many times. *Never be complacent*, the voice says. The voice is always right.

A last deep breath. A look to Simon. A silent acknowledgment back.

Yet we have cut a vital corner. I know it. But I do nothing.

I leap.

I am instantly taken by the speed. Normally I love it. This time I am worried.

I never feel worried in the moment.

I know something is wrong.

I am soon traveling at over 40 mph. Feet first down the mountain. The ice races past only inches from my head. This is my world.

I gain even more speed. The edge of the peak gets closer. Time to arrest the fall.

I flip nimbly onto my front and drive the ice axe into the snow. A cloud of white spray and ice soars into the air. I can feel the rapid deceleration as I grind the axe deep into the mountain with all my power.

It works like it always does. Like clockwork. Total confidence. One of those rare moments of lucidity.

It is fleeting. Then it is gone.

I am now static.

The world hangs still. Then—*bang*.

Simon, his heavy wooden sled, plus solid metal camera housing, piles straight into my left thigh. He is doing in excess of 45 mph. There is an instant explosion of pain and noise and white.

It is like a freight train. And I am thrown down the mountain like a doll.

Life stands still. I feel and see it all in slow motion.

Yet in that split second I have only one realization: a one-degree different course and the sled's impact would have been with my head. Without doubt, it would have been my last living thought.

Instead, I am in agony, writhing.

I am crying. They are tears of relief.

I am injured, but I am alive.

I see a helicopter but hear no sound. Then the hospital. I have been in a few since *Man vs. Wild* began. I hate them.

I can see them all through closed eyes.

The dirty, bloodstained emergency room in Vietnam, after I severed half my finger in the jungle. No bedside graces there.

Then the rockfall in the Yukon. Not to mention the way worse boulder fall in Costa Rica. The mineshaft collapse in Montana or that saltwater croc in Oz. Or the sixteen-foot tiger that I landed on in the Pacific versus the snakebite in Borneo.

Countless close shaves.

They all blur. All bad.

Yet all good. I am alive.

There are too many to hold grudges. Life is all about the living.

I am smiling.

The next day, I forget the crash. To me, it is past. Accidents happen, it was no one's fault.

Lessons learned.

Listen to the voice.

I move on.

"Hey, Si, I'm cool. Just buy me a piña colada when we get out of here. Oh, and I'll be sending you the evac, doc, and physio bills."

He reaches for my hand. I love this man.

We've lived some life out there.

I look down to the floor: at my ripped mountain bib pants, bloodstained jacket, smashed Minicam, and broken goggles.

I quietly wonder: when did all this craziness become my world?

PART 1

✠

IN THE GENES

The young do not know enough to be prudent, and therefore they attempt the impossible—and achieve it, generation after generation.

—Pearl S. Buck

CHAPTER 1

Walter Smiles, my great-grandfather, had a very clear dream for his life. As he breathed in the fresh, salty air of the northern Irish coast that he loved so dearly, he gazed out over the remote Copeland Islands of County Down. He vowed to himself that it would be here, at Portavo Point, on this wild, windswept cove, that one day he would return to live.

He dreamt of making his fortune, marrying his true love, and building a house for his bride here, on this small cove overlooking this dramatic Irish coastline. It was a dream that would shape, and ultimately end, his life.

⚜

Walter came from a strong line of self-motivated, determined folk: not grand, not high-society, but no-nonsense, family-minded, go-getters. His grandfather had been Samuel Smiles, who, in 1859, authored the original motivational book, titled *Self-Help*. It was a landmark work, and an instant bestseller, even outselling Charles Darwin's *The Origin of Species* when it was first launched.

Samuel's book *Self-Help* also made plain the mantra that hard work and perseverance were the keys to personal progress. At a time in Victorian society where, as an Englishman, the world was your oyster if you had the get-up-and-go to make things happen, his book *Self-Help* struck a chord. It became the ultimate Victorian how-to guide, empowering the everyday person to reach for the sky. And at its heart it said that nobility is not a birthright but is defined by our actions. It laid bare the simple but unspoken secrets for living a meaningful, fulfilling life, and it defined a gentleman in terms of character not blood type.

> Riches and rank have no necessary connection with genuine gentlemanly qualities.
>
> The poor man with a rich spirit is in all ways superior to the rich man with a poor spirit.
>
> To borrow St. Paul's words, the former is as "having nothing, yet possessing all things," while the other, though possessing all things, has nothing.
>
> Only the poor in spirit are really poor. He who has lost all, but retains his courage, cheerfulness, hope, virtue, and self-respect, is still rich.

These were revolutionary words to Victorian, aristocratic, class-ridden England. To drive the point home (and no doubt prick a few hereditary aristocratic egos along the way), Samuel made the point again that being a gentleman is something that has to be earned: "There is no free pass to greatness."

⚜

Samuel Smiles ends his book with the following moving story of the "gentleman" general:

The gentleman is characterized by his sacrifice of self, and preference of others, in the little daily occurrences of life . . . we may cite the anecdote of the gallant Sir Ralph Abercromby, of whom it is related, that, when mortally wounded in the battle of Aboukir, and, to ease his pain, a soldier's blanket was placed under his head, from which he experienced considerable relief.

He asked what it was.

"It's only a soldier's blanket," was the reply.

"Whose blanket is it?" said he, half lifting himself up.

"Only one of the men's."

"I wish to know the name of the man whose blanket this is."

"It is Duncan Roy's, of the 42nd, Sir Ralph."

"Then see that Duncan Roy gets his blanket this very night."

Even to ease his dying agony the general would not deprive the private soldier of his blanket for one night.

As Samuel wrote: "True courage and gentleness go hand in hand."

It was in this family, belief system, and heritage that Walter, my great-grandfather, grew up and dared to dream.

CHAPTER 2

During World War I, Great-grandpa Walter sought action wherever and whenever he could. He was noted as one of those "rare officers who found complete release in action."

He obtained a pilot's certificate but, realizing that action in the air was unlikely due to the lack of aircraft, he transferred as a sublieutenant to the Royal Naval Armoured Car Division, an early Special Forces organization formed by Winston Churchill.

Unlike the British officers on the Western Front, who were imprisoned in their trenches for months on end, he moved around many of the main theaters of war—and he was in his element. Even Walter's CO noted in an official report: "The cheerful acceptance of danger and hardship by Lieutenant Smiles is very noteworthy."

He was then seconded to the Czar's Russian Imperial Army, to fight the Turks on the Caucasian front. And it was here that Walter was promoted swiftly: lieutenant in 1915, lieutenant commander in 1917, and commander in 1918. He was highly decorated during this time, receiving a Distinguished Service Order (1916) and Bar (1917), a "Mention in Despatches" (1919), along with Russian and Romanian decorations.

The citation for his first DSO stated: "He was wounded on the

28th November, 1916, in Dobrudja. On coming out of hospital he volunteered to lead a flying squadron for special duty round Braila, and his gallantry on this occasion was the chief factor of success."

On one occasion, when in action with a light armored car, he got out twice to start it up under heavy fire. Being struck by a bullet he rolled into a ditch and fought on all day under attack. Despite the fact that Walter was wounded, within twenty-four hours he was back with his unit, chomping at the bit. As soon as he was on his feet, he was leading his vehicles into action again. Walter was proving himself both recklessly committed and irrepressibly bold.

An extract from the *Russian Journal* in 1917 stated that Walter was "an immensely courageous officer and a splendid fellow." And the Russian Army commander wrote to Walter's commanding officer, saying: "The outstanding bravery and unqualified gallantry of Lieutenant Commander Smiles have written a fine page in British military annals, and give me the opportunity of requesting for him the decoration of the highest order, namely the St. George of the 4th class." At the time this was the highest gallantry award given by the Russians to any officer.

To be honest, I grew up imagining that my great-grandfather, with a name like Walter, might have been a bit stuffy or serious. Then I discovered, after a bit of digging, that in fact he was wild, charismatic, and brave beyond the natural. I also love the fact that in the family portraits I have seen of Walter, he looks exactly like Jesse, my eldest son. That always makes me smile. Walter was a great man to be like. His medals are on our wall at home still today, and I never quite understood how brave a man my great-grandfather had been.

⚜

After the war, Walter returned to India, where he had been work-ing previously. He was remembered as an employer who "mixed freely with the natives employed on his tea plantations, showing a strong concern with the struggles of the 'lower' castes." In 1930 he was knighted, Sir Walter Smiles.

It was on a ship sailing from India back to England that Walter met his wife-to-be, Margaret. Margaret was a very independent middle-aged woman: heavily into playing bridge and polo, beau-tiful, feisty, and intolerant of fools. The last thing she expected as she settled into her gin and tonic and a game of cards on the deck of the transport ship was to fall in love. But that was how she met Walter, and that's how love often is. It comes unexpectedly, and it can change your life.

Walter married Margaret soon after returning, and despite her "advancing" years, she soon fell pregnant—to her absolute horror. It just wasn't "right" for a lady in her forties to give birth, or so she thought, and she went about doing everything she pos-sibly could to make the pregnancy fail.

My grandmother Patsie (who at this stage was the unborn child Margaret was carrying), recounts how her mother had "promptly gone out and done the three worst things if you were pregnant. She went for a very aggressive ride on her horse, drank half a bottle of gin, and then soaked for hours in a very hot bath."

The plan failed (thank God), and in April 1921 Walter and Margaret's only child, Patricia (or Patsie), my grandmother, was born.

On returning to Northern Ireland from India, Walter finally ful-filled his dream. He built Margaret a house on that very same point in County Down where he had stood so many years earlier.

With a diplomat's mind and a sharp intellect, he then entered the world of politics, finally winning the Northern Irish seat of North Down in Ulster, where he served loyally.

But on Saturday, January 30, 1953, all that was about to change. Walter was hoping to fly back home from Parliament in London, to Ulster. But that night a storm was brewing, bringing with it some of the worst weather the UK had experienced for more than a decade. His flight was duly canceled, and instead he booked a seat on the night train to Stranraer.

The next day, the storm building menacingly, Walter boarded the car ferry, the *Princess Victoria*, for Larne, in Northern Ireland. The passengers were reassured that the vessel was fit to sail. Time was money, and the ferry duly left port.

What happened that night has affected the towns of Larne and Stranraer to this very day. Preventable accidents—where man has foolishly challenged nature and lost—do that to people.

Note to self: Take heed.

CHAPTER 3

Walter and Margaret's house, on the shores of Donaghadee, was known simply as "Portavo Point."

The lovingly built house commanded sweeping views over the coastline, where on a clear day you could see over the distant islands and out to sea.

It was, and still is, a magical place.

But not on that night.

On board the ferry, Walter watched the Scottish coastline fade as the steel, flat-hulled ship slid out into the jaws of the awaiting tempest. The crossing became progressively rougher and rougher as the weather deteriorated even further until, only a few miles from her Northern Irish destination, the *Princess Victoria* found herself in the middle of one of the most ferocious Irish Sea storms ever witnessed.

Initially the ferry rode it, but a weakness in the ferry stern doors would prove disastrous.

Slowly the doors started to ship in water. As the sea-water poured in and the waves began to break over the freeboard, the ship began to lose her ability to maneuver or make headway.

The bilges also were struggling to cope. Leaking stern doors and an inability to clear excess water are a killer combination in any storm.

It was only a matter of time before the sea would overpower her.

Soon, swung broadside to the waves by the power of the wind, the *Princess Victoria* began to lurch and tilt under the weight of the incoming water. The captain ordered the lifeboats to be lowered.

A survivor later told the Ulster High Court, which investigated the incident, that Walter was heard instructing: "Carry on giving out life jackets to the women and children."

Over the roar of the wind and storm, the captain and his crew ushered the panic-stricken passengers into the lifeboats.

No one was to know that they were lowering the women and children to their deaths.

As the lifeboats were launched, the passengers were trapped in that "dead man's zone" between the hull of the steel ferry and the breaking white water of the oncoming waves.

In the driving wind and rain this was a fatal place to be caught.

The lifeboats lurched, then pitched repeatedly under the violence of the breaking waves. They were unable to escape from the side of the ferry. The crew were powerless to make progress against the ferocity of the wind and waves, until eventually, one by one, almost every lifeboat had been capsized.

Survival time would now be reduced to minutes in the freezing Irish January sea.

The storm was winning, and the speed with which the waves began to overpower the vessel now accelerated. The ferry was waging a losing battle against the elements; and both the captain and Walter knew it.

The Donaghadee lifeboat, the *Sir Samuel Kelly*, set out into the ferocious sea at approximately 1:40 P.M. on the Saturday, and managed to reach the stricken ferry.

Fighting gale force waves and wind, they managed to retrieve only thirty-three of the 165 passengers.

⚜

As a former pilot in World War I, Walter had always preferred flying as a means of travel, rather than going by sea. Whenever he was in the Dakota, flying over to Northern Ireland, he always asked for the front seat, joking that if it crashed then he wanted to die first.

It was bitter irony it wasn't a plane that was going to kill him, but the sea.

Everything he could possibly do to help had been done; every avenue exhausted. No lifeboats remained. Walter quietly retired to his cabin, to wait—to wait for the sea to deal her final blow.

The wait wasn't long, but it must have felt like an eternity. The glass in Walter's cabin porthole would have shattered into a thousand fragments as it succumbed to the relentless pressure of the water.

Walter, my great-grandfather, the captain of the *Princess Victoria*, and 129 other crew and passengers were soon swallowed by the blackness.

Gone.

They were only a few miles from the Ulster coast, almost within sight of Walter and Margaret's house at Portavo Point.

Standing at the bay window of the drawing room, watching as the coastguard flares lit up the sky, summoning the Donaghadee lifeboat crew to action stations, Margaret and her family could only wait anxiously and pray.

Their prayers were never answered.

CHAPTER 4

The Donaghadee lifeboat went to sea again at 7:00 A.M. on Sunday morning in eerie, poststorm, calm conditions—they found scattered bits of wreckage and took on board the bodies of eleven men, one woman, and a child.

There was not one soul found alive, and all the remaining bodies were lost to the sea.

That very same day, Margaret, in shock, performed the grisly task of identifying bodies on the quayside of Donaghadee harbor.

Her beloved's body was never found.

Margaret never recovered, and within a year, she died of a broken heart.

At a memorial service attended by more than a thousand people in the parish church at Bangor, the Bishop of Down said in his address that Walter Smiles died, as he lived: "a good, brave, unselfish man who lived up to the command: 'Look not every man to his own things, but every man, also, to the good of others.' "

⚜

Almost a hundred years earlier, to the day, Samuel Smiles had written the final pages of his book *Self-Help*. It included this moving tale of heroism as an example for the Victorian Englishman to follow. For the fate of my great-grandfather, Walter, it was poignant in the extreme.

The vessel was steaming along the African coast with 472 men and 166 women and children on board.

The men consisted principally of recruits who had been only a short time in the service.

At two o'clock in the morning, while all were asleep below, the ship struck with violence upon a hidden rock, which penetrated her bottom; and it was at once felt that she would go down.

The roll of the drums called the soldiers to arms on the upper deck, and the men mustered as if on parade.

The word was passed to "save the women and children"; and the helpless creatures were brought from below, mostly undressed, and handed silently into the boats.

When they had all left the ship's side, the commander of the vessel thoughtlessly called out, "All those that can swim, jump overboard and make for the boats."

But Captain Wright, of the 91st Highlanders, said, "No! If you do that, the boats with the women will be swamped." So the brave men stood motionless. Not a heart quailed; no one flinched from his duty.

"There was not a murmur, nor a cry among them," said Captain Wright, a survivor, "until the vessel made her final plunge."

Down went the ship, and down went the heroic band, firing a volley shot of joy as they sank beneath the waves.

Glory and honor to the gentle and the brave!

The examples of such men never die, but, like their memories, they are immortal.

As a young man, Walter undoubtedly would have read and known those words from his grandfather's book.

Poignant in the extreme.

Indeed, the examples of such men never die, but, like their memories, they are immortal.

CHAPTER 5

Margaret's daughter, Patsie, my grandmother, was in the prime of her life when the *Princess Victoria* sank. The media descended on the tragedy with reportage full of heroism and sacrifice.

Somehow the headlines dulled Patsie's pain. For a while.

In a rush of grief-induced media frenzy, Patsie found herself winning a by-election to take over her father's Ulster seat in Parliament.

The glamorous, beautiful daughter takes over her heroic father's political seat. It was a script made for a film.

But life isn't celluloid, and the glamour of London's Westminster Palace would exact a dreadful toll on Northern Ireland's youngest-ever female Member of Parliament (MP).

Patsie had married Neville Ford, my grandfather: a gentle giant of a man and one of seven brothers and sisters.

Neville's father had been the Dean of York Minster cathedral and Headmaster of the elite Harrow School. His brother Richard, a sporting prodigy, had died suddenly a day before his sixteenth birthday while a pupil at Eton, Harrow's rival; another brother, Christopher, had been tragically killed in Anzio during World War II.

But Neville survived, and he shone.

Voted the most handsome man at Oxford, he was blessed with not only good looks, but also a fantastic sporting eye. He played top-level county cricket and was feted in the newspapers as a huge "hitter of sixes," with innings becoming of his six-foot-three frame. But marrying the love of his life, Patsie, was where his heart lay.

He was as content as any man can hope to be, living with his bride in rural Cheshire. He took up a job with Wiggins Teape, the paper manufacturers, and together he and Patsie began to raise a small family in the countryside.

For Patsie to follow so publicly in her father's footsteps was a decision that troubled Neville, however. He knew that it would change all their lives drastically. But he consented all the same.

The glamour of Westminster was intoxicating for his young wife, and the Westminster corridors were equally intoxicated by the bright and beautiful Patsie.

Neville waited and watched patiently from their home in Cheshire. But in vain.

It wasn't long before Patsie became romantically involved with a fellow Member of Parliament. The MP vowed to leave his wife, if Patsie left Neville. It was a clichéd, empty promise. But the tentacles of power had firmly grasped the young Patsie. She chose to leave Neville.

It was a decision that she regretted until her dying day.

Sure enough, the MP never left his wife. Yet by now Patsie had burned her bridges, and life moves ever on.

But the damage, which would affect our family, was done; and for Neville and Patsie's two young daughters (Sally, my mother, and her sister, Mary-Rose), their world was turning.

For Neville it was beyond heartbreaking.

Patsie was soon wooed by another politician, Nigel Fisher, and this time she married him. But from early on in their marriage, Patsie's new husband was unfaithful.

Yet she stayed with him and bore the burden, with the flawed conviction that somehow this was God's punishment for leaving Neville, the one man who had ever truly loved her.

Patsie raised Sally and Mary-Rose, and she went on to achieve so much with her life, including founding one of Northern Ireland's most successful charities: the Women's Caring Trust, that still today helps communities come together through music, the arts and even climbing. (Climbing has always been in the family blood!)

Granny Patsie was loved by many and had that great strength of character that her father and grandfather had always shown. But somehow that regret from her early life never really left her.

She wrote a very poignant but beautiful letter on life to Lara, my sister, when she was born, that ended like this:

Savor the moments of sheer happiness like a precious jewel—they come unexpectedly and with an intoxicating thrill.

But there will also be moments, of course, when everything is black—perhaps someone you love dearly may hurt or disappoint you and everything may seem too difficult or utterly pointless. But remember, always, that everything passes and nothing stays the same . . . and every day brings a new beginning, and nothing, however awful, is completely without hope.

Kindness is one of the most important things in life and can mean so much. Try never to hurt those you love. We all make mistakes, and sometimes, terrible ones, but try not to hurt anyone for the sake of your own selfishness.

Try always to think ahead and not backward, but don't ever try to block out the past, because that is part of you and has made you what you are. But try, oh try, to learn a little from it.

It wasn't until the final years of her life that Neville and Patsie became almost reunited.

Neville now lived a few hundred yards from the house that I grew up in as a teenager on the Isle of Wight, and Patsie in her old age would spend long summers living with us there as well.

The two of them would take walks together and sit on the bench overlooking the sea. But Neville always struggled to let her in close again, despite her warmth and tenderness to him.

Neville had held fifty years of pain after losing her, and such pain is hard to ignore. As a young man I would often watch her slip her fingers into his giant hand, and it was beautiful to see.

I learned two very strong lessons from them: the grass isn't always greener elsewhere, and true love is worth fighting for.

CHAPTER 6

During the first few years of my life, all school holidays were spent at Portavo Point, in Donaghadee, on the Northern Irish coast—the same house where my great-grandfather Walter had lived, and so near to where he ultimately died.

I loved that place.

The wind off the sea and the smell of salt water penetrated every corner of the house. The taps creaked when you turned them and the beds were so old and high that I could only reach into mine by climbing up the bedstead.

I remember the smell of the old Yamaha outboard engine in our ancient wooden boat that my father would carry down to the shore to take us out in on calm days. I remember walks through the woods with bluebells in full bloom. I especially loved hiding and running among the trees, getting my father to try and find me.

I remember being pushed by my elder sister, Lara, on a skateboard down the driveway and crashing into the fence; or lying in a bed beside Granny Patsie, both of us ill with measles, quarantined to the garden shed to keep us away from everyone else.

I remember swimming in the cold sea and eating boiled eggs every day for breakfast.

In essence, it was the place where I found my love of the sea and of the wild.

But I didn't know it at the time.

❧

Conversely, the school term times would be spent in London, where my father worked as a politician. (It was a strange—or not so strange—irony that my mother married a future MP, after witnessing the dangerous power of politics firsthand growing up with Patsie as her mother.)

When my parents married, Dad was working as a wine importer, having left the Royal Marine Commandos, where he had served as an officer for three years. He then went on to run a small wine bar in London before finally seeking election as a local councillor and subsequently as a Member of Parliament for Chertsey, just south of London.

More important, my father was, above all, a good man: kind, gentle, fun, loyal, and loved by many. But growing up, I remember those times spent in London as quite lonely for me.

Dad was working very hard, and often late into the evenings, and Mum, as his assistant, worked beside him. I struggled, missing just having time together as a family—calm and unhurried.

Looking back, I craved some peaceful time with my parents. And it is probably why I behaved so badly at school.

I remember once biting a boy so hard that I drew blood, and then watching as the teachers rang my father to say they didn't know what to do with me. My father said he knew what to do with me, though, and came down to the school at once.

With a chair placed in the middle of the gym and all the children sitting cross-legged on the floor around him, he whacked me until my bum was black and blue.

The next day, I slipped my mother's hand in a busy London street and ran away, only to be picked up by the police some hours later. I wanted attention, I guess.

My mother was forever having to lock me away in my bedroom for troublemaking, but she would then get concerned that I might run out of oxygen, so had a carpenter make some airholes in the door.

They say that necessity is the mother of all invention, and I soon worked out that, with a bent-over coat hanger, I could undo the latch through the airholes and escape. It was my first foray into the world of adapting and improvising, and those skills have served me well over the years.

At the same time, I was also developing a love of the physical. Mum would take me every week to a small gymnasium for budding gymnasts, run by the unforgettable Mr. Sturgess.

The classes were held in a dusty old double garage behind a block of flats in Westminster.

Mr. Sturgess ran the classes with iron, ex-military discipline. We each had spots on the floor, denoting where we should stand rigidly to attention, awaiting our next task. And he pushed us hard. It felt like Mr. Sturgess had forgotten that we were only age six—but as kids, we loved it.

It made us feel special.

We would line up in rows beneath a metal bar, some seven feet off the ground, then one by one we would say: "Up, please, Mr. Sturgess," and he would lift us up and leave us hanging, as he continued down the line.

The rules were simple: you were not allowed to ask permission to drop off until the whole row was up and hanging, like dead pheasants in a game larder. And even then you had to request: "Down, please, Mr. Sturgess." If you buckled and dropped off prematurely, you were sent back in shame to your spot.

I found I loved these sessions and took great pride in determining to be the last man hanging. Mum would say that she couldn't bear to watch as my little skinny body hung there, my face purple and contorted in blind determination to stick it out until the bitter end.

One by one the other boys would drop off the bar, and I would be left hanging there, battling to endure until the point where even Mr. Sturgess would decide it was time to call it.

I would then scuttle back to my mark, grinning from ear to ear.

"Down, please, Mr. Sturgess," became a family phrase for us, as an example of hard physical exercise, strict discipline, and foolhardy determination. All of which would serve me well in later military days.

So my training was pretty well rounded. Climbing. Hanging. Escaping.

I loved them all.

Mum, still to this day, says that growing up I seemed destined to be a mix of Robin Hood, Harry Houdini, John the Baptist, and an assassin.

I took it as a great compliment.

CHAPTER 7

My favorite times from that era were Tuesdays after school, when I would go to my Granny Patsie's flat for tea, and to spend the night.

I remember the smell there as a mix of Silk Cut cigarettes and the baked beans and fish fingers she cooked me for tea. But I loved it. It was the only place away from home that I wasn't ever homesick.

When my parents were away, I would often be sent to spend the night in the house of an older lady who I didn't know, and who didn't seem to know me, either. (I assume it was a friendly neighbor or acquaintance, or at least hope it was.)

I hated it.

I remember the smell of the old leather photo frame containing a picture of my mum and dad that I would cling to in the strange bed. I was too young to understand that my parents would be coming back soon.

But it taught me another big lesson: Don't leave your children if they don't want you to.

Life, and their childhood, is so short and fragile.

Through all these times and formative young years, Lara, my sister, was a rock to me. My mother had suffered three miscarriages after having Lara, and eight years on she was convinced that she wasn't going to be able to have more children. But Mum got pregnant, and she tells me she spent nine months in bed to make sure she didn't miscarry.

It worked. Mum saved me.

The end result, though, was that she was probably pleased to get me out, and that Lara finally got herself a precious baby brother; or in effect, her own baby. So Lara ended up doing everything for me, and I adored her for it.

While Mum was a busy working mother, helping my father in his constituency duties and beyond, Lara became my surrogate mum. She fed me almost every supper I ate—from when I was a baby up to about five years old. She changed my nappies, she taught me to speak, then to walk (which, with so much attention from her, of course happened ridiculously early). She taught me how to get dressed and to brush my teeth.

In essence, she got me to do all the things that either she had been too scared to do herself or that just simply intrigued her, such as eating raw bacon or riding a tricycle down a steep hill with no brakes.

I was the best rag doll of a baby brother that she could have ever dreamt of.

It is why we have always been so close. To her, I am still her little baby brother. And I love her for that. But—and this is the big but—growing up with Lara, there was never a moment's peace. Even from day one, as a newborn babe in the hospital's maternity ward, I was paraded around, shown off to anyone and everyone— I was my sister's new "toy." And it never stopped.

It makes me smile now, but I am sure it is why in later life I craved the peace and solitude that mountains and the sea bring. I didn't want to perform for anyone, I just wanted space to grow and find myself among all the madness.

It took a while to understand where this love of the wild came from, but in truth it probably developed from the intimacy found with my father on the shores of Northern Ireland and the will to escape a loving but bossy elder sister. (God bless her!)

I can joke about this nowadays with Lara, and through it all she still remains my closest ally and friend; but she is always the extrovert, wishing she could be on the stage or on the chat show couch, where I tend just to long for quiet times with my friends and family.

In short, Lara would be much better at being famous than me. She sums it up well, I think:

Until Bear was born I hated being the only child—I complained to Mum and Dad that I was lonely. It felt weird not having a brother or sister when all my friends had them. Bear's arrival was so exciting (once I'd got over the disappointment of him being a boy, because I'd always wanted a sister!).

But the moment I set eyes on him, crying his eyes out in his crib, I thought: That's my baby. I'm going to look after him. I picked him up, he stopped crying, and from then until he got too big, I dragged him around everywhere.

One of the redeeming factors of my early years in smoky London was that I got to join the Scouts (the UK equivalent of the Boy Scouts of America) age six, and I loved it.

I remember my first day at the Scouts, walking in and seeing all these huge boys with neatly pressed shirts, covered in awards and badges. I was a tiny, skinny squirt in comparison, and I felt even smaller than I looked. But as soon as I heard the scoutmaster challenge us to cook a sausage with just one match, out on the pavement, I was hooked.

One match, one sausage . . . hmm. But it will never burn long enough, I thought.

Then I was shown how first to use the match to light a fire, then to cook the sausage. It was a eureka moment for me.

If anyone present during those Scout evenings had been told that one day I would hold the post of Chief Scout and be the figurehead to twenty-eight million Scouts worldwide, they would have probably died of laughter. But what I lacked in stature and confidence, I always made up for with guts and determination, and those qualities are what really matter in both the game of life and in Scouting.

So I found great release in Scouting, and great camaraderie as well. It was like a family, and it didn't matter what your background was.

If you were a Scout, you were a Scout, and that was what mattered.

I liked that, and my confidence grew.

CHAPTER 8

Soon my parents bought a small cottage in the Isle of Wight, and from the age of five to eight I spent the term times in London, which I dreaded, and school holidays on the island.

Dad's job allowed for this because as an MP he got almost school-length holidays, and with a constituency situated en route between London and the Isle of Wight, he could do his Friday drive-through "clinic" before heading down to the island. (It was probably not a model way to do his duties, but as far as I was concerned it worked great.)

All I wanted was to get to the island as quickly as possible. And for me it was heaven. Mum and Dad were continually building onto our small cottage, to try and make it ever so slightly bigger, and soon this would become our main home.

Life on the island ranged from being wild, windy, and wet in winter, to being more like a holiday camp in the summer, full of young people of my age, many of whom are still my closest friends today.

I felt, for the first time, liberated and free to explore and be myself.

⚜

The other great thing about the island was that my Grandpa Neville lived barely four hundred yards away from our house.

I remember him as one of the greatest examples of a man I have ever known, and I loved him dearly. He was gentle, kind, strong, faith-filled, and fun-loving; and he loved huge bars of chocolate (despite always angrily refusing them, if given one as a treat). Without fail, they would be gone within minutes, once you walked away.

He lived to ninety-three and did his daily exercises religiously. You would hear him in his bedroom mumbling: "Knee-beeend, touch tooes, reach up high, and breathe . . ." He said it was the key to good health. (Not sure where the chocolate or buttered toast fit into the regime but hey, you gotta live life as well.)

Grandpa Neville died, seated on a bench at the end of our road, near the sea. I miss him still today: his long, whiskery eyebrows, his huge hands and hugs, his warmth, his prayers, his stories, but above all his shining example of how to live and how to die.

My uncle Andrew summed Neville up beautifully:

Neville remained a schoolboy at heart; thus he had a wonderful rapport with the young. Enthusiasm, Encouragement, and Love were his watchwords.

He was an usher at Winston Churchill's funeral and moved easily among royalty, but was equally at ease in any company. He lived up to Kipling's: "If you can talk with crowds and keep your virtue, Or walk with kings—nor lose the common touch."

He was both a perfect sportsman and a perfect gentleman. I never heard him speak ill of anyone; I never saw him perform an unkind act. He was in all respects a wonderful man.

Granny Patsie was also a huge part of my upbringing on the island: a remarkable lady with an extraordinary life behind her.

She was kind, warm, yet fragile. But to us she was simply Granny. As she got older, she struggled, with tender vulnerability, against depression. Maybe it was, in part, due to guilt over her infidelity to Neville, when she was younger.

As an antidote, though, she developed a penchant for buying expensive, but almost entirely pointless objects, in the conviction that they were great investments.

Among these, Granny bought a fully decked-out, antique gypsy caravan, and a shop next to the village fish and chippie, two hundred yards up the road from our home. The problem was that the caravan rotted without proper upkeep, and the shop was turned into her own personal antiques/junk shop.

It was, of course, a disaster.

Add to that the fact that the shop needed manning (often by various members of our family, including Nigel, who for most of the time sat fast asleep in a deck chair outside the shop, with a newspaper over his head), and you get the idea that life was both unprofitable and characterful. But above all, it was always fun.

(Nigel was Granny's loveable rogue of a second husband, who actually also had been a very successful politician in his time. He had won a Military Cross [MC] during World War II, and went on to hold a junior ministerial post in government in later life. To me, though, he was a kindly, gentle grandfather figure, loved by us all.)

⚜

So growing up at home was always eventful, although it was also definitely chaotic. But that was typical of my parents—especially my mother, who, even by her own wacky standards, was, and remains, pretty offbeat, in the best sense of the word.

In fact I tend to sum my family up with the quote: "Families are like fudge—mostly sweet with a few nuts!"

The good side of this meant that, as a family, we were endlessly moving around and meeting streams of interesting characters from all over the world, who gravitated to Mum—this was all just part of life. Whether we were camping in an old van, traveling to listen to some American motivational speaker, or helping Mum in her new business of selling blenders and water filters.

Meals were eaten at varying times of the day and night; pork chops were pulled out of a bin with the immortal words: "These are absolutely fine." (Even if Dad had thrown them out the day before, as they had turned silvery.)

It seemed that the sole aim of my mother was to fatten her family up as much as possible. This actually has pushed me the other way in later life and given me a probably "unhealthy" obsession with being healthy. (Although I do probably have my mother to thank for my cast-iron stomach that has helped me so much filming my survival shows over the years. God bless those pork chops after all.)

Everyone around us tended just to see the fun side of Mum's wackiness, but the down side of it was that for us as a family it was, at times, quite draining. It meant that she was always right, despite some of her ideas or beliefs definitely bordering on the wacko.

We would often catch her wandering around the garden with a copper rod, assuring us that she needed "earthing" against the excessive electricity in the house. (Considering that we never had the heating on, and mainly burned candles instead of switching on lights, this kind of led us to suspect something wasn't entirely normal about our mother.)

But that was Mum for you; and with only the rare exceptions, my childhood was blessed with love and fun, both of which have remained driving forces for me in my life with my own family.

CHAPTER 9

My mother and father had met when Mum was twenty-one and Dad was twenty-nine. Theirs was a pretty crazy love affair, involving endless breakups and reunions, until eventually they eloped to Barbados and got married.

Their relationship remained one full of love, although in many ways Mum was a product of her parents' divorce. She had a deep-rooted fear of being left, and that often made her overprotective of Dad.

So for us to go out climbing or sailing involved Dad and me having to sneak out. (Which, of course, we both loved.) I guess it made every outing a mission. And we had masses of those missions in my early years.

But as I got older and could start to plan my own expeditions, however small they were, I felt sad that I didn't get to do more with my dad, just us two alone. I just know how much he loved our adventures, but he did feel that his loyalty was split between Mum and me.

Dad had never really experienced much intimacy with his own parents growing up.

His father was a hardworking, dedicated, but pretty stern army officer who reached the rank of brigadier. Maybe his rank was gained at the expense of a cozy family life; I know for certain that Dad struggled with his father's coldness.

As a kid, I was always a little scared of Grandpa Ted. (Almost entirely unfounded, as it happened. Yes, he was stern, but with hindsight, he was a kind, loyal man, loved by many.)

The scariest thing about Grandpa Ted was his big dogs.

On one occasion, when I was age six, one mauled me as I sat on the floor trying to play with it. The dog bit me straight down the center of my face, and my flesh split down my nose and lips.

I was raced to hospital for emergency suturing, where my mother decided the duty nurse was taking too long, so took the matter into her own hands and did the stitches herself.

She did a great job, by the way, and unless you look closely at my face you wouldn't notice the scars—although my nose does actually look pretty wonky. In fact, the editor of *Men's Journal* magazine, when I did the close-up for their cover, asked me laughingly if I had lost a lot of boxing matches when young. But the truth is that ever since the dog attack my nose has always been kind of squiffy.

If Grandpa Ted was very stern with my own father when he was growing up, then Dad's mother was even sterner still. She had a fierce reputation not only as a great character, but also as someone who did not tolerate foolhardiness—and foolhardiness was my own father's middle name. So Dad grew up with an equally fierce reaction to this serious, firm upbringing—and became a practical joker from day one.

I remember hearing endless stories, such as him pouring buckets of water over his elder sister and her new boyfriend as he peered down on them from his bedroom window above.

In many ways Dad never really grew up. It is what made him such a wonderful father, gentleman, and friend. And, in turn, I never had the ambition to grow up too fast, either.

I remember once, on a family skiing trip to the Alps, Dad's practical joking got all of us into a particularly tight spot.

I must have been about age ten at the time, and was quietly excited when Dad spotted a gag that was begging to be played out on the very serious-looking Swiss-German family in the room next door to us.

Each morning their whole family would come downstairs, the mother dressed head to toe in furs, the father in a tight-fitting ski suit and white neck scarf, and their slightly overweight, rather snooty-looking thirteen-year-old son behind, often pulling faces at me.

The hotel had the customary practice of having a breakfast form that you could hang on your door handle the night before if you wanted to eat in your room. Dad thought it would be fun to fill out our form, order 35 boiled eggs, 65 German sausages, and 17 kippers, then hang it on the Swiss-German family's door.

It was too good a gag to pass up.

We didn't tell Mum, who would have gone mad, but instead filled out the form with great hilarity, and sneaked out last thing before bed and hung it on their door handle.

At 7:00 A.M. we heard the father angrily sending the order back. So we repeated the gag the next day.

And the next.

Each morning the father got more and more irate, until eventually Mum got wind of what we had been doing and made me go around to apologize. (I don't know why I had to do the apologizing when the whole thing had been Dad's idea, but I guess Mum thought I would be less likely to get in trouble, being so small.)

Anyway, I sensed it was a bad idea to go and own up, and sure enough it was.

From that moment onward, despite my apology, I was a marked man as far as their son was concerned.

It all came to a head when I was walking down the corridor on the last evening, after a day's skiing, and I was just wearing my ski thermal leggings and a T-shirt. The spotty, overweight teenager came out of his room and saw me walking past him in what were effectively ladies' tights.

He pointed at me, called me a sissy, started to laugh sarcastically, and put his hands on his hips in a very camp fashion. Despite the age and size gap between us, I leapt on him, knocked him to the ground, and hit him as hard as I could.

His father heard the commotion and raced out of his room to find his son with a bloody nose and crying hysterically (and over-dramatically).

That really was the straw that broke the camel's back, and I was hauled to my parents' room by the boy's father and made to explain my behavior to Mum and Dad.

Dad was hiding a wry grin, but Mum was truly horrified, and I was grounded.

So ended another cracking family holiday!

CHAPTER 10

When I was growing up, my aunt Mary-Rose and uncle Andrew (another former army brigadier) would often come and stay for Christmas with us at home.

I remember once when Dad (with me in tow, and in training), stretched plastic wrap over their loo seat (always a great gag). But it went down terribly.

So Dad just tried another.

And eventually, after several other poorly received practical jokes, my aunt and uncle decided it was time to go home . . . early.

What they hadn't bargained on was that my father had anticipated that very move, and had removed their car's spark plugs ahead of time, so all they could do was sit in the car, fuming, all packed up, with the car engine turning over and over.

My aunt and uncle, though, have always been such close friends of our family, and looking back through my life they have been a wonderful, kind, constant for me. I cherish their friendship so much.

Despite the jokes, Dad always felt the same way. It is proof that love can tease its own.

⚜

Dad's cold upbringing bred in him a determination to do it differently. Where he lacked affirmation and cuddles, he gave both to Lara and me in spades.

Above all, Dad wanted to be a cozy father to us, and he was—the best. For that I am so grateful, and despite losing him all too early, when I was age twenty-six, the truth is that I could not have had better preparation and training for life than I received through his example.

He was a politician for more than twenty years, and was a loyal, hardworking, back-bencher MP; but he never reached the higher echelons of political office. He never really seemed to want that.

What he aspired to most in life was to be close to his family.

There was no doubt that he loved his work, and he worked to make a difference and to better people's lives, but his ambitions lacked that ruthless drive so common in politics, and our lives were so much richer for it.

I guess his career was being a good dad.

I remember, for example, the time at prep school when I was chosen for the under nines' rugby team. Well, to be more accurate, I was chosen to be linesman, as I wasn't good enough for the actual team.

Anyway, it was a cold, miserable winter's day, and there were no spectators out watching, which was uncommon. (Normally, at least a few boys or teachers would come out to watch the school matches.) But on this cold, blustery day the touchlines were deserted, except for one lone figure.

It was my dad, standing in the rain, watching me, his son, perform my linesman duties.

I felt so happy to see him, but also felt guilty. I mean, I hadn't even made the team and here he was to watch me run up and down waving a silly flag.

Yet it meant the world to me.

When the halftime whistle blew it was my big moment.

On I ran to the pitch, the plate of oranges in my hands, with Dad applauding from the touchline.

Lives are made in such moments.

Likewise, I remember Dad playing in the fathers-and-sons cricket match. All the other fathers were taking it very seriously, and then there was Dad in an old African safari hat, coming in to bat and tripping over his wicket—out for a duck.

I loved that fun side of Dad, and everyone else seemed to love him for it as well.

To be a part of that always made me smile.

CHAPTER 11

I remember vividly, as a young teenager, finding an old photograph of my father from when he was seventeen and a fresh-faced Royal Marines commando. He looked just like me . . . but much smarter and with a parting in his hair.

Next to this photograph in the album was a shot of him ice climbing with his fellow marines on the north face of Ben Nevis in winter: a treacherous place to be if things go wrong.

I asked him about the climb, and he told me how a rockfall had almost killed him outright that day, when a boulder the size of a basketball had been dislodged two hundred feet above him.

It had missed his head by less than a foot and smashed into a thousand tiny rock fragments just below him on a ledge.

He felt he had been handed his "get out of jail free" card that day, a moment of grace and good fortune. He always told me: "Never depend on those luck moments—they are gifts—but instead always build your own backup plan."

I use that thinking a lot in my job nowadays. Thanks, Dad, if you can read this from the other side.

⚜

As a young boy I used to love any trip away with him.

I look back now and can see how much my father also found his own freedom in the adventures we did together, whether it was galloping along a beach in the Isle of Wight with me behind him, or climbing on the steep hills and cliffs around the island's coast.

It was at times like these that I found a real intimacy with him.

It was also where I learned to recognize that tightening sensation, deep in the pit of my stomach, as being a great thing to follow in life. Some call it fear.

I remember the joy of climbing with him in the wintertime. It was always an adventure and often turned into much more than just a climb. Dad would determine that not only did we have to climb a sheer hundred-and-fifty-foot chalk cliff, but also that German paratroopers held the high ground. We therefore had to climb the cliff silently and unseen, and then grenade the German fire position once at the summit.

In reality this meant lobbing clumps of manure toward a deserted bench on the cliff tops. Brilliant.

What a great way to spend a wet and windy winter's day when you are age eight (or twenty-eight, for that matter).

I loved returning from the cliff climbs totally caked in mud, out of breath, having scared ourselves a little. I learned to love that feeling of the wind and rain blowing hard on my face. It made me feel like a man, when in reality I was a little boy.

We also used to talk about Mount Everest, as we walked across the fields toward the cliffs. I loved to pretend that some of our climbs were on the summit face of Everest itself.

We would move together cautiously across the white chalk faces, imagining they were really ice. I had this utter confidence that I could climb Everest if he were beside me.

I had no idea what Everest would really involve but I loved the dream together.

These were powerful, magical times. Bonding. Intimate. Fun. And I miss them a lot even today. How good it would feel to get the chance to do that with him just once more.

I think that is why I find it often so emotional taking my own boys hiking or climbing nowadays. Mountains create powerful bonds between people. It is their great appeal to me.

But it wasn't just climbing. Dad and I would often go to the local stables and hire a couple of horses for a tenner and go jumping the breakwaters along the beach.

Every time I fell off in the wet sand and was on the verge of bursting into tears, Dad would applaud me and say that I was slowly becoming a horseman. In other words, you can't become a decent horseman until you fall off and get up again a good number of times.

There's life in a nutshell.

CHAPTER 12

On one occasion we were on Dartmoor, a wild part along the UK's southwest peninsula, and were staying at a small inn, walking and riding each day.

It was in the depth of winter, with snow on the ground, and I can remember how freezing cold it was every day.

My young, boyish face felt as if it were literally about to freeze solid. I couldn't feel the end of my nose at all, which for someone with a big one like myself (even age ten) was a scary new physical phenomenon.

I started to cry; that usually worked to show Dad that things were serious and needed his attention. But he just told me to "cover up better and push through it. We are on a proper expedition now, and this is no time to whinge. The discomfort will pass."

So I shut up, and he was right, and I felt proud to have endured in my own little way.

Moments like that encouraged me to believe that I could persevere—especially (and more important), when I felt cold and rotten.

Nothing, though, was ever forced on me by him, but a lot was expected if I was to join in these adventures. As my own confidence grew, so did the desire to push myself, each time a little bit further.

We also spent a lot of days messing about together boating. Mum had been thoroughly put off boats by my dad early on in their marriage, due to what she called his "gung-ho attitude." I, though, loved the "gung-ho" bits, and craved for the weather to be bad and the waves to be big.

I had a real goal one day to own my own speedboat, to be able to drive around in it, and to tinker with the engine. Obviously a real speedboat was out of the question, but instead I got to build one with my dad: a very cool little eight-foot wooden rowing boat with a 1.5 hp engine on the back.

The boat was barely fast enough to make any progress against the incoming tides, but it was perfect for me. We rigged up an improvised cable system, linked to a steering wheel bolted into the bench, and I was away.

I would head off to meet my mum and dad at a small bay a few miles around the coast—I would go by sea, they would walk. I just loved the freedom that I found, being in charge of a boat on the sea.

I was always pushing Dad to allow me to take Lara's second-hand Laser sailing boat out on my own. (This was a single-handed racing dinghy, superprone to capsizing, and requiring substantially more weight than my puny eleven-year-old frame could offer.)

I just thrived off the challenge, the solitude, and the big waves and spray.

I loved the time alone, just nature and me—but only as long as I had that safety net of knowing that Dad was nearby on hand to help in a crisis. (Which was often the case.)

And I felt on top of the world as I sailed back into harbor, drenched like a drowned rat, grinning from ear to ear, hands and muscles burning from holding the lines so tightly, against the same strong wind that had driven all the other boats back to port.

It was a feeling that I could be a little different from everyone else of my age, and that, if pushed, I could battle against the forces of nature and prevail. Adventure felt the most natural thing in the world, and it was where I came alive. It is what made me feel, for the first time, really myself.

As I got older and the rest of my world got more complicated and unnatural, I sought more and more the identity and wholeness that adventure gave me.

In short, when I was wet, muddy, and cold, I felt like a million dollars, and when I was with the lads, with everyone desperately trying to be "cool," I felt more awkward and unsure of myself. I could do mud, but trying to be cool was never a success.

So I learned to love the former and shy away from the latter.

(Although I gave "cool" a brief, good go as a young teenager, buying winklepicker boots and listening to heavy metal records all through one long winter, both of which were wholly unsatisfying, and subsequently dropped as "boring.")

Instead, I would often dress up in my "worst" (aka my best) and dirtiest clothes, stand under the hosepipe in the garden, get soaking wet—in December—and then go off for a run on my own in the hills.

The locals thought me a bit bonkers, but my dog loved it, and I loved it. It felt wild, and it was a feeling that captured me more and more.

Once, I returned from one such run caked in mud and ran past a girl I quite fancied. I wondered if she might like the muddy look. It was at least original, I thought. Instead, she crossed the road very quickly, looking at me as if I were just weird.

It took me a while to begin to learn that girls don't always like people who are totally scruffy and covered in mud. And what I considered natural, raw, and wild didn't necessarily equal sexy.

Lesson still in progress.

CHAPTER 13

On one occasion, probably at about age eleven, I remember being dared by a local friend of mine from the Isle of Wight to attempt, with him, a crossing of the harbor at low tide.

I knew the reputation of the harbor, and I felt in my bones that it was a bad idea to attempt to beat the mud and sludge.

But it also sounded quite fun.

Now to cross the harbor at low tide would be no mean feat, as the mud was the worst thick, deep, oozy, limb-sucking variety . . . and in short, it was a damned stupid plan, flawed from the start.

Within ten yards of the shore I knew it was a bad idea, but foolishly, I just kept going. Sure enough, by the time we were about a third of the way out, we were stuck, and I mean really stuck.

I was up to my chest in black, stinking clay, slime, and mud.

We had used up so much energy in the short distance we had traveled that we were soon utterly beat, utterly stationary, and in utterly big trouble.

Each time we tried to move we got dragged down further, and I felt that awful sense of panic you get when you realize that you are into something beyond your control.

By the grace of God two things then happened. First of all, I found out, by experiment, that if I tried to "swim" on the surface of this mud and not to fight it, then I could make very slow progress. Well, at least, progress of sorts. So, slowly we both turned around and literally clawed our way back toward the shore, inch by inch.

The second thing that happened was that someone on the shore spotted us and called the lifeboat. Now I knew we were in trouble—whether we made it out or not.

By the time the lifeboat had arrived on the scene we had made it ashore, both looking like monsters from the deep, and we had scarpered.

My mother inevitably heard about what had happened, as well as the part about the lifeboat being launched to rescue us. I was made, rightly, to go around to the coxswain of the lifeboat's house and apologize in person, as well as offer myself to do chores for the crew in penance.

It was a good lesson: Know your limits, don't embark on any adventures without a solid backup plan, and don't be egged on by others when your instincts tell you something is a bad idea.

Apart from the odd disaster, I found that as I grew up I gravitated more and more to the outdoors. Because my mother never really enjoyed Dad and me going off on joint missions, as I got older those occasions of adventuring together with Dad sadly decreased.

As an aside, the one occasion I did get him out in the bigger mountains with me was a year after I passed the selection course to join the Special Air Service (SAS). I suggested we hike into the Brecon Beacons to climb some of the peaks in south Wales which had been the focal point of so many of my military marches and tests.

I arranged for Dad to be met at Merthyr Tydfil train station by Sgt. Taff, my troop sergeant.

"How will I recognize Taff?" Dad had asked.

"You'll recognize him," I replied. Taff looked military through and through: short, stocky, tight-haired, and with a classic soldier's handlebar mustache.

Taff collected Dad, and we all met up at the foot of the Brecon Beacons. The mountains were shrouded in a howling gale. We got halfway up the first peak, yet after an exciting river crossing of a raging torrent that was normally only ever a trickle of a stream, I noticed Dad's nose was bleeding badly.

He looked very pale and tired, so we headed down.

We had a fun few days together like this in the mountains, but by the time he got home to my mother she accused me of half-killing him and told us that there would be: "Strictly no more 'death expeditions.' "

I understood where she was coming from, but she kind of threw the baby out with the bathwater, and her blanket ban on our trips simply meant that Dad and I missed out on a load of fun adventures that I know he was so keen to do.

Now that Dad is no longer with us, I feel sad we didn't exploit those precious years together more. But that is life sometimes.

⚜

The final real adventure I had with Dad growing up was also my first taste of being in a life-threatening, genuine survival situation—and, despite the danger, I found that I just loved it.

This final mission also probably had something to do with my mother's ban on Dad and me undertaking any further escapades into the wild. Yet like all great adventures, it started off so innocently.

CHAPTER 14

We were on a family holiday to Cyprus to visit my aunt and uncle. My uncle Andrew was then the brigadier to all the British forces on the island, and as such a senior military figure I am sure he must have dreaded us coming to town.

After a few days holed up in the garrison my uncle innocently suggested that maybe we would enjoy a trip to the mountains. He already knew the answer that my father and I would give. We were in.

The Troodos Mountains are a small range of snowy peaks in the center of the island, and the soldiers posted to Cyprus use them to ski and train in. There are a couple of ski runs, but the majority of the peaks in winter are wild and unspoiled.

In other words, they are ripe for an adventure.

Dad and I borrowed two sets of army skis and boots from the garrison up in the hills and spent a great afternoon together skiing down the couple of designated runs. But designated runs can also be quite boring. We both looked at each other and suggested a quick off-piste detour.

I was all game . . . age eleven.

It wasn't very far into this between-the-trees deep-powder

detour that the weather, dramatically, and very suddenly, took a turn for the worse.

A mountain mist rolled in, reducing visibility to almost zero. We stopped to try and get, or guess, our directions back to the piste, but our guess was wrong, and very soon we both realized we were lost. (Or temporarily geographically challenged, as I have learned to call it.)

Dad and I made the mistake that so many do in that situation, and plowed on blind, in the vain hope that the miraculous would occur. We had no map, no compass, no food, no water, no mobile telephone (they hadn't even been invented yet), and in truth, no likelihood of finding our way.

We were perfect candidates for a disaster.

Trudging through deep snow, when you are young, cold, wet, and tired is hard. And the minutes became hours, and the hours began to rack up.

It was soon dark.

We pushed on; Dad was concerned, I could tell. He was a mountain man, but hadn't anticipated that we would be doing anything other than a quick couple of simple ski runs. He hadn't foreseen this. It was a simple mistake, and he acknowledged it. We kept going down; we were soon among deep forest, and even deeper snow.

We then reached a fork in the valley. Should we go left or right? Dad called it left. I had a very powerful intuition that right was the choice we should make. Dad insisted left. I insisted right.

It was a fifty-fifty call and he relented.

Within two hundred yards we stumbled across a snowy track through the woods and followed it excitedly. Within a mile it came out on a mountain road, and within ten minutes we had flagged down a lift from a car heading up the hill in the darkness.

We had found salvation, and I was beat.

The car dropped us off at the gates of the garrison thirty minutes later. It was, by then, late into the night, but I was suddenly buzzing with energy and excitement.

The fatigue had gone. Dad knew that I had made the right call up there—if we had chosen left we would still be trudging into the unknown.

I felt so proud.

In truth it was probably luck, but I learned another valuable lesson that night: Listen to the quiet voice inside. Intuition is the noise of the mind.

As we tromped back through the barracks, though, we noticed there was an unusual amount of activity for the early hours of a weekday morning. It soon became very clear why.

First a sergeant appeared, followed by another soldier, and then we were ushered into the senior officers' block.

There was my uncle, standing in uniform looking both tired and serious. I started to break out into a big smile. So did Dad. Well, I was excited. We had cheated a slow, lingering hypothermic death, lost together in the mountains. We were alive.

Our enthusiasm was countered by the immortal words from my uncle, the brigadier, saying: "I wouldn't smile if I was you . . ." He continued, "The entire army mountain rescue team is currently out scouring the mountains for you, on foot and in the air with the search-and-rescue helicopter. I hope you have a good explanation."

We didn't, of course, save that we had been careless, and we had got lucky; but that's life sometimes. And the phrase: "I wouldn't smile if I was you," has gone down into Grylls family folklore.

CHAPTER 15

Those were some of the many fun times. But life can't be all fun—and that leads me nicely on to school.

As a young boy, I was unashamedly open to the world and hungry for adventure, but I was also very needy for both love and for home. That in itself made me woefully unprepared for what would come next.

My parents decided the right and proper thing for a young English boy to do was to be sent away to boarding school. To me, age eight, it was a mad idea. I mean I was still hardly big enough to tie my own shoelaces.

But my parents both felt it was the best thing for me, and so with the best of intentions, they sent me away to live and sleep at a school far from home, and I hated it.

As we pulled up at the big school gates, I saw tears rolling down my dad's face. I felt confused as to what part of nature or love thought this was a good idea. My instinct certainly didn't; but what did I know? I was only eight.

So I embarked on this mission called boarding school. And how do you prepare for that one?

In truth, I found it really hard; there were some great moments like building dens in the snow in winter, or getting chosen for the tennis team, or earning a naval button, but on the whole it was a survival exercise in learning to cope.

Coping with fear was the big one. The fear of being left and the fear of being bullied—both of which were very real.

What I learned was that I couldn't manage either of those things very well on my own.

It wasn't anything to do with the school itself, in fact the headmaster and teachers were almost invariably kind, well-meaning and good people, but that sadly didn't make surviving it much easier.

I was learning very young that if I were to survive this place then I had to find some coping mechanisms.

My way was to behave badly, and learn to scrap, as a way to avoid bullies wanting to target me. It was also a way to avoid thinking about home. But not thinking about home is hard when all you want is to be at home.

I missed my mum and dad terribly, and on the occasional night where I felt this worst, I remember trying to muffle my tears in my pillow while the rest of the dormitory slept.

In fact I was not alone in doing this. Almost everyone cried, but we all learned to hide it, and those who didn't were the ones who got bullied.

As a kid, you can only cry so much before you run out of tears and learn to get tough.

I meet lots of folk nowadays who say how great boarding school is as a way of toughening kids up. That feels a bit back-to-front to me. I was much tougher before school. I had learned to love the outdoors and to understand the wild, and how to push myself.

When I hit school, suddenly all I felt was fear. Fear forces you to look tough on the outside but makes you weak on the inside. This was the opposite of all I had ever known as a kid growing up.

I had been shown by my dad that it was good to be fun, cozy, homely—but then as tough as boots when needed. At prep school I was unlearning this lesson and adopting new ways to survive.

And age eight, I didn't always pick them so well.

CHAPTER 16

I remember all of us in our dormitory counting down the days, (like prisoners!) until the next exeat, or weekend at home.

Boy, they took a long time to come around, and man, then the glorious weekends would go past quickly.

It was unbridled joy on the day we broke up, seeing my mum and dad arrive first out of all the parents, and have Dad press his huge nose against our classroom window, pulling a silly face. It was embarrassing but heavenly.

Conversely, those Sunday-night drives back to school were truly torturous. Give me SAS Selection any day . . . and that was bad, trust me.

Dad seemed to find dropping me back to school even worse than I did, which was at least some consolation. But it also just added to my confusion as to why I was being sent away.

But what made me most scared wasn't just being away from home—it was the bullying.

A few poor and entirely innocent boys just seemed to get picked on by one or two bullies. These bullies would truly make life hell for their hapless victims. Not only physically but also emotionally; systematically alienating their victims and teasing them relentlessly and heartlessly.

It has made me detest bullying in adult life. If I see it anywhere I go mad.

I was lucky to avoid being on the receiving end of this bullying at that young age, but it meant that I had to learn to cower and keep off the radar. And cowering and hiding are bad emotions for a kid.

Like most of the fears we all carry into later life, they are so often based on what could or might happen, rather than what actually did.

But bullying and absent parents aside, boarding school really wasn't all bad, and in truth I was so lucky to get an amazing education in the best ones around.

The headmaster and his wife at the school were real gems, and they genuinely cared and looked after every boy as best they could. But a school is a school, and the heart of a school is what happens when the teachers' backs are turned.

In the school's favor, I learned so much more than how to hide from bullies, and we were genuinely encouraged to be real little people, with real interests.

We were allowed to make camps in the woods with our buddies, and a blind eye was turned when we sneaked off to build even better secret camps in the out-of-bounds areas. The once-a-term table-tennis competition was treated like Wimbledon itself.

Each Saturday night the whole school would crowd into the hall, perched on benches to watch a classic old World War II film on an old, flickery cine-reel, and afterward we each got one chocolate bar as our weekly treat.

I would cut this up into segments and ration it for as many days as I could manage.

All that was brilliant fun. It was like living in a different century, and I am certain the school intended it to be like that.

It was old-school in the best of ways.

We skated on the frozen lake in winter, which was tested for strength by the poor Latin teacher on a horizontal ladder, and I was allowed to go cross-country, whatever the weather, which I always loved. And Health and Safety was kept healthily at bay.

Above all, we were taught to look out for one another and to think big, and those are pretty vital life skills, which I am still so grateful for today.

By the end of my five years at prep school, though, I was also getting pretty naughty, and, on one occasion I—with a few buddies—pushed my luck a little far. I was caught red-handed with beer cans in my rugby boots, cigarettes under my pillow, and attempting a break-in and entry to the deputy headmaster's house to steal his cigars.

The headmaster told us in no uncertain terms that: "Enough is enough. One more slipup and you'll all be out."

The straw that broke the camel's back was when I was caught French-kissing the daughter of another headmaster, whose school we were staying at on our way back from a field trip. The irony is that I wasn't entirely to blame, either.

Fifteen of us were sleeping on the floor of a gym in this school we were staying at for a night, and during the evening I had spotted the young teenage daughter of the headmaster looking us all up and down. That night, she crept into our dormitory in the dark. (Brave girl for venturing into a room full of thirteen-year-old boys.) And she then volunteered to snog one of us.

My hand shot up like a rocket, and she came straight over and slapped her mouth over mine. Age thirteen, I didn't realize that it was possible to breathe and kiss at the same time, so thirty seconds later I had to break free, gasping frantically for breath. She looked at me like I was some weirdo, and then ran out.

But she ran straight out and bumped into her father on his

headmaster patrol, and, of course, made up the story that we had lured her into our dormitory, and that I had then tried to kiss her!

It was the final straw.

I was politely asked to leave the school, along with a few of the other troublemakers who had been alongside me in most of these misadventures.

As it was so close to the end of the summer term, though, no sooner had we all been "expelled," than we were then all summoned back. Somehow, all of our parents had gotten together and agreed that the best punishment would be to send us *back* to school after the term had ended, and make us spend a week of our summer holiday copying out Latin textbooks.

It worked.

That was the nail in the coffin for me. I left prep school with a determination that no child of mine would ever be forced to go away against their will, and that I would do all I could to help them grow up without fear.

Surely public school couldn't be any worse? I thought. ("Public" school is the British term for what the rest of the world would call expensive private schools.)

At least there wouldn't be any more randy headmaster's daughters out to snitch on me.

CHAPTER 17

Eton College has the dubious honor of being the most famous school on the planet; and that makes it both a privileged and a pretty daunting place to go.

But like most things in life, it is all about what you make of it.

In my case, yes it was scary, but in many ways, it was also the making of me.

Unlike many public schools, Eton has more in common with a university than a high school. It gives you great freedoms as long as you prove yourself trustworthy of them. I liked that. I felt empowered and free to explore and pursue those things I was good at.

But it wasn't like that at the beginning.

❧

Eton has to be one of the most intimidating places to turn up as a nervous thirteen-year-old.

I was excited but terrified.

(I have since become pretty familiar with such emotions through many expeditions and missions, but at the time it was new territory.)

The redeeming factor was that I wasn't the only soul who felt like this when I arrived. I was really fortunate to go into a popular house with fun people, and it made all the difference to my time at Eton.

Very quickly, I made a few great friends, and they have remained my closest buddies ever since. But they were friendships formed in the trenches, so to speak, and there is nothing that forms friendships faster than facing off or escaping from bullies together.

It is amazing quite how small and insignificant you can feel turning up at Eton as a new boy. The older pupils look like gods and giants.

Shaving, masturbating, testosterone-fueled giants.

Each house is made up of fifty boys spanning across all the years, from thirteen to eighteen, and they all live in that house together.

Early on, each new boy is summoned individually to the top year's common room (called library), and made to perform a bizarre series of rituals, determined by the older boys and their whims and perversions.

One by one we were called in.

I was one of the first. This was a good thing—it meant the older pupils had yet to get into full flow. I escaped relatively unharmed, with only having to demonstrate how to French-kiss a milk bottle.

As I had only ever kissed one person (the prep-school headmaster's daughter some months earlier, and that in itself had been an unmitigated disaster), I wasn't exactly showing this milk bottle much of a virtuoso performance. The older boys soon got bored of me and I was dismissed; passed and accepted into the house.

I soon found my feet, and was much less homesick than I was at prep school. Thank God. I learned that with plenty of free time on our hands, and being encouraged to fill the time with "interests," I could come up with some great adventures.

A couple of my best friends and I started climbing the huge old oak trees around the grounds, finding monkey routes through the branches that allowed us to travel between the trees, high up above the ground.

It was brilliant.

We soon had built a real-life Robin Hood den, with full-on branch swings, pulleys, and balancing bars high up in the treetops.

We crossed the Thames on the high girders above a railway bridge, we built rafts out of old Styrofoam and even made a boat out of an old bathtub to go down the river in. (Sadly this sank, as the water came in through the overflow hole, which was a fundamental flaw. Note to self: Test rafts before committing to big rivers in them.)

We spied on the beautiful French girls who worked in the kitchens, and even made camps on the rooftops overlooking the walkway they used on their way back from work. We would vainly attempt to try and chat them up as they passed.

In between many of these antics we had to work hard academically, as well as dress in ridiculous clothes, consisting of long tailcoats and waistcoats. This developed in me the art of making smart clothes look ragged, and ever since, I have maintained a life-long love of wearing good-quality clothes in a messy way. It even earned me the nickname of "Scug," from the deputy-headmaster. In Eton slang this roughly translates as: "A person of no account, and of dirty appearance."

CHAPTER 18

The school regime refused to make it easy for us on the dress side of things, and it dictated that even if we wanted to walk into the neighboring town of Windsor, then we had to wear a blazer and tie.

This made us prime targets for the many locals who seemed to enjoy an afternoon of beating up the Eton "toffs."

On one occasion, I was having a pee in the loos of the Windsor McDonald's, which were tucked away downstairs at the back of the fast-food joint. I was just leaving the Gents when the door swung open, and in walked three aggressive-looking lads.

They looked as if they had struck gold on discovering this weedy, blazer-wearing Eton squirt, and I knew deep down that I was in trouble and alone. (Meanwhile, my friends were waiting for me upstairs. Some use they were being.)

I tried to squeeze past these hoodies, but they threw me back against the wall and laughed. They then proceeded to debate what they were going to do to me.

"Flush his head down the toilet," was an early suggestion. (*Well, I had had that done to me many times already at Eton*, I thought to myself.)

I was okay so far.

Then they suggested defecating in the loo first.

Now I was getting worried.

Then came the killer blow: "Let's shave his pubes!"

Now, there is no greater embarrassment for a young teenager than being discovered to not *have* any pubes. And I didn't.

That was it.

I charged at them, threw one of them against the wall, barged the other aside, squeezed through the door, and bolted. They chased after me, but once I reached the main floor of the McDonald's I knew I was safe.

I waited with my friends inside until we were sure the thugs had all left, then cautiously slunk back across the bridge to school. (I think we actually waited more than two hours, to be safe. Fear teaches great patience.)

There were a few other incidents that finally encouraged me to take up karate and aikido, the two martial arts that they ran at Eton.

One of those incidents involved one of the sixth-form boys in our house. I won't name him, bully though he was, as he is probably a respectable married man and businessman now. But at the time, he was mean, aggressive, and built like a bodybuilder.

He had these wild eyes, and after one of his heavy glue-sniffing sessions, he would tend to go insane.

His veins would look as if they were going to explode from the muscles in his arms, neck, and forehead, and he had a nasty habit of announcing he was on the warpath by blasting on a foghorn that he had somehow acquired.

For a while, his chosen targets to beat up were both me and my next-door roommate, Ed, and when that foghorn blew you knew it was time to scarper.

Once, I remember hearing it blast, and Ed and I ran into my room, frantically looking for a place to hide. We opened the closet, crouched inside . . . and hoped like hell he wouldn't find us.

The foghorn got louder and louder, until finally my study door swung open with a bang . . . then there was silence.

We held our breath as this wild man turned the room upside down, breathing heavily and cursing us under his breath.

Finally there was a pause in the room's destruction. Then we heard his footsteps move toward the closet. Another pause.

Then the closet door was torn open violently, and we were both suddenly staring into the wild, frenzied eyes of our nemesis.

We screamed.

He grabbed our heads and whacked them together, and after that the rest was a bit of a blur. He threw us around the room for a while and finished with putting us both in half nelson armlocks so hard that I was convinced my shoulder would snap.

Finally, bored, he kicked us, demonstrating what he said was a "ninja jack-kick," then left.

That's it, I thought to myself, *I have to learn how to defend myself properly.*

Apart from the odd occasion like that, and a few bog-flushings—oh, and quite regularly being winched up by your boxer shorts and hung off the clothes peg on the back of your door—the days passed busily.

The difference between the fear and bullying at Eton to what we experienced at prep school is that at least I didn't have to face those demons alone. There was generally someone to share those negative experiences with.

This time round, it was my buddies and me together, taking flak in the trenches.

And, somehow, I found I thrived on our misadventures.

CHAPTER 19

I signed up as soon as I could for the karate and aikido clubs, and found that I loved the martial arts way—the focus, the camaraderie, and above all the acquiring of an art that requires the use of guile over power, technique over force.

And I stuck with it. That was the real key to getting good at martial arts: time and motivation—and I certainly had the motivation, thanks to the foghorn.

A few of my friends also signed up with me, and came along to the early classes. In actual fact they were invariably much better than me when we started—often stronger, fitter, and more flexible—but after a few weeks they all began to drop out.

It was hard sometimes on a Sunday evening, when everyone else was messing around playing table tennis or watching TV, to drag yourself out into the winter's darkness and head off to get battered for two hours in the gym by some maniacal martial arts teacher.

But I kept going and kept going, and I guess I did a bit of a Forrest Gump on it: I just stuck at it—and I am so pleased I did.

One summer I got the chance to tour as part of the Karate Union of Great Britain (KUGB) team to Japan. It was a dream come true.

I remember being dropped off at the bus station in London by my mother, and nervously waving her good-bye. I was neatly dressed in a blazer and tie, with my karate team badge neatly sewn in place on my lapel.

The bus was filled with the rest of the karate squad, gathered from all over the UK—none of whom I had met before.

I could instantly see that they were all bigger, tougher, and louder than me—and I was pretty scared. Japan felt a frighteningly long way away.

I took a deep breath and sat down in the bus, feeling very small and insignificant.

The team was an eclectic mix of karate experts—from London taxi drivers to full-time professional fighters. (The only other Etonian who had been selected as part of the team was Rory Stewart, the MP who went on to become known for his epic walk through Afghanistan, as well as governing a province of occupied Iraq age only thirty.) *This is going to be an interesting trip,* I thought.

But I had nothing to fear.

The squad completely took me under their wing as their most junior member, and arriving in Tokyo as a fresh-faced teenager, away from home, was eye-opening for me.

We headed up to the mountains outside of Tokyo and settled into the training camp.

Here we began to study and train under Sensei Yahara, one of the most revered karate grandmasters in the world. Each night we slept on the floor in small wooden Japanese huts, and by day we learned how to fight—real and hard.

The training was more exacting and demanding than anything I had previously encountered. If our positions or stances weren't pinpoint accurate, we would receive a firm crack from the bamboo "jo" cane.

We quickly learned not to be lazy in our stances, even when tired.

In the early evenings when we finished training I would walk the two miles down the mountain to a small roadside hut and buy milk bread, a form of sweet milk cake, and I would slowly eat it on my way back to the camp.

Then I would bathe in the natural hot volcanic springs and soak my tired muscles. And I loved it all.

On our return to Tokyo, en route back to the UK, we got to witness a private training session of the top twenty karate fighters in the world. It was intense to watch. Fast, brutal at times, yet like poetry in motion.

I was even more hooked than I had been before.

One day I would be that good, I vowed.

⚜

I will never forget the day I finally got awarded my black belt, and the pride I felt.

The day of the grading had taken three years to arrive, and for those three years I had given it my all: training at least four or five times a week, religiously.

The final examination came and my mother came down to watch it. She hated watching me fight. (Unlike my school friends, who took a weird pleasure in the fights—and more and more so as I got better.)

But Mum had a bad habit.

Instead of standing on the balcony overlooking the gymnasium where the martial arts grading and fights took place, she would lie down on the ground—among everyone else vying to get a good view.

Now don't ask me why. She will say it is because she couldn't bear to watch me get hurt. But I could never figure out why she just couldn't stay outside if that was her reasoning.

I have, though, learned that there is never much logic to my wonderful mother, but at heart there is great love and concern, and that has always shone through with Mum.

Anyway, it was the big day. I had performed all the routines and *katas* and it was now time for the *kumite,* or fighting part of the black-belt grading.

The European grandmaster Sensei Enoeda had come down to adjudicate. I was both excited and terrified—again.

The fight started.

My opponent (a rugby ace from a nearby college), and I traded punches, blocks, and kicks, but there was no real breakthrough.

Suddenly I found myself being backed into a corner, and out of instinct (or desperation), I dropped low, spun around, and caught my opponent square round the head with a spinning back fist.

Down he went.

Now this was not good news for me.

It was bad form and showed a lack of control.

On top of that, you simply weren't meant to deck your opponent. The idea was to win with the use of semicontact strikes, delivered with speed and technique that hit but didn't injure your opponent.

So I winced, apologized, and then helped the guy up.

I then looked over to Sensei Enoeda, expecting a disapproving scowl, but instead was met with a look of delight. The sort of look that a kid gives when handed an unexpected present.

I guess that the fighter in him loved it, and on that note I passed and was given my black belt.

I had never felt so proud as I did finally wearing that belt after having crawled my way up the rungs of yellow, green, orange, purple, brown—you name it—colored belts.

I had done this on my own and the hard way; you can't buy your way to a black belt.

I remember being told by our instructor that martial arts is not about the belts, it is about the spirit; and I agree . . . but I still couldn't help sleeping with my black belt on that first night.

Oh, and the bullying stopped.

CHAPTER 20

By the end of my time at Eton I had become one of the youngest second dan black belts in the country, a rank one higher than black belt.

I had started training also in aikido, which I loved, as a more lock-and-throw martial art, in comparison to the more physical punches and kicks of karate. But as a teenager I thrived off that physical side of karate.

After school, and during my time in the army, I stopped training in karate every week, mainly on the grounds that I was always so tired by the time I got back from some army exercise. The prospect of another additional "beasting" session became a bridge too far for me to maintain at that level.

Instead I have kept up my martial arts ever since by practicing in either ninjutsu or aikido, as well as yoga, as often as I can. All of these are less physical than karate, but feel like more of a life journey to master as an art form. And on that journey I am still at the very beginning.

But it all began with the foghorn and those relentlessly physical Sunday-night training sessions.

The only other karate story worth telling from school days is my dubious claim to fame of kicking a mass murderer in the balls.

The Crown Prince Dipendra of Nepal was a pupil at Eton at the same time as me, and he also loved his karate. We would often train together, and he became a good friend in many ways, despite being quite an unusual character at times.

Fighting with him did, though, require a degree of respect, as he was, after all, royalty and a semideity in his home country.

Having said that, he was also pretty wild, and was not only older and stronger than me, but also a terrifying fighter, with his deep black moustache and ponytail. So I felt quite free to give it my all.

On one occasion, a hard front kick from me aimed at his stomach ended up ricocheting off and planting itself firmly in his groin.

Ow.

All my apologies didn't help the fact that he couldn't walk properly for a week.

Some ten or so years later, back in his home country, he went completely insane and, in a fit of drug- and alcohol-induced rage, driven by some family dispute, he shot dead almost the entire royal family as they sat at dinner.

It was the Kingdom of Nepal's darkest hour.

CHAPTER 21

The karate gave me a great avenue to be able to push myself physically—and I thrived on the challenge.

I wanted more.

I started to run, but not normally. I would load up a backpack with weights and run at night for long distances, pouring with sweat. I pushed myself hard—sometimes until I vomited. I was exploring my limits, and I felt alive on that edge. I was never the fastest, the strongest, or the best at anything, but that only served to fire me.

I had a hunger to push myself, and I found out that I could dig very deep when I needed to. I don't really know where or how this hunger came about, but I had it. I call it "the fire."

Maybe it was trying to seek an identity in this big new world. Maybe it was frustration from my younger years. I don't really know; but I realized that I was beginning to be able to do stuff that no one else at school could do, and it felt good.

One of those things was climbing. Not just normal climbing. I developed a taste for climbing the highest school buildings and steeples at night.

And I loved it.

I would explore all the forbidden areas of the school and

grounds, and I knew I was faster and more agile than any of the security guards who patrolled the college.

I remember one night attempting an ascent of the school library dome, which stood about a hundred and twenty feet high on top of a huge classical library building.

The top dome was lead-lined and as smooth as marble, but with a classic line of weakness—the lightning conductor wire running up the dome's side.

The legendary explorer Sir Ranulph Fiennes, as a pupil at Eton, had wrestled with the problem of scaling this dome as well, and had finally conquered it by improvising a stepladder made with many small carpentry clamps he had "borrowed" from the school's woodwork shed.

I knew it would be possible to do it without such climbing aids if only the lightning conductor held my weight.

The night of the first ascent was clear, and the sky bright with stars, and I moved nimbly from garden to garden, over walls, down passageways, and across tree limbs to reach the rear foot of the building. I had one accomplice with me, my good friend Al.

A series of rooftops, then drainpipes, put us within fifteen feet of the library roof, at which point the dome started. But to get onto the roof itself, some sixty feet up, involved first climbing an overhanging, classical-looking narrow ledge.

Standing, balanced precariously on the narrow top of a drain-pipe, you had to give a good leap up to grab hold of the narrow ledge, and then swing your whole body up and over.

It took some guts, and a cool head for heights.

Get it wrong and the fall was a long one, onto concrete.

In an attempt to make it harder, the school security officers had put barbed wire all around the lip of the roof to ensure such climbs were "impossible." (This was probably installed after Ran Fiennes's escapades onto the dome all those years earlier.) But in actual fact the barbed wire served to help me as a climber. It gave me something else to hold on to.

Once on the roof, then came the crux of the climb.

Locating the base of the lightning conductor was the easy bit, the tough bit was then committing to it.

It held my weight; and it was a great sense of achievement clambering into the lead-lined small bell tower, silhouetted under the moonlight, and carving the initials BG alongside the RF of Ran Fiennes.

Small moments like that gave me an identity.

I wasn't just yet another schoolboy, I was fully alive, fully me, using my skills to the max.

And in those moments I realized I simply loved adventure.

I guess I was discovering that what I was good at was a little off-the-wall, but at the same time recognizing a feeling in the pit of my stomach that said: *Way to go, Bear, way to go.*

My accomplice never made it past the barbed wire, but waited patiently for me at the bottom. He said it had been a thoroughly sickening experience to watch, which in my mind made it even more fun.

On the return journey, we safely crossed one college house garden and had silently traversed half of the next one.

We were squatting behind a bush in the middle of this housemaster's lawn, waiting to do the final leg across. The tutor's light was on, with him burning the midnight oil marking papers probably, when he decided it was time to let his dog out for a pee. The dog smelled us instantly, went bananas, and the tutor started running toward the commotion.

Decision time.

"Run," I whispered, and we broke cover together and legged it toward the far side of the garden.

Unfortunately, the tutor in question also happened to be the school cross-country instructor, so he was no slouch.

He gave chase at once, sprinting after us across the fifty-meter dash. A ten-foot wall was the final obstacle and both of us, powered by adrenaline, leapt up it in one bound. The tutor was a runner but not a climber, and we narrowly avoided his grip and sprinted off into the night.

Up a final drainpipe, back into my open bedroom window, and it was mission accomplished.

I couldn't stop smiling all through the next day.

CHAPTER 22

I had gained another nickname at school (apart from "Bear," which I had had since I was a baby, courtesy of my sister Lara), and that was "Monkey."

Stan started that one, and I guess my love of climbing both buildings and trees was behind the name. Whether it was Bear or Monkey, I never minded, as I really didn't like my real name of Edward—it felt so stuffy and boring. Monkey or Bear was okay by me—and they have both stuck into adult life.

During my time at Eton, I led regular nighttime adventures, and word spread. I even thought about charging to take people on trips.

I remember one where we tried to cross the whole town of Eton in the old sewers. I had found an old grill under a bridge that led into these four-foot-high old brick pipes, running under the streets.

It took a little nerve to probe into these in the pitch black with no idea where the hell they were leading you; and they stank.

I took a pack of playing cards and a flashlight, and I would jam cards into the brickwork every ten paces to mark my way.

Eventually I found a manhole cover that lifted up, and it brought us out in the little lane right outside the headmaster's private house.

I loved that. "All crap flows from here," I remember us joking at that time.

But I also sought to pursue some more legal climbing adventures, and along with Mick Crosthwaite, my future Everest climbing buddy, we helped resurrect the school's mountaineering club.

Eton's great strength is that it does encourage interests—however wacky. From stamp collecting to a cheese-and-wine club, mountaineering to juggling, if the will is there then the school will help you.

Eton was only ever intolerant of two things: laziness and a lack of enthusiasm. As long as you got "into something," then most other misdemeanors were forgivable. I liked that: it didn't only celebrate the cool and sporty, but encouraged the individual, which, in the game of life, matters much more.

Hence Eton helped me to go for the Potential Royal Marines Officer Selection Course, age only sixteen. This was a pretty grueling three-day course of endless runs, marches, mud yomps, assault courses, high-wire confidence tests (I'm good at those!), and leadership tasks.

At the end I narrowly passed as one of only three out of twenty-five, with the report saying: "Approved for Officer Selection: Grylls is fit, enthusiastic, but needs to watch out that he isn't too happy-go-lucky." (Fortunately for my future life, I discarded the last part of that advice.)

But passing this course gave me great confidence that if I wanted to, after school, I could at least follow my father into the commandos.

⚜

I was also really fortunate at Eton to have had a fantastic house-master, and so much of people's experience of Eton rests on whether they had a housemaster who rocked or bombed.

I got lucky.

The relationship with your housemaster is the equivalent to that with a headmaster at a smaller school. He is the one who supervises all you do, from games to your choice of General Certificate of Secondary Education (GCSE), and without doubt he is the teacher who gets to know you the best—the good and the bad.

In short, they are the person who runs the show.

Mr. Quibell was old-school and a real character—but two traits made him great: he was fair and he cared. And as a teenager those two qualities really matter to one's self-esteem.

But, boy, did he also get grief from us.

Mr. Quibell disliked two things: pizzas and the town of Slough.

Often, as a practical joke, we would order a load of Slough's finest pizzas to be delivered to his private door; but never just one or two pizzas—I am talking thirty of them.

As the delivery guy turned up we would all be hidden, peeping out of the windows, watching the look of both horror, then anger, as Mr. Quibell would send the poor delivery man packing, with firm instructions never to return.

The joke worked twice, but soon the pizza company got savvy.

One of the optional subjects that we could study at Eton was motor mechanics, roughly translated as "find an old banger, pimp it up, remove the exhaust, and rag it around the fields until it dies."

Perfect.

I found an exhausted-looking, old brown Ford Cortina station wagon that I bought for thirty pounds, and, with some friends, we geared it up big-time.

As we were only sixteen we weren't allowed to take it on the road, but I reckoned with my seventeenth birthday looming that it would be perfect as my first, road-legal car. The only problem was that I needed to have it pass inspection, and to do that I had to get it to a garage. This involved having an adult drive with me.

I persuaded Mr. Quibell that there was no better way that he could possibly spend a Saturday afternoon than drive me to a repair garage (in his beloved Slough). I had managed to take a lucky diving catch for the house cricket team the day before, so was in Mr. Quibell's good books—and he relented.

As soon as we got to the outskirts of Slough, though, the engine started to smoke—big-time. Soon, Mr. Quibell had to have the windshield wipers on full power, acting as a fan just to clear the smoke that was pouring out of the hood.

By the time we made it to the garage the engine was red-hot and it came as no surprise that my car failed its inspection—on more counts than any car the garage had seen for a long time, they told me.

It was back to the drawing board, but it was a great example of what a good father figure Mr. Quibell was to all those in his charge—especially to those boys who really tried, in whatever field it was. And I have always been, above all, a trier.

I haven't always succeeded, and I haven't always had the most talent, but I have always given of myself with great enthusiasm—and that counts for a lot. In fact my dad had always told me that if I could be the most enthusiastic person I knew then I would do well.

I never forgot that. And he was right.

I mean, who doesn't like to work with enthusiastic folk?

CHAPTER 23

Two final stories from my school days:

The first involves my first-ever mountaineering expedition, done in winter to Mount Snowdon, the highest peak in Wales, and the second is winning my first girlfriend. (Well, when I say girlfriend, I mean I kissed her more than once and we were together almost a week.)

But first the Snowdon mission.

As the planned expedition was in wintertime, Watty, one of my best school buddies, and I had two months to get excited and pack for it. When the trip finally came around our backpacks were so heavy that we could hardly lift them.

Lesson one: Pack light unless you want to hump the weight around the mountains all day and night.

By the time we reached Snowdonia National Park on Friday night it was dark, and with one young teacher as our escort, we all headed up into the mist. And in true Welsh fashion, it soon started to rain.

When we reached where we were going to camp, by the edge of a small lake halfway up, it was past midnight and raining hard. We were all tired (from dragging the ridiculously overweight packs), and we put up the tents as quickly as we could. They were the old-style A-frame pegged tents, not known for their robustness in a Welsh winter gale, and sure enough by 3:00 A.M. the inevitable happened.

Pop.

One of the A-frame pegs supporting the apex of my tent broke, and half the tent sagged down onto us.

Hmm, I thought.

But both Watty and I were just too tired to get out and repair the first break, and instead we blindly hoped it would somehow just sort itself out.

Lesson two: Tents don't repair themselves, however tired you are, however much you wish they just would.

Inevitably, the next peg broke, and before we knew it we were lying in a wet puddle of canvas, drenched to the skin, shivering, and truly miserable.

The final key lesson learned that night was that when it comes to camping, a stitch in time saves nine; and time spent preparing a good camp is never wasted.

The next day, we reached the top of Snowdon, wet, cold but exhilarated. My best memory was of lighting a pipe that I had borrowed off my grandfather, and smoking it with Watty, in a gale, behind the summit cairn, with the teacher joining in as well.

It is part of what I learned from a young age to love about the mountains: They are great levelers.

For me to be able to smoke a pipe with a teacher was priceless in my book, and was a firm indicator that mountains, and the bonds you create with people in the wild, are great things to seek in life.

(Even better was the fact that the tobacco was homemade by Watty, and soaked in apple juice for aroma. This same apple juice was later brewed into cider by us, and it subsequently sent

Chipper, one of the guys in our house, blind for twenty-four hours. Oops.)

If people ask me today what I love about climbing mountains, the real answer isn't adrenaline or personal achievement. Mountains are all about experiencing a shared bond that is hard to find in normal life. I love the fact that mountains make everyone's clothes and hair go messy; I love the fact that they demand that you give of yourself, that they make you fight and struggle. They also induce people to loosen up, to belly laugh at silly things, and to be able to sit and be content staring at a sunset or a log fire.

That sort of camaraderie creates wonderful bonds between people, and where there are bonds I have found that there is almost always strength.

Anyway, now for the second story: and to the subject of girls.

Or lack of them.

CHAPTER 24

Eton, for all its virtues, seriously lacked girls. (Well, apart from the kitchen girls who we camped out on the roof waiting for night after night.)

But beyond that, and the occasional foxy daughter of a teacher, it was a desert. (Talking of foxy daughters, I did desperately fancy the beautiful Lela, who was the daughter of the clarinet teacher. But she ended up marrying one of my best friends from Eton, Tom Amies—and everyone was very envious. Great couple. Anyway, we digress.)

As I said, apart from that . . . it was a desert.

All of us wrote to random girls whom we vaguely knew or had maybe met once, but if we were honest, it was all in never-never land.

I did meet one quite nice girl who I discovered went to school relatively nearby to Eton. (Well, about thirty miles nearby, that is.)

I borrowed a friend's very old, single-geared, rusty bicycle and headed off one Sunday afternoon to meet this girl. It took me hours and hours to find the school, and the bike became steadily more and more of an epic to ride, not only in terms of steering but also just to pedal, as the rusty cogs creaked and ground.

But finally I reached the school gates, pouring with sweat.

It was a convent school, I found out, run entirely by nuns.

Well, at least they should be quite mild-natured and easy to give the slip to, I thought.

That was my first mistake.

I met the girl as prearranged, and we wandered off down a pretty, country path through the local woods. I was just summoning up the courage to make a move when I heard this whistle, followed by this shriek, from somewhere behind us.

I turned to see a nun with an Alsatian, running toward us, shouting.

The young girl gave me a look of terror and pleaded with me to run for my life—which I duly did. I managed to escape and had another monster cycle ride back to school, thinking: *Flipping Nora, this girl business is proving harder work than I first imagined.*

But I persevered.

One good way of meeting girls was to join Eton's Strawberry Cricket Club, which was a school team for people who were meant to be half-decent at cricket but who didn't want to take it very seriously.

Instead of playing other schools, it was designed to play local clubs. This mainly consisted of pub teams and their female supporters, and the concept was brilliant fun, made even better by the fact that we had bright pink sweaters and it was all considered a bit of a joke.

It was just my sort of team, and I signed up at once.

One custom that we had was that the first person on the team to go into bat had to drink a certain quantity of liquor that the team had begged, borrowed, or stolen en route to the venue beforehand.

On this particular match I was in first; a supersized can of cider was produced from the depths of someone's cricket bag. I drank it down, walked in to bat, took my crease, and steadied myself.

The first ball of the day came thundering down and I took a

giant swipe at it, belted it for miles. *Brilliant,* I thought. *Now let's do that again.*

The second ball came, and attempting another monster shot, I missed it completely, spun around, fell over and landed on my stumps. Out!

As I returned to the pavilion, I noticed, sitting on the sideline, a beautiful girl in a flowing summer dress sipping a can of Coke and smiling at me. If my legs weren't like jelly from the cider, they definitely were now.

We got chatting, and I discovered that she was called Tatiana, and that her brother was playing for the opposition. She had also found my batting saga quite amusing.

To top it all, she was age twenty—two years older than me—and didn't go to a convent school, but to a German university.

Now, there was a weekend out of school coming up the next day, and I had planned to head down home to the Isle of Wight with about ten school friends, all together. I boldly asked Tatiana if she might like to join us. (I was buzzing on adrenaline and cider, and couldn't believe I had actually dared to invite her out.)

She accepted and, before I knew what was happening, we were at home in the Isle of Wight, my parents away, and with all my friends and this beautiful girl—who for some unknown reason couldn't get enough of me.

This was indeed very new territory.

We had an amazing weekend, and I got to kiss Tatiana nonstop for thirty-six hours, and she even shared my bed for two whole nights.

Unbelievable.

Sadly she then returned to university in Germany, and that was the end of that. I guess she just moved on.

But the truth is that such good fortune didn't come around very often at an all-boys school. When it did, you had to thank your lucky stars.

Top: Granny Patsie at her beloved Portavo Point, in Northern Ireland.
Bottom: Dad *(back row, fourth from right)* at the Royal Marines Commando Training Centre, Lympstone.

Left: Family portrait, at home together in London. Guess who the good-looking baby is . . .

Below left: Granny and me, age seven (about the only time I've ever worn a bow tie!).

Right: Dad and me in the mountains together.

Below right: On holiday in France—that cheeky grin beginning to shine through.

Above: Age ten, at home on the Isle of Wight and ready for adventure.

Right: Me, Dad, and my sister, Lara, in the garden on the Isle of Wight.

Below left: My first school portrait, age seven.

Below right: Lara, age eighteen—always beautiful.

Right: Mick Crosthwaite and me getting ready for a sailing expedition on the island, both age eleven.

Below right: Winning the shield for the best karate student, age sixteen, before leaving for Japan.

Left: House cricket team at Eton, age seventeen. I'm second from left in the front row.

Below left: Charlie Mackesy and me, age eighteen, messing around as always.

Right: Having just passed SAS (R) Selection, doing our parachute training.

Below: Me and soldiers from my SAS (R) squadron in the North African desert.

Above: Gritting it out in bad weather in the mountains—one of the great loves of my life.

Left: Mick and me at Everest base camp before the climb.

CHAPTER 25

Girls aside, the other thing I found in the last few years of being at school was a quiet but strong Christian faith—and this touched me profoundly, setting up a relationship, or faith, that has followed me ever since.

I am so grateful for this. It has provided me with a real anchor to my life and has been the secret strength to so many great adventures since.

But it came to me very simply one day at school, age only sixteen.

As a young kid, I had always found that a faith in God was so natural. It was a simple comfort to me: unquestioning and personal.

But once I went to school and was forced to sit through somewhere in the region of nine hundred dry, Latin-liturgical chapel services, listening to stereotypical churchy people droning on, I just thought that I had got the whole faith deal wrong.

Maybe God wasn't intimate and personal but was much more like chapel was . . . tedious, judgmental, boring, and irrelevant.

The irony was that if chapel was all of those things, a real faith is the opposite. But somehow, and without much thought, I had thrown the beautiful out with the boring. If church stinks, then faith must do, too.

The precious, natural, instinctive faith I had known when I was younger was tossed out with this newly found delusion that because I was growing up, it was time to "believe" like a grown-up.

I mean, what does a child know about faith?

It took a low point at school, when my godfather, Stephen, died, to shake me into searching a bit harder to refind this faith I had once known.

Life is like that. Sometimes it takes a jolt to make us sit and remember who and what we are really about.

Stephen had been my father's best friend in the world. And he was like a second father to me. He came on all our family holidays, and spent almost every weekend down with us in the Isle of Wight in the summer, sailing with Dad and me. He died very suddenly and without warning, of a heart attack in Johannesburg.

I was devastated.

I remember sitting up in a tree one night at school on my own, and praying the simplest, most heartfelt prayer of my life.

"Please, God, comfort *me*."

Blow me down . . . He did.

My journey ever since has been trying to make sure I don't let life or vicars or church overcomplicate that simple faith I had found. And the more of the Christian faith I discover, the more I realize that, at heart, it is simple. (What a relief it has been in later life to find that there are some great church communities out there, with honest, loving friendships that help me with all of this stuff.)

To me, my Christian faith is all about being held, comforted, forgiven, strengthened, and loved—yet somehow that message gets lost on most of us, and we tend only to remember the religious nutters or the God of endless school assemblies.

This is no one's fault, it is just life. Our job is to stay open and gentle, so we can hear the knocking on the door of our heart when it comes.

The irony is that I never meet anyone who doesn't want to be loved or held or forgiven. Yet I meet a lot of folk who hate religion. And I so sympathize. But so did Jesus. In fact, He didn't just sympathize, He went much further. It seems more like this Jesus came to destroy religion and to bring life.

This really is the heart of what I found as a young teenager: Christ comes to make us free, to bring us life in all its fullness. He is there to forgive us where we have messed up (and who hasn't?), and to be the backbone in our being.

Faith in Christ has been the great empowering presence in my life, helping me walk strong when so often I feel so weak. It is no wonder I felt I had stumbled onto something remarkable that night up that tree.

I had found a calling for my life.

I do owe so much of my faith to a few best friends at school who, especially in the early days, nurtured that faith in me. They helped me, guided me, and have stood beside me ever since as my buddies: the great Stan, Ed, and Tom.

As for my other great buddies at school, like Mick, Al, Watty, Hugo, and Sam, they simply considered this newfound Christian faith of mine was a monumental waste when it came to getting girls!

Talking of getting girls, in case you were wondering, it was because of my faith that I only kissed that beauty of a German girl I met, and didn't end up making love. (Although, I must admit, it took all my strength at the time to resist that one!)

Despite all my friends thinking I was utterly mad, deep down I felt a determination to try to keep my virginity for my wife one day.

But that really is another story.

CHAPTER 26

So that was Eton for me, and I look back now with a great sense of gratitude: gratitude that I got to have such a great education, and gratitude that my father had worked so damned hard so as to be able to afford to send me there.

I never really thanked him as I should have—but I just hope somehow he knows how grateful I am for all he gave me.

Eton did, though, teach me a few key lessons: it showed me the value of a few close friends, and how those friendships really matter as we walk through our days. It also taught me to understand that life is what you make of it. And with that there comes responsibility.

No one will do it all for you. That is left to each of us: to go out, to grab life, and to make it our own.

⚜

My time at Eton did develop in me a character trait that is essentially, I guess, very English: the notion that it is best to be the sort of person who messes about and plays the fool but who, when it really matters, is tough to the core.

I think it goes back to the English Scarlet Pimpernel mentality:

the nobility of aspiring to be the hidden hero. (In fact, I am sure it is no coincidence that over the years, so many senior SAS officers have also been Old Etonians. Now explain that one, when the SAS really is the ultimate meritocracy? No school tie can earn you a place there. That comes only with sweat and hard work. But the SAS also attracts a certain personality and attitude. It favors the individual, the maverick, and the quietly talented. That was Eton for you, too.)

This is essentially a very English ethos: work hard, play hard; be modest; do your job to your utmost, laugh at yourself; and sometimes, if you have to, cuff it.

I found that these qualities were ones that I loved in others, and they were qualities that subconsciously I was aspiring to in myself—whether I knew it or not.

One truth never changed for me at Eton: however much I threw myself into life there, the bare fact was that I still really lived for the holidays—to be back at home with my mum and dad, and Lara, in the Isle of Wight.

It was always where my heart really was.

⚜

As I got older, the scope of my world increased.

My mum helped me buy a secondhand moped (in fact it was more like eighthhand, thinking about it), and was also an "elderly person's" model—and in purple. But it was a set of wheels, despite only being 50 cc.

I rode it everywhere: around our little village to see friends and into town to go to the gym. (I had found a gritty weightlifters' gym that I loved going to as often as I could.) I rode the moped on the beach at night, and I ragged it up the dirt tracks (as much as one can rag an elderly person's purple moped).

I felt free.

Mum was always so generous to Lara and me growing up, and it helped me develop a very healthy attitude to money. You could never accuse my mum of being tight: she was free, fun, mad, and endlessly giving everything away—always. Sometimes that last part became a bit annoying (such as if it was some belonging of ours that Mum had decided someone else would benefit more from), but more often than not we were on the receiving end of her generosity, and that was a great spirit to grow up around.

Mum's generosity ensured that as adults we never became too attached to, or attracted by money.

I learned from her that before you can get, you have to give, and that money is like a river—if you try to block it up and dam it (that is, cling to it), then, like a dammed river, the water will go stagnant and stale, and your life will fester. If you keep the stream moving and keep giving stuff and money away, wherever you can, then the river and the rewards will keep flowing in.

I love the quote she once gave me: "When supply seems to have dried up, look around you quickly for something to give away." It is a law of the universe: to get good things you must first give away good things. (And of course this applies to love and friendship, as well.)

Mum was also very tolerant of my unusual aspirations. When I found a ninjutsu school through a magazine, I was determined to go and seek it out and train there. The problem was that it was at the far end of the island in some pretty rough council estate hall. This was before the moped, so poor Mum drove me every week . . . and would wait for me. I probably never even really thanked her.

So, thank you, Mum . . . for all those times and so much more.

By the way, the ninjutsu has come in real handy at times.

CHAPTER 27

One of the many great things about growing up on the Isle of Wight was that during the wintertime the community was quiet: the weather was blowy and the sea was wild.

I loved that—it gave me time to climb, train, and do all the outdoorsy stuff I had started to need so badly.

Then in summertime, it would go crazy, with families from London and beyond coming down and renting cottages for the holidays. Suddenly the place would be teeming with kids my age with whom to mess about, sail, and hang out. I loved it then even more.

I would arrange with friends to sneak out after dark and meet on the beach for barbecues, fires, and to drink as much illegally bought alcohol as could be found. (At fifteen, this was more often than not a big bottle of cider "borrowed" from one of our parents, in the hope that they wouldn't notice it was missing.)

We would sit on the beach, swig from the bottle, throw stones into the sea, and stoke up a big fire. I loved these times so much.

Mick Crosthwaite was one of my closest friends down on the island during these summers, and he was also at Eton with me. We eventually went on to join the military, climb Everest, and cross the North Atlantic Arctic Ocean together. But really the friendship started on the beach.

Sneaking out of home was relatively easy. A sloping roof from my bedroom window led to a drainpipe, and from there it was a simple twelve-foot slither down onto the lawn.

A breeze compared with school.

Mum and Dad would come and say good night, they would leave, switch the light out, close the door, and I would be gone.

Life on the beach at night was great. I had my first real teenage kiss with a girl I really liked, on a bench overlooking the sea—and the world was all good.

If we weren't on the beach we would be in one of each other's houses. (It had to be someone's house whose parents were more liberal than mine and didn't mind a load of kids watching films until 4:00 A.M. upstairs. My folks, kind of rightly, would never have allowed that.)

I remember, one week, we all started playing strip poker.

This is more like it, I thought.

It wasn't really even poker, but was more like: pick an ace and lose an item of clothing. I tried one night to rig the cards so that I could end up naked with Stephie, this girl I really fancied.

I carefully counted out the cards and the aces, and rather unsubtly made sure I was sitting next to her, when we started playing. Annoyingly, she then swapped places when someone else came to join us and I ended naked next to Mick, embarrassed and self-conscious. (That will teach me to cheat.)

Most of the time my attempts to get a girl fell pretty flat.

In fact, whenever I really liked a girl I would always end up losing her to someone else, mainly because I found it so hard to make my feelings known and to pluck up the courage just to ask her out.

I remember a friend coming down to the island to stay at the end of one summer, and within twenty-four hours he was in bed with the girl I had been chasing all holidays!

I couldn't believe it. What the hell did he have that I didn't?

I noticed that he wore these brown suede cowboy boots, so I went out and bought a secondhand pair, but I just looked stupid in them. To make matters worse, this friend then went on to describe to me in great detail what they had got up to in that bed.

Aarrgh.

It kind of summed up my attempts at womanizing.

CHAPTER 28

One of the very strong memories for me, from growing up on the island, was reading my school reports and opening my exam results.

I would always grab the official letter before anyone could open it "accidentally" before me, and I would sprint down the end of our garden where there was this gorgeous big sycamore tree.

It had amazing limbs, perfectly spaced for monkey-style climbing. Over the years, I had got it down to a fine art, being able to reach the highest limbs of this tree in a matter of seconds, and from there I would have a commanding view over the whole village.

None of my friends ever went to the very top of this tree with me as it always began to sway and wobble precariously as you reached the very last few branches.

But I loved that part.

Opening the reports or exam results up here meant that whatever the outcome, I had time and space to keep things in perspective.

Okay, so I flunked another maths exam and the Latin teacher says I must stop "sniggering like a puppy in class," but from up here, the world looks pretty all right.

By the time I came down I would be ready to face the music.

I never had anything to fear, though, from Mum and Dad when it came to school reports. The reports weren't ever all bad, but they definitely weren't ever all good. But Mum and Dad just loved me, regardless, and that has helped me so much in my life: to have the confidence to just be myself and to go for things.

I have never minded risking failure, because I was never punished for failing.

Life was about the journey—and the fun and adventure along the way. It was never just about the destination, such as getting perfect exam results or making the top team. (Dad had always been pretty hopeless at sports and academia, yet he had done well and was greatly loved—so that was good enough for me.)

He would always say that what really matters in life is to "Follow your dreams and to look after your friends and family along the way." That was life in a nutshell for him, and I so hope to pass that on to my boys as they grow up.

On that note, I would slip the school reports in the bin and get a big hug.

⚜

The other final memory from growing up on the island is of going on a monster run one day, and getting very bad groin rub on the last mile toward home.

I had endured the rubbing for the previous eight miles, but it was now becoming agony. No one was around, the village was deserted, it was a warm summer's evening, so I took my shorts off and continued the final leg of the run naked.

No sooner had I run a hundred meters than I heard a police siren right behind me.

I could not believe it.

I mean, in all my life growing up on the island, I had never even seen a police car. There was a station in the village, but it always just sat empty, acting only as a staging post if ever needed—and it certainly didn't have its own police car. The nearest permanent station was thirty minutes away.

This was bad luck in the extreme.

The car pulled me over, and the officer told me to get in the back: "Sharpish!"

I jumped in, tried to explain, but was told to be quiet. I was nicked.

I did eventually make it home after doing some serious explaining that I was not a streaker or a pervert. I even showed them my blood-red groin rub as proof.

Finally, they let me off with a caution.

So there you have it: I had been arrested for nudity, flunked my exams, and failed at getting a girlfriend—but I had a hunger for adventure and the love of a great family in my soul.

I was as ready as I could ever be for my entrance into the big bad world.

CHAPTER 29

My first summer after leaving school I realized that my priority, if I were to get to travel and adventure and see something of the world, was to earn some money.

I had always been encouraged to be an entrepreneur from when I was very young, whether it was getting paid to do a paper route in the Isle of Wight or trying to sell home-brewed cider made from apple juice at school. (Great recipe—thanks, Watty.)

So I set out to make a buck . . . selling my mother's water filters door to door. It was hard, thankless work, but I found that a sufficient number of my parents' friends were encouraging enough at least to give me half an hour of their time, to demonstrate the benefits of nonchlorinated water.

Ill-fitting tap attachments that squirted water over many an immaculate kitchen cost me a considerable amount of my profits, but I persevered, and over a summer I managed to earn enough money to get a ticket to go InterRailing around Europe.

I slept on trains and explored many of the European cities. But I soon got quite depressed by the traffic and noise of one city after another.

In Berlin, not wanting to carry my heavy backpack into the city center after dark, I had hidden my belongings behind a row of dustbins, while I went for an explore. Upon returning, I found a tramp huddled over in the dark, rifling through my bags.

I shouted at him and ran toward both my pack and him.

At this point he pulled out the diving knife that I had in my bag and started brandishing it at me wildly. Luckily he was far too drunk to be able to use the knife, and I managed to disarm him and recover it in one relatively tidy move. But the fear and adrenaline of the situation then hit me, and I grabbed my pack and just ran.

That was the final straw for me. I had had it with gray, northern European cities, and sleeping on train station platforms.

I reckoned it was time to hit the beach.

I asked around for where the best beach resort in Europe was, accessible by train, and the name St. Tropez kept coming up.

Perfect.

St. Tropez is a small French town, renowned as the beach hangout for the rich and famous, on the southern coast of France. At this stage I was definitely not rich (in fact I was getting poorer by the day now), and was definitely not famous; but undeterred, I headed south—and instantly felt better.

As I pulled into town, the gray of Berlin felt a million miles away. My funds, though, were by now running severely low, and I soon discovered that St. Tropez was not the place to find cheap lodgings. But I was determined that this was the place to hang out for the last week, until I headed home again.

I found a quiet back street, running behind the town's church bell tower.

I glanced up.

A solid-looking drainpipe ran up to the first level of roofing, and from there a lightning conductor ran straight up the vertical wall to the bell tower itself.

How I love lightning conductors.

I checked that no one was watching, then steadily shimmied up the drainpipe and the lightning conductor, before wriggling over into the bell tower itself, some hundred feet up—high above the town.

It was the perfect campsite. I had a spectacular view over the coastline, and could watch and listen to the hustle and bustle of the seaside restaurants below. There was just about enough room to lie down, and I carefully unpacked and made the eight foot by eight foot concrete space my new home.

The two flaws in my plan were, first of all, the many pigeons that had also made the bell tower their dwelling, and, second, the bell that rang every hour, two inches from my head. The former I just had to live with (in fact, I thought at least I could find dinner easily, in the form of a pigeon, if my money completely ran out), but the latter, the tolling of the bells, became unbearable.

At 3:00 A.M. on the first night, with the help of my flashlight, I found the fuse box for the automatic bell and put a temporary end to the town's clock, and from then on slept like a baby.

By day, I swam for hours around the beautiful bays and along the beaches, and I then wandered aimlessly through the small streets and drank tea in cafés.

It was heaven.

But soon my funds really did run out, and I kind of knew that it was time to head back to the UK.

⚜

I had promised I would first join my good friend Stan on a road trip to Romania to help a small church build an orphanage there. Romania was a firmly Eastern European country at that stage, and poverty was both widespread and visible.

The mission was life-changing for me in many ways, and was such an eye-opener to how fortunate we are in the UK.

We were welcomed as brothers into the homes of members of the church and by day we helped physically build the orphanage. We laid bricks and shifted sand, and in the evenings we helped with local outreach events to support the small church. This was mainly geared at helping and welcoming in the local gypsies, who were treated as outcasts by most of the resident population.

I learned during this trip that I had no right ever to grumble at my own circumstances and that I should always try to be grateful and hospitable wherever I can. Above all, I will always remember the kindness and warmth I was shown from those who had so little.

I have since witnessed so much of this generosity and kindness from people all over the world, and it never fails to bring me up short.

It tends to shine a light on my own all too often self-inflated ego.

Guilty as charged.

CHAPTER 30

One of my closest friends in my life is someone I met age sixteen, and we just kind of always got on.

Charlie Mackesy is a good few years older than me but you would never have known it from the antics we got up to.

During this first year after school, when I rented a small room in my sister's flat, Charlie and I hung out a lot together in London.

We endlessly messed about, hanging upside down at the local parks' monkey bars, making giant bacon, avocado, and tomato sandwiches, and devouring Ribena juice cartons by the multitude—in an effort to win the £5,000 prize you got if you happened to drink the carton that contained the magic "Harry the Lime" toy inside.

And that has kind of been our friendship ever since.

He is godfather to my first son, Jesse, and he was the best man at Shara's and my wedding. (I am still waiting to be his—come on girls, get with the program—he is a serious catch!)

Charlie helped me, at a very formative age, to understand that there are no prizes for taking either yourself or life too seriously, and that life should be lived freely. Charlie was the first buddy I had met who really lived the way I enjoyed. He also wore messy clothes, slept outside a lot, laughed at ridiculous things, and hung upside down in trees.

Not much has changed really, over the years—we both have maybe a few more gray hairs, and I hope we both behave marginally better, but through it all, our friendship has grown stronger as we have both been rolled and rocked by the boat of life.

Old friends are wonderful, aren't they? There is nothing to explain.

I recently asked Charlie to try and remember some of his favorite stories from that year after school we spent together. And they vary from the sublime to the very ridiculous.

Like the time we built our own circus trapeze swing in the garden, and I hung by my legs upside down, and then had the rope snap, dropping me down right on my head from quite some height. (Charlie said he heard the loud crack of vertebrae crumpling and was certain I was dead—but somehow I walked away from it.)

Then there was the day we both raided my sister Lara's very expensive Dead Sea mud pack, that she had bought several years earlier but had never been able to bring herself to use. We covered ourselves head to toe in this gloop and fell asleep on the grass, waking with a start when she came back, red with rage.

Charlie and I would find giant hedges in London parks and repeatedly leap into them from high branches of trees, using them as natural crash mats.

We dressed up in gorilla suits and sat on the rocks that overlooked a central London park café mainly frequented by the local old folk. Their faces were priceless.

I also remember managing successfully to push both Charlie's knees through the railings of that same lakeside café, and then leaving him there, to repay him for some other gag he had played on me. He tried everything to get free—from olive oil to being pulled and manipulated by passersby—and it was only as the café was calling the fire brigade that I relented and managed to pry him free.

Together we climbed across the giant River Thames by crossing under, rather than on top of, one of the big bridges. It was exciting climbing and brilliant fun—until Charlie's car and house keys fell out of his pocket into the river.

We even fell through the ice of a frozen lake together in Ireland, one New Year, barely making it out alive. The girls we were with soothed our wounds with hot drinks and warm blankets for hours afterward. And we milked their sympathy for days.

The list goes on and on, and I am proud to say it continues today. He is still one of my most lovely, loyal, and fun friends, and I am so grateful for that friendship.

Oh, and by the way, he is the most insanely talented artist on the planet, and makes an incredible living touching people's lives through art. I thought I should mention that.

⚜

Anyway, I had one more trip planned for my year out, and after that I decided that I should probably (reluctantly) go to university.

But first I needed some more money.

I tried being a barman but was fired for being scruffy, and then finally Ed, one of my old school friends, said why didn't I start some self-defense classes in London, and make them exclusive to girls?

It was an inspired idea.

I had some flyers printed and persuaded a few health clubs to allow me to run classes in their aerobics studios. I loved it from the very start. (Although, sadly, the clubs dissuaded me from making the classes exclusively for girls!)

Invariably I would get the occasional macho lad who would turn up determined to prove to everyone how tough they were. Luckily these types never lasted long, as I basically taught the ethos of minimal force, and the art of using an aggressor's force against himself. The machos soon got bored of this passivity.

On the whole the folk who signed up were committed, well-meaning people who just wanted to learn how to defend themselves if they were ever in a tough spot.

Soon the number of clubs I taught at was growing, and I was beginning to earn some half-decent money. But it had always been a means to an end—the end being to travel.

It was time to move on.

I felt a bit guilty when I stopped teaching the classes, as the regulars were so much fun, but I made sure I handed the clubs on to other good instructors I knew.

I had loved the camaraderie of it all, but I had bigger dreams that I wanted to follow.

CHAPTER 31

I soon had enough money saved to take my old school friend Watty up on his offer of traveling through northern India together, hiking and exploring.

His family knew a retired Indian Army officer who wanted to start a trekking company for young school leavers; and we were to be his English guinea pigs, upon whom he could test various different treks and adventures.

It was a dream opportunity.

We spent a month hiking through the Indian Himalayas, around Darjeeling and beyond. We traveled on the roofs of trains, slept on wooden beds in remote mountain villages, and rode the white waters down mountain rivers.

We also got to explore the spectacular regions of western Bengal and northern Sikkim, both of which were then restricted zones for tourists due to the border disputes with Pakistan, but for which the Indian Army officer had arranged special permits.

We visited the Himalayan Mountaineering Institute, outside of Darjeeling, where they ran a winter mountaineering school run by Indian Himalayan guides, and I was hooked. The place was like a shrine to the great mountaineers, and the stories of death and adventure on the highest peaks on earth had me entranced.

Meanwhile, Watty had fallen in love with a local Indian girl, which proved a massive distraction to adventure, as far as I could see. He announced he was off to go and visit her family; but all I wanted to do was hike the mountains in the distant hope of getting to see Everest herself.

When I rose early one freezing cold mountain morning, woefully ill-equipped in terms of appropriate clothing, footwear, or sleeping bag, I finally got to watch the sun rise over Everest in the distance, looming like a giant across the horizon.

Now, like Watty, I too was in love.

On our return to lower altitudes, I bought a large, rolled-up, laminated poster of Everest (which was a bigger version of the one that my father had given me when I was a young boy, after one of our climbing forays), and I vowed to myself that one day I would risk it all and attempt to climb the biggest, highest mountain on earth.

The truth is that, at that stage of my life, I had no idea what such an expedition would really involve. I had minimal high-altitude experience and, according to all the books, I was far too young to make a serious high-altitude mountaineer.

But I had a dream, and that always makes people dangerous.

Dreams, though, are cheap, and the real task comes when you start putting in place the steps needed to make those dreams a reality. I had never been one for idle threats, and I made my Everest intentions clear to all who were close to me.

To a man, they thought I was mad.

⚜

Before leaving India I had one more ambition I longed to fulfill— I had always dreamt of meeting Mother Teresa.

I discovered that her mission of mercy headquarters was based in Calcutta, so we routed by train into the huge, terrifying, sprawling metropolis of one of the world's biggest cities. And that alone is an experience.

The station was a seething mass of hurrying, scurrying, hustling bodies; it was physically impossible to move faster than a slow shuffle, and you just got taken in whichever direction the crowd was moving. The noise, and the smell of feces and sweat, was overpowering. There were no other Westerners as far as I could see.

Little could have prepared me for what I saw on the squalid streets of Calcutta, beyond the main drag and city center. I had never seen people dying on a street in front of my eyes before. I had never seen legless, blind, ragged bodies lying in sewers, holding their arms out begging for a few rupees.

I felt overwhelmed, inadequate, powerless, and ashamed—all at once.

Watty and I finally found the small hospital and nunnery that was Mother Teresa's mission. Among a city of suffering, we had found a haven of love, cleanliness, calm, and care.

We returned there every day we were in Calcutta, we gave the remaining notes we had in rupees into her collection box, and I wrote Mother Teresa a folded, hand-written note to say how her work had moved me.

I just wanted to thank her and encourage her.

I never expected any reply.

Knock me down, if two months later I didn't get a personal letter from her saying thank you. I still have it to this day. Believe me when I say that all we gave were a few pounds in total.

Her response is called grace, and it amazed me.

Her being, and her whole way of life (even though we never even met her), was a living, breathing example of God's presence on this earth, and it changed how I saw both myself and the world around me very powerfully. I realized that I had been given privileges beyond those any person could ever hope for, and that we, in turn, have a duty of care toward the world and her people.

But I wasn't yet sure what this meant for me.

I just know that I left the squalor, dirt, and suffering of Calcutta with a sense that, in Mother Teresa's life, we had experienced a brush with God that was both beautiful and very real.

There is a simple Bible verse, Matthew 23:12, which says: "Whoever exalts himself will be humbled, and whoever humbles himself will be exalted." This speaks pretty strongly to how I feel about the whole fame issue, and it has colored so much of what I see in people nowadays.

The more I live, the more aware I become of the greatness of the everyday man (and I don't mean this in any sycophantic way). I witness tough people doing tough jobs every day, as we travel to the many extremes of the world, filming.

Maybe it's a lone worker digging a roadside ditch in the middle of the night in the pouring rain on a small jungle track in a remote part of China; or someone more "regular" (whatever that means), like a coffee vendor in some unsung town in middle America, just doing the daily grind.

Whichever extreme it is, I find myself admiring these people more and more. Unsung. Uncelebrated. Uncomplaining.

But we are getting ahead of ourselves. At this stage, I was still a young, wide-eyed pup with bleached-blond, ponytailed hair, freshly home from a hiking trip to India, with a determination to live life to the max.

CHAPTER 32

The vigor with which I wanted to get on and live life was countered by the slumberlike crawl I adopted to the prospect of returning to "higher education."

I had only scraped by on my final school exams, gaining the grades ACDC. (I did, though, love the fact that they spelled the name of a cool rock band.)

I also noted the irony of the fact that the only exam for which I had done literally no revision, and for which I had been told the key ingredient was common sense, I had gained an A grade in.

General Studies is a subject where the questions are like: "Describe how a sailing boat might be sailed backward." "Explain how trees might be shown to 'communicate.' " I was good at those, but bad at knuckling down to academic study.

Anyway, having only just escaped from years of academic learning, I had little motivation to apply to go to university. At the same time, though, I lacked the confidence to ditch the idea of university completely. *Oh, God, did I really have to go to uni?*

In a desperate bid for a fun alternative, I spent three days in the month leading up to the start of the university year sitting in the foyer of MI5, the British counterespionage service, asking to interview for a job.

I had initially written to MI5, and had received a succinct reply saying thank you for my letter, but there were no posts currently available for me. The letter was signed off by a Miss Deborah Maldives.

Now, I might have been born at night but it wasn't last night, and even I could tell that Miss Deborah Maldives was a fake name.

I made up my mind to go and offer myself in person.

In hindsight, I quite admire the balls that I showed to go to each of the many entrances of MI5 HQ in central London, over and over again, day after day, asking to speak directly to Miss Deborah Maldives.

Each time, I told the security guard that I had a meeting booked with her, and waited.

Each time I was politely told that no one of that name worked there and that my name certainly wasn't down for any meeting.

So, I would leave, and try the next entrance along.

Eventually, on the umpteenth attempt, I was told to my surprise, that Miss Deborah Maldives was coming down to see me.

I suddenly wasn't quite so sure what to do with myself, as I waited anxiously in MI5's marble foyer. *Oh, God, Bear. What have you done, you idiot?*

Finally a stocky-looking gentleman, who definitely didn't look like a Deborah Maldives, appeared at the other side of the revolving, security-controlled glass doors. He beckoned me forward and the door started to turn for me.

Moment of truth, I thought, and walked through.

Mrs. (or Mr.) Deborah Maldives sat me down in an interview room and told me that there were proper channels to apply for MI5, and sitting in each entrance's foyer, day after day, was not one of them.

He then smiled.

He admitted that I had shown the sort of spirit that was required for counterespionage work and suggested I reapply, direct to him, when I had a university degree. I took the card, shook his (her) hairy hand, and scarpered.

So there is some better motivation to go to university, after all, I thought.

Frantically, I applied late, in the vain hope that somewhere, anywhere, might accept me.

CHAPTER 33

The Royal Marines description of me as "happy-go-lucky" is good for many things, but somehow it doesn't wash with university applications.

And with my mediocre A level results I was getting a hefty number of rejections winging my way.

A lot of my good friends were heading to Bristol University. But I had as much chance of getting in there with my ACDC grades as Deborah Maldives had of winning a beauty pageant. Yet I really wanted to be with my buddies.

I finally persuaded the University of the West of England (UWE) (which was the less academic version of Bristol University) to offer me a place studying modern languages. (Incidentally, I had only pulled this off by going down there in person and begging the admissions lady for a place, face-to-face, after sitting outside her office all day. This was becoming a familiar pattern. Well, at least, I have always been persistent.)

I wasn't allowed to study purely Spanish, which I loved, so I had to do German and Spanish. My run-in with the beautiful German Tatiana had led me to believe that the German language might be as beautiful as her.

Boy, was I wrong.

The language is a pig to learn.

This became the first nail in the coffin of my university experience.

The up side was that me and my best friends, Eddie, Hugo, Trucker, Charlie, Jim, and Stan, all got to share a house together.

Now when I say house, I use the term loosely. It was actually an old disused hotel called the Brunel. Situated in the roughest, cheapest part of Bristol, where call girls and drug dealers cruised the streets, the Brunel soon developed somewhat of a legendary status among our circle of friends as an outpost, full of eccentric Old Etonians living in bohemian squalor.

I quite liked the reputation.

We would breakfast on the street, smoke pipes in our dressing gowns, and race each other up the steep hills, carrying books under our arms en route to lectures.

We had all sorts of strange visitors endlessly coming in and out uninvited, including several regular homeless guys off the street.

Neil was one such guy, and he loved coming round leading us on daytime raids of the industrial bins around the back of the local supermarket. We would sneak round in our car (as subtly as we could with an old, smoky Ford full of students crammed in the back). One of us would then leap out, diving headfirst into the compressor before throwing out great sides of salmon and bundles of out-of-date hot cross buns, to the eagerly awaiting arms below.

We also went a couple of times a week to help out in the soup kitchen at the homeless center down the road from us, and got to know ever-increasing numbers of colorful folk around us.

Sadly, Neil died soon after, of a drug overdose, and I suspect not many of those Brunel homeless characters are still alive today. But it was a formative time for us as friends living together and taking our first tentative steps in the outside world, away from school.

Highlights of the Brunel featured the likes of Mr. Iraci, our landlord, coming around and being greeted by myself, stark naked, painting cartoons on my bedroom wall to liven the place up a bit; or Eddie showing another pretty girl his technique for marinating venison in a washing-up bowl full of Bordeaux wine.

Our housekeeping kitty of funds would miraculously evaporate due to Hugo's endless dinner parties for just him and up to ten different girls that he had been chatting up all week.

Stan developed a nice technique for cooking sausages by leaving them on the grill until the hundred decibel smoke alarm went off, indicating they were ready. (On one occasion, Stan's sausage-cooking technique actually brought the fire brigade round, all suited and booted, hoses at the ready. They looked quite surprised to see all of us wandering down in our dressing gowns, asking if the sausages were ready, while they stood in the hall primed for action, smoke alarm still blaring. Happy days.)

I also fondly remember Mr. Iraci coming round another time, just after I had decided to build a homemade swimming pool in the ten-foot-by-ten-foot "garden" area out the back.

I had improvised a tarpaulin and a few kitchen chairs and had filled it optimistically with water. It held for about twenty minutes . . . in fact just about until Mr. Iraci showed up to collect his rent.

Then it burst its banks, filling most of the ground floor with three inches of water, and soaking Mr. Iraci in the process.

Truly the man was a saint.

CHAPTER 34

Trucker and I did quite a bit of busking together on our guitars, doing the rounds at various Bristol hot spots.

This included the local old people's home, where I remember innocently singing the lyrics to "American Pie." The song culminates with the spectacularly inappropriate claim that this would be the day that I'd die.

A long, awkward pause followed, as we both realized our predicament.

The home wasn't a long-standing gig after that.

We also played together with another friend of ours called Blunty, who went on to become a worldwide singing sensation after he left the army, under his real name of James Blunt. I am not sure Blunty will consider those jamming sessions as very formative for him, but they make for fun memories now all the same.

Good on him, though. He always had an amazingly cool singing voice.

During this first year at the Brunel, though, two key events happened.

The first was finding such a good buddy in Trucker. We had hit it off at once. We laughed together masses and found that we had so much in common: our faith, a thirst for adventure, and a love of the fun, quirky things and people in life.

Together, we signed up for the university OTC (Officer Training Corps), which was a marginally more professional outfit than the Army Cadets. It was, though, full of overserious military-minded students, hoping to join the real army after university.

To our great amusement, these students invariably overacted the military card, whereas we had just joined for a bit of fun and to meet foxy GI Janes. It was total pleasure pulling the well-pressed legs of all these military stiffs by intentionally wearing our berets like chef's hats and turning up late and in pink socks.

In turn, they looked down their raised noses at us as two incompetent jokers, wasters, and buffoons. Neither of us minded at all. It was all way too much fun!

It was something about guys of our age pretending to be something that they weren't that made playing the fool so totally irresistible. I suspect that my dad would have behaved the same. (Taking yourself too seriously, in whatever field, was always dangerous around him.)

During that OTC year, though, we did develop a marked respect for one of the genuine soldiers, a senior officer we met who had been in the SAS in his younger years. He walked with a quiet confidence, he laughed a lot, and never took himself too seriously.

Correspondingly, we never felt the urge to mess around when he was there. Instead, he inspired us to be more like him: to have done something difficult, real, and lasting. That is ultimately what good leadership does. It inspires us to reach higher.

So was quietly born in both Trucker and myself a quickening of the heart that said: *I wonder if one day we might ever attempt Selection for the SAS?*

And that was the second life-altering thing that happened—and it started off a ride that was to take me to the very edge.

Literally.

CHAPTER 35

Two things motivated me to join the Special Air Service Reserves.

One was the determination to achieve something special and lasting in my life. To find that pride that lasts a lifetime; to have endured, to have been tested—and to have prevailed.

It is a hard feeling to explain, but it was very real inside me.

The other motivator was less worthy.

It was to outclass all those OTC military-stiffs who had so looked down their noses at me. A totally flawed reason, I know! But I wanted to show them what I was actually capable of. To show them that real soldiering was about work, work, and work—not smart, smart, and smart.

Both these motivations may sound a bit warped, but if I'm honest they are probably accurate reasons why I initially wanted to attempt SAS(R) Selection.

Above all, it was about wanting to achieve something special, that so few people pull off.

The flip side was that the task did feel like an almost insurmountable challenge for me.

I knew that out of the many already toughened soldiers that applied each year for 21 SAS Selection, only a tiny handful regularly passed. It is a brutal attrition rate to embark on, especially when you feel very average physically. But big challenges inspire me. I think we are all made a little like that.

I also believe strongly in the powerful words: "I took the road less traveled, and that has made all the difference." They are good ones to live by.

The big, final motivator was that I really wasn't enjoying my university studies.

I loved the Brunel and our small group of buddies there, but the actual university experience was killing me. (Not the workload, I hasten to add, which was pleasantly chilled, but rather the whole deal of feeling like just another student.)

Sure, I liked the chilled lifestyle (like the daily swim I took naked in the ornamental lake in the car park), but it was more than that. I just didn't like being so unmotivated.

It didn't feel good for the soul.

This wasn't what I had hoped for in my life.

I felt impatient to get on and do something.

(Oh, and I was learning to dislike the German language in a way that was definitely not healthy.)

So I decided it was time to make a decision.

Via the OTC, Trucker and I quietly went to see the ex-SAS officer to get his advice on our Special Forces Selection aspirations.

I was nervous telling him.

He knew we were troublemakers, and that we had never taken any of the OTC military routine at all seriously. But to my amazement he wasn't the least bit surprised at what we told him.

He just smiled, almost knowingly, and told us we would probably fit in well—that was if we passed. He said the SAS attracted misfits and characters—but only those who could first prove themselves worthy.

He then told us something great, that I have always remembered.

"Everyone who attempts Selection has the basic mark-one body: two arms, two legs, one head, and one pumping set of lungs. What makes the difference between those that make it and those that don't, is what goes on in here," he said, touching his chest. "Heart is what makes the big difference. Only you know if you have got what it takes. Good luck . . . oh, and if you pass I will treat you both to lunch, on me."

That was quite a promise from an officer—to part with money. So that was that.

Trucker and I wrote to 21 SAS HQ, nervously requesting to be put forward for Selection. They would do their initial security clearances on us both, and then would hopefully write, offering us (or not) a place on pre-Selection—including dates, times, and joining instructions.

All we could do was wait, start training hard, and pray.

I tossed all my German study manuals unceremoniously into the bin and felt a million times better. And deep down I had the feeling that I might just be embarking on the adventure of a lifetime.

On top of that, there was no Deborah Maldives saying I needed a degree to join the SAS. The only qualification I needed was inside that beating heart of mine.

PART 2

✦

AMONG THE FEW

Many are called, but few are chosen.

I would like to preface this chapter with the following note:

As a former Special Forces soldier, I signed the Official Secrets Act, which rightly restricts me from revealing details, places, names, and operational procedures of the Special Air Service.

The following account has been modified to ensure that I comply with this, and it remains important for me personally to honor that brotherhood.

The aim of the next part of the book is to give you a taste of what I went through to have earned the right to be part of the family that is the SAS.

CHAPTER 36

This is how the BBC summed up the Special Air Service (SAS) in one of their broadcasts:

> The reputation of the SAS stretches worldwide. It has a reputation for ruthless efficiency and military professionalism. Other Special Forces units model themselves on the SAS, whose selection procedures are arduous and protracted. Around nine in every ten hopefuls fail . . .

Like so many boys growing up, I had always heard about the famed SAS. The shadowy figures that formed what is widely acknowledged as the toughest, most elite Special Forces fighting unit on earth.

In quiet moments, I had always wondered what it would be like to try their selection course to join.

Would I be one of those who had the "right stuff," or, more likely, would I be among the majority who attempt it . . . and fail?

I wondered what it would really take to be one of those few who had earned the right to wear that famous sand-colored beret with its winged dagger.

What toll would it exert to be part of this Special Forces (SF)

Unit, and would I have what it required to join the elite, the best?

Barely age sixteen, I had passed my Potential Officers Course to join the Royal Marines Commandos as a young officer after school; I was all set to join up—just like Dad had done.

But part of me just wondered, should I not at least try Selection for the SAS Reserves, before committing to the marines?

Just to see.

The rational answer that came back to me was that I should be honest with myself. I was fit and strong and determined, but I wasn't a totally natural athlete—I had always had to work at it, and hard.

I had many friends who were naturally much stronger and fitter than me (and they didn't even have to train at all), and deep down, that made me doubt myself. Yet somehow, because I wasn't naturally gifted athletically, I had developed this ability to fight, and to push myself hard, physically and mentally.

It was this fight and determination that would become the key ingredient to attempting Selection—much more than any natural ability.

If SAS Selection does one thing, it ensures that everyone, over the many months, reaches that stage where they are physically dead on their feet. Utterly spent.

However fit you are.

What the SAS is looking for is spirit and fight: those soldiers who, when every bone in their body is screaming for rest, will dig deep, and start moving, again and again and again. That isn't natural fitness, it is heart, and it is this that Selection demands of all who attempt it.

At this stage, though, I maybe didn't have the confidence in myself to understand that we all have that spirit in us.

I felt a little more comfortable with the marines. I had experienced a small taste of what would be asked of me as a potential Royal Marines officer.

I knew it would be tough, but I felt I could do it.

I was good at push-ups and pull-ups and yomping with a backpack (a staple of life in the marines); could I manage the ultralong marches over the high mountains, carrying seriously huge weights on your back, which is such a core part of SAS Selection?

That somehow felt beyond what I believed I could do.

Yet still the voice niggled.

In the end I concluded, nothing ventured, nothing gained. (A vital ethos to follow if life is to have flavor, I have since learned.)

I knew I should at least attempt Selection.

If I failed, well at least I would fail while trying. Facedown in the dirt. Knowing that I had given it my all. (Oh, and what's more, I knew that the SAS required secrecy from anyone attempting Selection, which was perfect. If I failed, I concluded, at least no one would know!)

So that was the plan; but in truth, if I could have had any idea of the pain and battering that my body would go through on Selection, I would have realized it was insane to continue with this mad dream.

But luckily, we never really know what the future holds.

CHAPTER 37

Normally, for a soldier to attempt SAS Selection, it first requires several years of service in the regular army. But the SAS is comprised of three regiments, with 21 and 23 being reserve regiments to 22 SAS.

Both 21 and 23 SAS tend to be made up of former paratroopers or commandos who have left the regular army, but still want a challenge and an outlet for their hard-earned skills.

The SAS then take these ex-soldiers and put them through a rigorous selection course, designed to separate the best. Then they take those few and train them up in all the skills of a covert, combat operative.

But 21 and 23 SAS are also open to any civilians who can prove themselves capable of the exacting high standards demanded by the SAS. The route in is longer and more spread out, but it is a potential route in, all the same.

What I liked about the SAS(R) (Reserve) was that it gave you a degree of flexibility in how you lived your life.

You weren't a full-time soldier, yet many of the SAS Reserve soldiers did it as their main job. They could be deployed anywhere in the world at little notice, were highly trained and specialized, yet they could pick and choose how much time they dedicated to the regiment.

I loved the idea of that.

Joining straight in from being a civilian meant a very steep learning curve, but if you were successful you could join the SAS(R) without all the tedious process of having to learn conventional, boot-cleaning soldiering first.

And I never had any ambitions to be a conventional anything.

Quite a few of my friends had set out after school to join a regular tank or infantry regiment, as officers. It would invariably involve a lot of ceremonial duties and high living in London. But despite the fun that they would surely have, I found the thought of that lifestyle, at barely twenty years old, totally unappealing.

I wanted adventure, and I was looking for the less trodden path.

If I were to join 21 SAS, I could only do it as a trooper, in other words at the lowest military rank available. I wouldn't be an officer like my public-school friends, but would be joining at the very bottom of the pile as a "grunt" (as troopers or private soldiers were often derogatively called).

But "grunt," to me, sounded much more challenging and much more fun.

What's more, among SAS troopers, Old Etonians were very thin on the ground.

CHAPTER 38

In the Brunel Hotel, Trucker and I had often discussed SAS Selection long into the night. To go for it was a decision we very much took together.

It proved one of the best decisions we ever made, and it forged in us a friendship (formed through shared hardship) that I could never have anticipated.

For the rest of our days we will be the best of friends because of what we went through together on SAS(R) Selection over the next year and beyond.

We did, though, recognize that if only a very small number of those who applied eventually went on to pass 21 SAS Selection, then the likelihood of us both passing together was very small.

It was an unspoken subject.

Also, deep down, I did worry, as Trucker was so much stronger than me. In fact, he was the most naturally fit man I'd ever met, and I so envied this. He was so effortlessly strong when we ran and trained together—so different from me—and this just fueled my fear that he would pass Selection, and I would, in reality, never make it.

⚜

On March 23, 1994, we both arrived at the barrack gates, call-up papers in hand, tense and very nervous.

We were beginning a journey that would effectively take us from enthusiastic civilians to highly trained Special Forces operatives in just under twelve long months.

It was a daunting prospect.

To be transformed from a total amateur to a total pro, skilled in everything from demolitions to covert maritime and airborne insertions, would be a journey that would stretch us to our limits. But before we could get anywhere near anything exciting we would have to prove ourselves fit and determined, way beyond the normal.

The only way to do that was through graft—sweat and bloody hard work.

We had both been assigned to what I believe was one of the best squadrons in 21 SAS. It had a strong reputation within the SAS family as being made up of tough, no-nonsense, down-to-earth soldiers. They were mainly Welsh, fiercely protective of their own, and utterly professional.

But their reputation was hard earned and well guarded.

We would have to work twice as hard to earn a place there.

The first evening, along with an eclectic mix of other hopefuls, we were issued with kit, taken on a steady run up and down the nearby hills, interviewed on what our motivations were, and then briefed on what to expect.

Commitment seemed to be the watchword.

I went home relieved—just to have started this damned thing.

That is often the hard bit of any long, daunting journey.

Trucker and I then returned for one evening every week, for what was called a drill night. These evenings were designed to familiarize us with what we could expect over the year ahead.

Selection itself would take place over many weekends, over

many, many months—but these two-day training tests and exercises were not to start for another few weeks.

First they wanted to sieve out those who wouldn't stand a chance.

The weekly drill nights were spent being put through progressively harder and harder physical training.

Often these consisted of very fast, lung-bursting runs, followed by hill sprints and fireman's carries—up and down, up and down—until every recruit was on his knees, often covered in vomit.

One particularly nasty trick they played was to line us all up at the top of this steep two-hundred-foot hill. They would then send us to the bottom, tell us to lift up our partner on our backs, and then announce that the last two back to the top would be RTU'd, or returned to unit—failed.

We would all stagger to the top, fighting not to be last, only then to be sent back down, minus the last two, to repeat it again—then again.

Eventually only a few of us would remain—all reduced to crawling wrecks.

Sometimes they carried out their threat and the weakest would be RTU'd; sometimes they then just ran all of us back to camp and no further action was taken. But you never knew.

That was how they played it.

You were only ever safe if you gave 150 percent, stayed near the front, and never gave up.

It was becoming apparent that this was the hallmark needed to still be there the next week.

Or they might get us to do some "milling." Two-minute bouts, in full gloves, where the aim was to punch your opponent with everything you could throw at him. No technique, just blood and guts.

I always got paired with the six-foot-four bruiser. And came off worse.

Then more push-ups. And lifts. Until we could no longer stand.

At this stage it wasn't about even passing Selection—it was about just not getting thrown off the course—today.

Yet after each "beasting" session the exhilaration always surpassed the doubt, and I was slowly learning to get used to the pain.

That seemed to be the key to survival here.

CHAPTER 39

Finally, our first pre-Selection weekend was approaching.

I arrived at the barracks at around 5:30 P.M., Friday night—we were to be driven to the SAS HQ for what they called the pre-Selection tests.

These were simply intended to ensure we were "serious about doing this course, and aware of what would be required." This was what the SAS officer told us as we sat huddled on the cold concrete floor of a semisubmerged hangar that first night.

He added, "I hope that you will all pass, trust me, the regiment always needs more numbers, but it won't happen like that. I can guarantee that out of all of you here, I will be able to count on just two hands the number who'll eventually join."

I hardly slept at all that night. Instead I lay awake, waiting for 5:30 A.M., on that hard concrete floor, in that dark, dank hangar, that I was to get to know so well in the months ahead.

At 0600 we set off running as a large squad. (All of the 21 SAS Squadrons had come together for this pre-Selection weekend.)

This was the first simple test: an eight-mile hill run in under an hour. I dug deep as the forest track wound up the hill and we all went up it for the fourth time.

The rest of the morning was spent on basic skills lessons from the directing staff (DS), and a briefing about the afternoon's activities ahead.

We then got run down to the assault course.

I'd done a few tough assault courses before with the Royal Marines. This somehow felt different. Before, the assault courses had been fun; this one had a sense of impending pain.

What the DS wanted to see was total commitment and real effort, and there was always an officer or DS watching your every lurch and move.

Occasionally they would swiftly step in and drag some poor person off and quietly tell them to start all over again, saying, "Do it properly, and with three times the speed and effort."

After two hours of nonstop rolling, crawling, climbing, and diving, I was dead on my feet. We all were.

Legs and arms screaming for rest.

Before we had a second to recover we were run through the woods, fast, to a small clearing. Manhole covers peppered the whole area. They were the hidden entrances to a covered network of underground tunnels.

If you hated confined spaces, this was going to be a bad place to find out.

But we weren't given a chance to think about it. We were just each pushed individually down into these tiny manholes—then the covers were locked above us.

On our own, we each negotiated our way round this dark, underground, and cramped maze of narrow passages only three feet high.

Each was semisubmerged in six inches of water and mud. I crawled and crawled, feeling with my hands stretched out in front of me to probe the way ahead. Whenever I reached another manhole cover and some light, seeping through the cracks, I would hear heavy army boots stamping on the metal grate above me.

"Keep moving," one of the DS would shout, "faster."

Claustrophobia was a big no-no in the regiment. You needed to be able to work in close, confined conditions, you needed to be able to control your emotions and feelings, and to learn to channel them.

If you couldn't do that, then it was best that the regiment found out now, before you started out on Selection itself.

Eventually we were released from our rat holes—tired, cramped, and exhausted. We were then run round the assault course again—just for good measure.

This was all about the DS having a chance to see each of our default characters: Was I a sticker, a worker, was I calm under pressure, could I maintain my control in a crisis?

Still there was no rest.

We were then escorted off to a large, heavy steel artillery cannon that sat, sunk in the mud, in the middle of a field.

"Well, get pulling, lads—and fast."

We heaved at the towlines and strained to move it, and slowly the wheels started to turn.

"We will tell you when to stop . . . and if you stop before, then you will be off the course . . ."

The DS rarely shouted, but tended quietly just to watch—they were looking for self-discipline. This was their mantra throughout: "You push yourselves, lads—if you are too slow, then you've failed yourself. Is that clear?"

It was clear and it was hard, but I liked it.

Such self-reliance was strangely empowering.

A lot of other soldiers who I encountered on Selection found such an attitude difficult. Many recruits were used to being shouted at, endlessly driven on by their color sergeants.

But the SAS way was different, and those who needed shouting at in order to perform would soon fall by the wayside.

You had to be able to push yourself, and be able to do it alone. And as I learned, in the case of the SAS, it was "always a little further."

Eventually, as dusk fell, utterly exhausted, we were stood down. It had been a long, hard day, and I collapsed into my sleeping bag on the hangar's concrete floor.

It was still dark when I could hear the corporals hovering outside the hangar like quiet, prowling lions. I fumbled to get ready. At 0550 I lugged my heavy backpack on and shuffled out into the predawn light. It felt even colder outside than it had in the damp, open hangar.

I was stood on parade five minutes early, ready.

We had been told very clearly that if we were told to be on parade at 6:00 A.M., then that really meant 5:55 A.M. A minute late and you were warned. Late again and you were off the course.

We weighed in our packs on the makeshift scales—35 lbs minimum plus webbing, weapon, water, and food. It felt heavy. (Little did I know what was in store over the next year ahead, and the sort of weights I'd finally be carrying.)

We set off as a squad at a fast walk that quickly became a forced stride, and then a jog, as we followed the same track round the same hills, all over again.

The same eight miles—over four laps of the wooded hill—but this time in full kit.

"Come on—one lap done—three more to go."

Halfway through the second we lost several more recruits who slipped behind the group, unable to maintain the pace. If the speed was too fast and the weight too great now, then it was best they were taken off the course at this early stage—for their own sake.

By the third lap I was really struggling, gasping for more oxygen, snot smeared down my face, any humor or romance firmly gone, replaced by burning leg muscles and burning lungs.

Just fight, Bear. Come on, one more lap. Don't waste all that hard work now.

At last the finish point, and I turned around to see a diminished group and a load of stragglers behind. The stragglers were taken aside. I never heard what was said to them, but they looked utterly dejected and spent.

They were sent to pack their bags.

Another eight had been failed, but the real fear in me was whether I could keep pushing that hard.

I mean, this was still only pre-Selection. And it was tough.

What on earth would SAS Selection itself be like?

CHAPTER 40

Before we got even close to the stage of being trained in all the skills of a Special Forces soldier, we would have to pass the hill phase of Selection.

This was simply the SAS's way of whittling down the numbers from the masses to the few. It was always against the clock and invariably against the elements.

Only when the few remained would the SAS begin to teach and train those recruits in the real Special Forces skills.

Such training is very time- and money-intensive for the regiment, and there was no point spending such valuable resources on people who didn't, underneath it all, have the right attitude and required fitness.

So phase one was to whittle; phase two was to train.

⚜

We had lost almost a quarter of the recruits from our squadron already, since starting pre-Selection; we were now officially about to start Selection proper.

In the squadron barracks, we were escorted into the main campus area, where all the bulk of the squadron buildings were.

We were no longer just confined to a side block and the gymnasium.

This was at least progress.

We were briefed on what would be expected of us from now onward, and then kitted out with our first military fatigues and basic equipment.

We were then shown our recruit locker room, lined with metal mesh lockers and red-painted concrete floor. This was to be our home for as long as we lasted on the course.

The message they kept drumming into us was clear: "If you want it bad enough, you'll pass."

This whole first hill phase of Selection would be carried out in the wild Welsh peaks of the Brecon Beacons.

For the next six months the bulk of my time was to be spent sweating and slogging round these mountains: sometimes in soaring heat and blazing sun, surrounded by plagues of mosquitoes and drenched in sweat; then, later on in the year, plowing through thigh-deep thick snow, cold and wet; and at times being near blown over by the force of the wind on the high peaks.

At times, we would be carrying up to 75 lbs in total—roughly the weight of an average eight-year-old kid.

Both hypothermia and exhaustion were going to become the ever-present enemy, along with the timed clock. It's a constant battle as your boots fill with water and your clothing turns stiff in the gale-force wind that sweeps across the Welsh mountains. Can you keep moving—and fast?

The whole Selection process is about so much more than just physical fitness. It requires navigational skills, mental agility, self-discipline, and a fierce determination to push on when your legs and whole body are screaming to rest.

The SAS can afford to be tough when recruiting. There'll

always be more people willing to test themselves by trying for the regiment.

Our first exercise in the Brecon Beacons was what they call a "guided tour"—it sounded worryingly mundane.

We were to be escorted in small groups round the mountains, to show, practically, that we had a good grasp on the fine art of day and night mountain navigation.

Only then could they let us loose on our own.

As we climbed higher into the mountains, the DS gave us their advice and tips, learned the hard way. Advice on how to navigate effectively, and how to cover ground efficiently.

I absorbed it all.

We took it in turns to navigate each leg, and we burned up the miles.

About ten hours later, we had covered roughly eighteen miles, up and down the remote valleys and peaks.

Everyone was feeling the weight on their backs, and our feet were aching—but we were working hard and together, and it felt good.

We also got our first taste of one particularly high Welsh mountain that we'd get to know intimately. A peak synonymous with SAS Selection, and known to all recruits so well.

Finally, we stopped in some woods and rested for two hours at the foot of this mountain. I was wet through from the all-day drizzle and sweat, but I was excited.

We awaited darkness.

The next stage would be the first of many night navigation exercises.

CHAPTER 41

As night fell, we headed off in small groups into the darkness, in search of the first checkpoint or RV (rendezvous).

Moving at night through high mountain terrain was hard, and we were all soon fumbling around, stumbling into ditches and unseen bogs.

Night navigation is an art that we were soon to become experts in, but as of yet our feet, eyes, and instinct were new and uncertain.

I noticed, though, that the DS, who were with us, would never trip or stumble. It was only the recruits who would be tripping over clumps of grass or potholes in the dark.

It was as if the fully badged SAS guys had learned this game long ago.

I so wanted to develop that level of confidence and skill, and I knew it would come with practice; and practice at moving at night was something we would have no shortage of.

We finally traipsed into the last checkpoint in the mountainous forest, tired, wet, and exhausted. I tied my poncho between two trees, laid out my bivvy bag, and fell fast asleep.

Two hours later, at 0555, we were lined up along the track leading up to one of the high peaks, some six miles away. Standing high above us, the summit was barely visible in the early morning half-light.

Looking down the ragged line of recruits to my left, I could see that everyone was buttoned up against the chill.

Army-green woollen hats, damp combat clothes, hands clasped in fists at our sides to try to keep warm, and packs neatly laid in front of us on the ground.

Each soldier's breath was steaming in the cold air.

My feet were sore, and felt tight in my new army boots. I could feel that they had started to swell with the bruising.

The RSM (regimental sergeant major) shouted out, "Stick with me if you want to pass this course." Then he was off at a pace.

We raced off after him, hauling our packs on as we moved.

Recruits were fighting to barge past each other in an attempt to get to the front. But keeping up with this pace meant going at almost a full run—a task that I knew would be impossible to maintain.

Each step up was hard-fought, and as the gradient increased so I could feel my energy draining. My body was running on reserve, and I was already pouring with sweat and sucking for air.

This is where it counts, this is the time to shine, I kept telling myself. *Do not slip back, even one step.*

I knew that to slip back would be fatal.

I would be swallowed by the other recruits, and would never be able to keep the pace.

It was the energy of this front pack that was keeping me there, despite the punishing pace and gradient.

I found myself among the few who had managed to keep up with the RSM by the time we reached the summit, and I fought hard to maintain that position all the way down the other side.

Running all the way down the steep mountain paths.

By the time we reached the bottom, we were a good twenty minutes ahead of most of the straggle of recruits.

When the whole group were assembled, the officer announced that our performance had been an embarrassment, and that if we were serious about passing we'd all have to start putting some effort in.

With that comment, he told us to stay where we were. He then ordered the trucks to start up, and we watched as they all pulled away, driving off down the main road, empty.

"Turn round, lads—the trucks will be waiting for you back on the other side. That took you a pathetic two hours seventeen minutes to complete. You all now have two hours to retrace your steps back over the mountain to make the trucks. Those outside of that time are failed . . . and will walk home."

Bleary-eyed, I turned to start the climb up again.

I pushed to the front of the group, determined to make a good start and keep ahead, and headed back up the mountain.

As we cleared the first false horizon, some twenty minutes later, a corporal was stood there waiting, noting silently who was up the front and who had dropped behind already.

He quietly pointed back down the steep slope.

"Get back down, lads—the trucks are coming back. Good to see who was prepared to put in the effort, though," he said, nodding at the front-runners, which included Trucker and myself.

We turned, and started down, exhausted and drained.

We all collapsed silently in the back of the four-ton lorries, and heaved a sigh of relief as the engines started up and we pulled out onto the road and headed south.

It had been just another little tester. A tester with a purpose.

Are you the sort of person who can turn around when you have nothing left, and find that little bit extra inside you to keep going, or do you sag and wilt with exhaustion?

It is a mental game, and it is hard to tell how people will react until they are squeezed.

All I cared, though, was that weekend one of Selection was done.

The squeezing had begun.

CHAPTER 42

How on earth could lying on the metal floor of an army truck, cramped, exhausted, and inhaling diesel fumes, be the best feeling on earth?

But somehow, such moments, curled up in our bivvy bags, having survived and passed another weekend exercise, made all the effort and pain worthwhile.

The weekly drill nights kept the same momentum—running, PT (or physical training, which consisted of log runs, grueling strength circuits, fireman's lifts, and general beastings), map-reading lessons, medic-training, and weapon-handling.

As the new recruits we dressed in green, standard-army uniform. You couldn't help but notice the confident, purposeful air that the SAS fully badged soldiers wandering around camp possessed.

In contrast, we recruits knew nothing and were nothing. We were just numbers.

Nothing more, nothing less.

I looked with hidden admiration at the carefully molded berets and wing-daggered belts that the SAS guys wore. I was also beginning to appreciate the work that had gone into earning them.

Our next Selection weekend in the mountains was soon looming over me again.

No sooner had my body begun to recover from one test than the fear and stress of what was to come next was upon me again.

I mean, no one looks forward to being driven physically to their knees—over and over again.

⚜

The four-ton green army truck pulled into a quiet turnout at the foot of another cold, windswept mountain, at about 1:00 A.M. It was raining hard.

In pairs, we tried to find a small patch of flat ground to sleep. But sleep was impossible, and tucked into the side of a gully in what was fast becoming a soaking-wet bog, we made what we could of the five hours until dawn.

At 5:55 A.M. we were all stood to attention in the marsh, in the pouring rain. The SAS officer in charge told us that this was our last accompanied set of marches, and to remember the importance of learning key lessons from the DS with us.

He handed over to the corporals, then turned and walked away.

No sooner was the briefing over, than the DS just turned and shouted at us to follow them.

They stormed ahead across the steep, marshy "moon grass," and within minutes they were what seemed like miles ahead of us all. They then stopped and waited—looking back, as we slowly reached them in a heaving gaggle spread out across the bogland.

We were all wet, muddy, and looking like an utter shambles, heaving along under the weight of our packs.

In contrast, the DS looked crisp, fit, and composed. They were never loud or aggressive, they were just indifferent. And they had been fast—very fast.

I had no idea how they had managed to cover almost a mile of steep, boggy ground in so little time—and look so unaffected.

They calmly told us that this was the sort of pace we would need to be doing as a minimum speed later, during Selection. I tried not to think about that, but just told myself to keep up with them at all costs.

It was obvious that the gulf between a recruit and a badged SAS soldier was vast.

We started moving again and soon I began to feel stronger as I got into my rhythm.

Under the DSs' guidance, we practiced crossing swollen streams with full kit, as well as carefully getting the feel of traversing the steep and exposed mountain faces with the weight of pack, webbing, and rifle.

At 1:30 P.M. we had a short break to take on food and water, and we sat huddled in a group in a small gulley. But the stop didn't last long, and soon we set off again for the next leg of the march, the final fifteen miles of the day.

As we headed up the next peak, I noticed all the other recruits alongside me: heads down, straining, with sweat pouring off their foreheads. No one spoke. We were all just busting our backsides to keep up the pace.

The last few miles along the ridge and down the other side of the mountain dragged on, until we finally reached the day-march's end. We were told to rest up for an hour in the woods, check our feet, and take on board some food and water.

But this rest was made truly miserable by the swarms of summer midges that enveloped each of us.

I had never known them so thick in the air.

The army mosquito-repellent was utterly useless against them, and all it did was give the midges something to stick to, leaving you to wipe off swarms of them with your hands.

All we wanted now was to get marching again, and to get the wind through our hair and the midges off our backs.

We were soon lined up again on parade, in the woods, and told: "Stand still and do not move."

The air was so thick with midges that each breath you took you inhaled a mouthful of the brutes. All you wanted to do was scratch and brush them away from your face, and standing there, immobile, enveloped in the swarms, was truly hellish.

"Stop moving," shouted one of the DS, who we had unofficially named "Mr. Nasty."

He then proceeded to stand in front of us, covered in midges as well, and to watch us—waiting for one of us to quit.

I kept blinking my eyes and twitching my nose in a futile attempt to deter the midges that circled relentlessly around our heads. It felt like some old form of medieval torture, and the seconds went by like hours.

It was morale-sapping and miserable, but eventually after about forty-five minutes of this head messing, we were stood down to await orders for the night-march.

It had been a simple reminder that mental strength was something that had to accompany the physical. And the physical is always driven by the mental.

It was a lesson that every one of us on that godforsaken, midge-infested forest track was taught that day.

CHAPTER 43

The DS came forward and told us that the night's march ahead would be an "educational introduction" to the infamous moon-grass. This consisted of bogland—riddled with mile-upon-mile of tufts of clumpy grass, and ankle-twisting divots, that made any sort of progress almost impossible.

Over the following months we would learn to dread and hate this moon grass. (Or "baby-heads," as many of the recruits called it, as it resembled millions of small heads sticking out of the ground.)

That night I expected the worst, and I wasn't disappointed.

Wading across mile after mile of these melon-sized clumps of weed tussocks was hellish. It was made worse by the fact that, in the darkness, each step you placed was a lottery as to whether you tripped or not.

Add to this the fact that much of the moon grass also had razor-sharp, chest-high reeds growing out of it, and you can see why all the soldiers learned to hate it so much.

In the pitch black my legs buckled and twisted on each step, and occasionally I'd slip in up to my thighs in stinking black, oozing mud.

Finally, as we came off the high plateau, we arrived at the perimeter fence of a farm beneath us.

We were warned to stay silent—the farmer had been known to chase lads on Selection off his land with a shotgun. This all just added to the excitement as we skirted cautiously round his house and over the fence.

After a final fast-and-furious speed march along forestry tracks in the dark, we reached our destination at about 3:00 A.M.

Three hours of precious rest lay ahead of us now, huddled in the woods.

These times of sleepless, wet, cold waiting constituted some of the worst parts of Selection for me.

Physically your body was in bits: your knees and the soles of your feet would be swollen and stiff, and your body would be crying out for decent rest. But we rarely got more than three hours in between marches—and it was neither long enough to rest, nor short enough to stay fired up on that exercise high.

Instead, you would just get cold and stiff, and even more sleep-deprived and exhausted—it was a killer combination.

The SAS directing staff knew this.

The self-will needed to get back up, time and time again, to keep slogging over the mountains in the dark, while being soaking wet and cold, was just what they were looking for.

In those few hours' reprieve, I would busy myself, sorting out my blistered feet, eating some food, and heating up a hot drink. But after that I could only lie there waiting for that dreaded call to muster on parade for morning battle physical training (PT).

Each weekend this battle PT got more and more unpleasant, and harder and harder.

The next morning, in full kit, we paraded in the predawn light. Everyone was shuffling around with stiff, aching legs, and we all looked drained and exhausted. In contrast, the instructors were pacing around us. Hungry for blood.

Then at 0555 on the dot, the order went out.

"Follow us, and keep up. This weekend your performance has been appalling, and now you will pay."

The DS set off at a pace down one of the forestry tracks, and we pulled on our packs and set out after them. Then the pace quickened to a level where we had to run to keep up—but running under so much weight was near impossible.

Within twenty minutes each of us was gasping and pouring with sweat, as we fought to keep up. An hour and a half later, that pace hadn't eased one notch.

We had become this long straggle of moaning, exhausted bodies—disheveled and in no order—with about a mile between the front and last man. It was now broad daylight, and each and every man was dead on their feet.

I dragged myself along the final track, and finished somewhere in the middle of the group. But I was completely spent. I had nothing more I could give. Nothing.

If you had asked me to walk another fifty yards I would have struggled to manage it.

As I stood there, my sweat-drenched body steaming, one of the recruits started cursing and muttering quietly to himself.

"I've had enough of this shit," he grumbled under his breath. "It's bollocks. This isn't soldiering, it's sadism."

Then he looked at me. "No one should be made to do this," he continued. "We are treated like pack mules, and even pack mules would eventually die under this workload."

I told him to hang on in there and that he would have forgotten about all this by the end of the day, when he was in a warm shower. He then turned and just stared at me.

"You know the difference between you and me, Bear? You're just dumber than me." And with that, he turned, dropped his pack in a heap, walked over to the DS, and said he wanted out.

The DS quietly directed the guy toward the trucks.

The recruit climbed aboard one and I never saw him again. That was how it always happened.

They beat you down by quietly raising the bar ever higher and higher, until either you snapped or you failed to make the time.

As they always told us: "We don't fail you, you fail yourself. If you beat the clock, and keep going, you will pass."

On the journey back, huddled in the four-tonner, I thought about what that recruit had said: "You're just dumber than me."

Maybe he had a point.

I mean, getting thrashed senseless did feel pretty dumb—and then getting paid only £27 a day for the privilege of being thrashed felt even dumber.

But that guy who quit also missed the real point. Good things come through grit and hard work, and all things worthwhile have a cost.

In the case of the SAS, the cost was somewhere around a thousand barrels of sweat.

Was it a price I was prepared to pay?

It was a question that Selection would give me plenty of time to ask myself.

CHAPTER 44

Selection had seemed to take over my every waking moment.

I'd been told this would happen, and had never really believed it—but it was true. Something that you put so much effort and time into is hard to switch off from.

The excitement of what had passed, and the trepidation of what was to follow, consumed me in the days off we had in between.

Trucker and I would return to our student life in Bristol, where friends wandered casually between lectures and the canteen.

We would tag along and hang with them, but we would also maintain a little distance.

We avoided the drunken late nights and long, lazy lie-ins that so many of our student buddies seem to enjoy. Instead we would be up early training or prepping kit for what was always looming ahead.

Simply put, we both had a different purpose in our lives.

⚜

Our next exercise was in the Black Mountains in Wales. For some reason the dreaded midges were not out—maybe the altitude and wind. Whatever the reason, it came as a great relief.

This, now, was to be our first march in pairs, and not as a group, and I made sure I got coupled with Trucker (by doing some nifty maneuvering in the lineup).

Each pair was set off at timed intervals, and Trux and I got away early at 6:30 A.M.

The sun was out, the morning flew by, and we made fast, but hot, progress across the mountains. Visibility was good, which made navigation a breeze, and we were full of confidence.

We soon reached a dam and had to make a decision.

We knew it was forbidden to cross a dam, in the same way that it was forbidden ever to use a footpath or forestry track. (Unless it was part of the dreaded morning battle PT.)

This was a simple rule on Selection to make sure that you got used to navigating properly and that the going underfoot was always hard, which it inevitably always was. (In fact I, still to this day, feel a bit guilty if I go hiking on a footpath—old habits die hard.)

But not crossing the dam meant that we would have to drop down and up the other side of the four-hundred-foot ravine beneath the dam.

Are we being watched by a DS, or can we risk it?

In the regiment's spirit of "Who Dares Wins" and all that, we climbed carefully over the locked gate and ran across the two-hundred-meter dam at a sprint.

All clear.

We then set about climbing the steep face up to the next DS checkpoint some seven miles away.

Six hours into the march, though, we were both starting to wane.

The heat had been relentless, and when you are burning through six thousand calories a day carrying a heavy pack, belt kit, and rifle up and down steep mountains, then you need to make sure you are drinking enough.

We hadn't been.

We had both been in that zone where we were moving well, feeling good, and probably got a little overconfident. That would nearly cost us our chance of passing Selection.

We had one last climb up over a two-thousand-foot ridge before dropping down to the final checkpoint. But already I was struggling. I wasn't sweating any longer, despite the heat and the exertion. That was a bad sign.

Each step up that steep face felt like I was carrying the world on my back. I felt dizzy, I felt delirious, and I had to keep sitting down.

In short, I had heat exhaustion.

I had never experienced this deliriousness and weakness before. The feeling of semiconsciousness, as if in a drunken stupor—and time and time again, I kept falling to my knees.

All you want to do is to stop and lie down, somewhere dark, quiet and cool. But you can't. You have to drink, then get on and get moving—and hope the rehydration will take effect.

Eventually I crawled over the summit and let my body tumble down the other side toward the final RV. I checked in and then collapsed in the woods with the other recruits.

I had a screaming migraine headache, and felt nauseated and light-headed. I needed to start rehydrating and getting a grip of myself, and fast.

Meanwhile, five other recruits had failed to complete the route, and two others had been picked up, all suffering from heatstroke. All were removed from the course.

Part of me envied them as I saw them sprawled in the medic's truck, being well looked-after. It looked like welcome relief from what I was feeling.

But I knew that all I had to do was hang on in there. By this time the next day, it would be another test down and another step closer to my goal.

So I sat down and started to brew myself some warm, sweet tea, and hoped I would soon be able to open both eyes beyond a squint.

Before the night march started, we were all called on parade early. This boded badly.

As we stood there, two recruits' names were read out, and the individuals were called forward.

These two guys had been spotted crossing the dam earlier on in the day, and they were both quietly, and without fuss, RTU'd—or in our language, "binned."

Trucker and I had got lucky, but we had also learned another valuable lesson: If you are going to risk it all on an act of daring, then pick your moment and don't get caught.

By the time we both set off for the night march I was feeling a little stronger. I still had a headache, but I could stand without feeling faint. This was progress at least.

Trucker was also feeling like death, which was some consolation.

Luckily the route was relatively straightforward, and finally, at 3:00 A.M., and with a growing sense of strength (and also pride that I had come through this and was feeling stronger again), I arrived back at our base camp in the woods.

I lay back and rested, awaiting the battle PT at 5:55 A.M.

The battle PT started out relatively straightforward—a three-mile pack run down a track along the valley floor.

Once again the group spread out as the DS set a blistering pace, but we soon reached the end of the track where all the trucks were waiting for us.

I was feeling strong again now, and was almost enjoying the

161

fact that I was managing to keep up, whereas almost everyone else was dragging behind.

At the point where I reckoned the DS should turn left toward the waiting four-tonner wagons, I saw the DS turn hard right and head straight up the sheer thousand-foot face to the ridge line.

It was then that the shouting really began, and this had hardly ever happened before.

CHAPTER 45

The DS always prided themselves on the fact that they never needed to shout. Selection was hard enough as it was.

They were there, as they often told us, simply to run the course and observe.

But suddenly there had been a tempo change, and the shouting was now firm, directed, and serious.

"Move—now!" the DS shouted. "If we see any one of you walking, you are out, get it? This hill is to be run up!"

I did as I was told, turned away from the enticing trucks, and headed up the steep hill, following in the DS's footsteps. I had to pace myself, I knew that.

This was a big hill, and with the weight of a heavy pack, it was going to be near impossible to run up it all the way.

I just had to make sure that I was not the first to be seen to slow. I dug in and started to breathe harder and harder.

Halfway up, the DS stopped, turned, and watched us. I determined to keep running, however slowly, until I reached him, whatever the fatigue I felt.

Finally I reached him, somewhere in the middle of the group. My legs and shoulders felt like they were on fire, and my heart and lungs felt as if they would explode.

I looked down beneath us, to see the last few stragglers pulling themselves up the hill toward us. Two guys had been reduced to only a slow shuffle. I knew they were in trouble.

The DS had told us the parameters—run, you pass; walk, you fail.

"Right, you lot, get back down to the track and into the four-tonners. And you," he barked, pointing at the last two men, "you follow me." Back at the track, as we all piled into the wagons in the muddy car park, relief swept over me. I watched out of the back of my Bedford truck as these two recruits who had faltered were led off to another truck.

That was the way it worked: Once someone was failed they were kept apart from the rest of us. It helped build us together into a team, and it gave those of us still hanging on in there a certain pride that we were still in the right truck.

It wasn't much, but it meant a lot to us.

⚜

For the next three weekends, the pace continued to build: the distances got longer, the weights got heavier, and the pressure mounted.

Routinely we would be covering up to thirty miles, across the mountains, carrying up to 50 lbs of weight. On top of this, we were now doing every march on our own—during the day and night.

The SAS were beginning to test our ability to work alone. Could we motivate ourselves to keep going, navigate effectively, and look after ourselves, even when we were cold, wet, and tired?

The strange thing was that I was thriving.

We rarely got shouted at, and, for now, we were only asked to do these three basic tasks: navigate across the mountains; carry the weight; be within the time.

The soldiering stuff would come later on, but only to those who had first proved themselves capable of working to the max, whatever the conditions.

I liked this whole ethos.

Pretty soon, the number of recruits in our squadron was down to under ten men, and we'd only just completed half of the mountain weekends. Trucker was still there, but many of the muscle guys had long since fallen by the wayside.

What was clear was that Selection was taking its toll on us all physically.

After each weekend my feet and my bruised body would take days to recover. I would hobble about on tender feet and aching limbs.

My body still felt relatively virgin for this level of mountain endurance work. I was still only twenty and significantly younger than any of the other soldiers on Selection. Endurance comes with age.

It was no surprise that so few young guys passed and that the optimum age was late twenties.

It would be a long journey, and getting used to the strain took time. The key was that I had to learn to recover quickly.

This skill would end up taking me months to develop.

In the early days, my calves would be in agony after one of the long, repeated, fireman's lift hill sessions, and my shoulders would start to burn after just a few hours of carrying the heavy pack around the mountains—but steadily, over time, I hardened.

Another vital lesson I learned, during this first phase of Selection, was how to listen to and prepare my body properly: the right food, the right rest, the right training.

To what level of intensity should I train at in between the tests, and how often?

A big mistake that soldiers often made in preparing for

Selection, was to overtrain and then get hurt—and with an injury, Selection becomes virtually impossible.

It is an intricate balance and requires you to listen carefully to your own body.

This skill has helped me so much in my life since.

CHAPTER 46

One thing that I have always found annoying is that when I most need sleep, I often find it hardest to achieve.

It is a horrible, pit-of-the-stomach feeling: lying wide awake in bed, scared of what is ahead, knowing that your body needs rest, yet unable to switch off.

My head is constantly racing, and the less sleep I get the more it bothers my already troubled mind.

And what was ahead was troubling me—a lot.

Our first make-or-break big physical test. Fail this and you were off the course.

No questions asked.

Infamous in SAS circles as a real tester of character, this mountain test is a grueling eighteen-mile "speed march" (run) in full kit, almost three thousand feet up and then down the other side of one particular high peak, then all the way back to the start.

One minute outside of the set time and you were RTU'd—no second attempts.

At the foot of the mountain on a mild, clear-skied morning, I was more nervous awaiting the setoff time for this than I had been about anything so far.

Do I have enough food in me? Am I going to be strong today? Will I be able to maintain the pace?

Within minutes of starting up the steep track, Trucker and the front group had pulled ahead of me.

Come on, Bear, push harder—you can rest all you want at the end, but go for it now.

Weighed down under 45 lbs of backpack, belt kit, rifle, food, and water, moving at that speed wasn't easy. After an hour, all my clothes were drenched in sweat, and I was striving with all I had to push my body on, faster and faster.

At the halfway mark, I took a quick gulp of water, and then I was off again—back up the long track through the foothills, toward the distant summit.

But I was behind time, and I knew it.

I was angry with myself.

Trucker had looked so in control as he had passed me on his way back: running confidently, looking strong. In contrast, I knew that I looked as I felt: a wreck. My head was down, my eyes were down, and I was breathing wildly through spit-drenched, clenched teeth.

I had to make up time, and fast, or I would fail.

Somehow, I found my strength on the next leg, and I overtook long lines of recruits who were beginning to flag. This gave me more confidence, and I pushed on harder still.

At the summit, I set off almost at a sprint, down to the foot of the peak and the end.

I could see the DS at the gate far beneath me—tiny specks—one and a half thousand feet below, and still three miles away.

I gave it everything I had and ran for the finish.

I made it. With only three minutes to spare.

As I sat on my pack, head hung between my legs, exhausted, the relief swept over me.

I knew that almost all those that I had overtaken would be failed.

Sure enough, thirty minutes later, when all the stragglers had crawled back in, a parade was called.

"The following names, take your kit and put it in the back of the near truck."

It was clinical: cold and unapologetic.

You fail yourself. Remember?

That day sixteen people were returned to their unit.

The bar was being raised ever higher, and, if truth be told, I was struggling.

CHAPTER 47

The night march was a long one.

It started at dusk and wouldn't finish until 3:30 A.M.

The weather had taken a turn for the worse as it had gotten dark, and was making the navigation especially hard.

On the way to the second-to-last checkpoint, among this high, windy, boggy terrain, I had to pass through a dense forest on the steep side of a mountain.

On the map it looked straightforward, but in reality it was a nightmare: thick, dense pine, piles of cut timber, and endless thickets of gorse.

After a few hundred yards I realized this was going to turn into a battle.

I was exhausted already from five hours of night march through boggy moon grass, and this was the last thing I now needed.

I just wanted to reach the other side of the wood.

In the pitch black, navigating through this insanely dense wood required pinpoint accuracy and a total dependence on your compass bearing. But the trees were unending.

Finally, I broke through and hit the steep track on the far side of the forest, and spotted the lone DS tent, silhouetted against the skyline.

The routine when arriving at a checkpoint was rigorously enforced. You approached the checkpoint, crouched down on one knee, map folded tightly in one hand, compass in the other, and weapon cradled in your arms.

Then you announced yourself. Name. Number.

The DS would then give you your next six-figure grid reference, which you had to locate rapidly on the map, and then point out to him with the corner of the compass or a blade of grass. (If we were caught pointing at a map with a finger, instead of a blade of grass or something sharp, we had been threatened, by the unforgettable Sgt. Taff, that he would "Rip that finger off and beat you to death with the soggy end!" It's a threat that I enjoy passing on to my boys when we are reading a map together nowadays.)

As soon as the grid reference was confirmed, it was time to "pack up and f*** off," as we were so often told.

That was your cue to get moving.

I moved away twenty yards from the tent and crouched down in the pitch black. I pulled out my head lamp, which was covered in masking tape with just a small pinprick of light shining through, and carefully studied my laminated map.

The map was always kept folded tightly in my thigh pocket, and the compass was attached to a lanyard from my jacket chest pocket. Lose either and you failed.

I shuffled my back round against the wind, and with a long blade of grass between my fingers, I traced out what I reckoned would be the best route to take across the moorland.

Make a bad choice and it could cost you precious hours.

But errors can come so easily when you are wet through, sleep-deprived and struggling to see a map in low light and strong winds.

I turned into the wind and headed up the steep track alongside the wood, and then across the last two miles of moon grass.

Come on. Let's finish this one now.

It was now 2:00 A.M.

I was so exhausted going along this track that I actually fell asleep walking. I'd never done that before.

It was a horrible feeling, having this intense desire to lie down and sleep, yet needing to fight to suppress that and just push ever onward.

An hour and a half later I reached this small, remote quarry cut into the mountainside. As bleak a reward for finishing a night march as you can imagine.

It was raining hard now, and there was no tree cover to tie a poncho to. I lay down on the marshy ground, pulled my poncho across the top of me, and fell asleep.

I was soon shivering with the cold and utterly soaked through. I just longed to get this miserable test weekend over with.

After being so cold, the battle PT was a welcome relief. I felt I had gone into a different zone in my head now. I no longer cared about the cold or wet or my aching limbs. I just wanted to get it all done.

After two hours of running up and down this steep-sided quarry, as well as doing endless push-ups in the mud, those of us remaining were stood down.

Totally beat up, totally filthy, totally drenched.

Totally wired.

I collapsed in the truck. The first test was complete.

CHAPTER 48

Our next test weekend was in a particularly hellish area of the Welsh mountains—remote, godforsaken, and full of even more boggy, ankle-twisting moon grass.

The area became known affectionately by the other recruits as simply: "The asshole of the world."

The first march started badly for me.

I just couldn't sustain the pace that I knew was required. Soon everyone was passing me.

Why did I so often feel like this at the start of a march? Was it nerves?

I was so frustrated with myself as I neared the first RV. And I knew I was slow.

To make matters worse, twice I found myself lost in this vast quagmire of boggy wetland only to have to use up valuable time moving off course to higher ground in order to reorient myself.

I was just having a bad day. I couldn't understand why I was tired when I should be firing, and why I was flustered when I should be keeping my calm. I didn't know how to stop myself from sliding like this, and I knew that each minute I was falling further behind the required time.

At the second RV I made a bad navigational decision. It cost me vital time. Time I didn't have to spare.

The navigational error was selecting to contour round a mountain, rather than go up and over it. It was a weak decision to try and save me energy—and it proved a disaster.

If anything, choosing the longer, less steep, route only served to exhaust me further.

Tentative holds no power. Sometimes you have just got to tackle these mountains head-on.

As I arrived at the next checkpoint, the DS made me do endless push-ups in the mud, pack still on, as a punishment for approaching the last thirty yards on a track, instead of along the ditch.

He delayed me a full fifteen minutes with this impromptu beasting, and I was now pretty beat-up.

When I finally made it out of the checkpoint, the DS made me wade across a fast-flowing, waist-deep stream instead of allowing me to use the small footbridge. It was a parting gesture from him to piss me off.

I was now soaking wet and struggling big-time. I staggered on for a hundred yards to get out of the DS's view, and then collapsed in a heap to sort myself out. I just needed to rest for a few minutes. I was beat.

The DS had been watching. He shouted and called me back.

"Do you want to pull yourself off the course, mate?" he asked.

He wasn't being unpleasant; he was simply being straight. He knew, from looking at me, that I was in a mess.

"No, Staff."

I staggered to my feet, turned, and staggered on.

"Then go for it, and make up some time," he shouted after me.

A big part of me simply longed for someone else to make the decision. I half-hoped he would shout again and just pull me off the course. But he didn't. You fail yourself.

Yet something deep inside said: *Keep going*.

I knew that nothing good in life ever came from quitting; that there would be plenty of time for rest when the hard work was finished. But such thoughts are easier said than done when you are being broken.

The next climb up that moon-grassed, boggy, interminable mountainside, I will never forget. I was utterly spent. I stumbled forward a couple of paces then would collapse to my knees under the weight of the pack.

I was feeling faint, light-headed, and very, very weak—just like when you have a bad fever and try and get up from your bed to walk.

Down to my knees I went again.

At the summit, I felt a little stronger. Just a little. I tried desperately to push on and make up some time.

Finally, I could see the four-ton trucks below me, parked in a small turnout next to a dam at the foot of the mountains.

I raced down to the dam and clocked in.

I knew I was slow, as I could see all the other recruits huddled in the woods next to the dam's entrance.

Wispy trails of smoke drifted up from the many little self-contained army Hexi stoves, each heating individual mugs of sweet tea. I knew the score. Each recruit quietly working in their own little world, trying to rehydrate and sort their kit out under their basha or camp, before the night march.

The DS didn't say anything. They simply sent me to join the others, and await the orders for the night-march.

As dusk approached, we all stood on parade.

Once more they announced: "Okay, the following will not start the night march. You have not passed today's test."

I stood and waited. Four names were read out.

Then the DS looked up at me. Cold. Unemotional.

". . . And Grylls."

CHAPTER 49

There were several other names read out after mine, but they were a blur.

I'd been failed because I was too slow. There was no fanfare, no quiet words of comfort; just the DS coldly ushering those of us who had failed to the woods to wait for dawn.

It was the worst sinking feeling I had ever felt.

Everything I had worked for—gone. Just like that.

All that sweat and effort and pain—for nothing.

A failure. A loser. A "scug."

In the twilight I sat on my pack in the woods, with ten of the other failed recruits, and I couldn't hold back the silent tears from rolling down my cheeks.

I didn't care who saw me.

Never had I worked so hard for something—never had I given so much of myself, and all for nothing.

Through my tears, I could see the distant figures of Trucker and the few remaining others, silhouetted on the skyline as they climbed into the darkness at the start of their night march.

Trux had put his arm around me earlier. He looked so sad for me. But there was nothing he could do or say.

That night I just lay there feeling utterly alone. I was tucked under the shelter of my bivvy, safe from the driving rain. Yet all I wanted was to be out there—out in that rain, out in the mountains, doing what I had set out to do. Passing. Not failing.

I never knew that being dry and warm could feel so awful.

So much of my life had been privileged. I'd never really had to work that hard for anything. I had grown up with loving parents, with food on the table, warmth, and clothing in abundance.

Yet I had felt uneasy with all that, almost guilty.

I wanted to work hard. I wanted to prove myself somehow worthy of the good things I had known.

If only to know that I possessed some grit and fortitude.

All I had done was remind myself that I had neither.

And that hurt.

⚜

The next few weeks were a real struggle.

Mental turmoil was a new emotion for me, and not a fun one.

I felt I had let myself down, and that I had wasted four months of my life to hard, cold misery, and all for nothing.

I was depressed and I felt useless. And that was on a good day.

The only silver lining was that my squadron training team had invited me back to try once more—if I wanted to.

It would involve going all the way back to the start. Day one.

It was a truly horrendous concept.

But they didn't invite people back who they didn't feel potentially had the right attitude or abilities to pass.

That was some small glimmer of hope, at least.

At this point, my greatest enemy was myself. Self-doubt can be crushing, and sometimes it is hard to see outside the black bubble.

I tried to look at the situation objectively—I'd failed Selection only a third of the way through the course—what chance did I really have of passing if I tried again?

My family said that maybe it wasn't meant to be and that I had gained an invaluable experience from it. This just made me feel worse.

Yet through it all, a little part of me, deep down, believed that I could do this—that I was capable of passing. It wasn't a big part of me, but it was an ember.

Sometimes an ember is all we need.

CHAPTER 50

Our achievements are generally limited only by the beliefs we impose on ourselves.

If we tell ourselves often enough that we don't have what it takes, then that will inevitably become our reality.

But I also knew if I could somehow replace my doubt with hope, my fear with courage, and my self-pity with a sense of pride, then I just might be able to do this.

It would involve paying a huge price in sweat and hard work; it would involve having to train longer and harder than ever before.

And the mind would have to drive it all.

It was a decision I had already made years earlier.

⚜

Ed Amies, one of my oldest and closest friends, told me simply that: "So often, God's callings have a birth, a death, and then a resurrection."

I had had the birth, and had got stuck into Selection; I had had the death, at that fateful dam in the Welsh mountains—now was a logical time for the resurrection.

If my faith stood for anything it was this: miracles really can happen.

So I made the decision to try again.

This time, though, I would be doing this alone.

I knew that support from my family and friends would be much less forthcoming, especially from Mum, who could see the physical toll that just four months had taken.

But I felt deadly serious about passing this properly now and I somehow knew that it was my last chance to do it.

And no one was going to do it for me.

Some two weeks later I listened to a mumbled message on my answering machine from Trucker.

He'd got lost on the final part of a march. After hours of wandering aimlessly in the dark, and out of time, he had finally been found by a DS in a Land Rover, out to look for stray recruits.

Trucker was dejected and tired. He, too, had failed the course.

He went through the same struggle over the next few weeks that I had, and like me, he was invited by the squadron to try again. We were the only two guys to have been asked back.

With greater resolve than ever, we both threw ourselves into training with an intensity that we had never done before. This time we meant business.

We both moved into an old, secluded, rented farm cottage some six miles out of Bristol. And, *Rocky*-style, we started to train.

The next Selection course (of which two are run annually) was just about to start. And just like in *Groundhog Day*, we found ourselves back in that old dusty gymnasium at the squadron barracks, being run ragged by the DS.

There was another whole bunch of hopefuls. They would diminish down at a startling rate. We had seen it happen before.

This time, though, we were there as the "old hands." And it helped.

We knew what to expect; the mystique had gone, and the prize was up for grabs.

That was empowering.

It was now wintertime, and winter Selection is always considered the tougher course, because of the mountain conditions. I tried not to think about this.

Instead of the blistering heat and midges, our enemies would be the freezing, driving sleet, the high winds, and the short daylight hours.

These made Trucker and me look back on the summer Selection days as quite balmy and pleasant! It is strange how accustomed you become to hardship, and how what once seemed horrific can soon become mundane.

The DS had often told us: "If it ain't raining, it ain't training."

And it rains a lot in the Brecon Beacons. Trust me.

(I recently overheard our middle boy, Marmaduke, tell one of his friends this SAS mantra. The other child was complaining that he couldn't go outside because it was raining. Marmaduke, age four, put him straight. Priceless.)

The first few weekends progressed, and we both shone.

We were fitter, stronger, and more confident than many of the other recruits, but the winter conditions were very real.

We had to contend with winds that, on one weekend exercise, were so strong on the high ridges that I saw one gust literally blow a whole line of soldiers off their feet—including the DS.

Our first night march saw one recruit go down with hypothermia. Like everyone else, he was wet and cold, but in the wind and whiteout he had lost that will to look after himself, and to take action early.

He had forgotten the golden rule of cold, which the DS had told us over and over: "Don't let yourself get cold. Act early, while you still have your senses and mobility. Add a layer, make shelter, get moving faster—whatever your solution is, just do it."

Instead, this recruit had just sat down in the middle of the boggy moon grass and stopped. He could hardly talk and couldn't stand. We all gathered round him, forming what little shelter we could. We gave him some food and put an extra layer of clothing on him.

We then helped him stagger off the mountain to where he could be picked up by Land Rover and taken to base camp, where the medics could help him.

For him, that would be his last exercise with 21 SAS, and a harsh reminder that the struggles of Selection go beyond the demons in your head. You also have to be able to survive the mountains, and in winter that isn't always easy.

One of the other big struggles of winter Selection was trying to get warm in the few hours between the marches.

In the summer it didn't really matter if you were cold and wet—it was just unpleasant rather than life-threatening. But in winter, if you didn't sort yourself out, you would quickly end up with hypothermia, and then one of two things would happen: you would either fail Selection, or you would die.

Both options were bad.

CHAPTER 51

Second time around, I could sense that I was stronger.

I found my mind and body coping better in comparison to my first attempt—and I was often now one of the front-runners at the end of a march.

As the Selection tests and weekends progressed, we were taken to more and more difficult and mountainous terrains around Wales: black, featureless peaks, endless bogs, and desolate old quarries.

I spent hour after hour, day after day, slogging around these mountains in the cold and driving rain. I would have the hood of my army-issue jacket wrapped up tight as I steadily plodded onward toward the next checkpoint.

Mumbling to myself, humming to myself, and pushing ever onward.

The worse that the conditions got, the more I had to learn to ride them out.

It is a learned skill to roll with the punches and keep going.

I made that my mantra.

⚜

All of this was slowly becoming second nature to me.

Here I am again: waist-deep in another swollen mountain stream, wading through fierce white water. Or I am kicking my boots into the cold mud of another steep mountainside as I carefully traverse a sheer face in the dark.

I am negotiating a narrow, slippery log across a gorge. It is dark and wet, and I am weighed down under my pack, belt kit, and weapon.

I am tired, but I keep going.

But the worst bit was always the waiting: lying in the cold, wet marshland trying to snatch a few hours' rest in between the marches.

Keep wiggling those toes, keep smiling, keep focused on the next task. You can do this, Bear.

And slowly I did.

Week after week after week.

By the end of the final test of the hills phase, there were only a handful of us left from our squadron. It included both Trucker and myself, plus several others.

We'd done, and been through, so much together—and we all felt like brothers. It was a powerful feeling.

We'd seen each other at our lowest ebb, but somehow the five of us had prevailed. Each of us had waged a private battle, and that had forged in us a pride and a togetherness that is hard to find in civvy street.

But all of this had only really been preparing us for the rigors of Test Week.

This was a week of back-to-back cross-mountain marches that were the culmination of all the physical tests for both the regular and the reserve SAS—and it was a brute.

But pass it, and you were through the first phase of Selection.

For the duration of this Test Week, we would be based from SAS HQ, and all three SAS regiments, 21, 22, 23 SAS, would converge together for it.

We would have to cover a crazy number of miles across mountainous terrain, carrying ever-increasing weights, and always against the clock. Test conditions.

For the regular SAS, Test Week is where they lose the majority of recruits, and it is 100 percent effective in testing even the fittest soldier to their limit. Each and every day the numbers dwindle, as more and more hopefuls fail to make the time required.

Bearing in mind that after each weekend so far, I had invariably been hobbling for a day or so afterward on swollen feet, the prospect of doing six marches back-to-back over much greater distances and with much greater weight, filled me with terror.

I just had no idea whether I could manage it.

At the end of Test Week would come the hardest test of all.

After five days of solid marching, I would have to complete the mother of all marches, nicknamed "Endurance."

It is a good description.

The distance of the march was far, far greater than anything we had ever done before. And it was measured as the crow flies, not taking into account elevation and steepness of terrain. (A "map mile" is very different to an actual mile, which involves going up and over three-thousand-foot mountains, through bogs, and across rivers.)

We would also have to carry 55 lbs of pack, plus weapon, water, food, and belt kit.

No wonder I was scared.

I had some idea what it would really mean.

⚜

That Friday, the five of us sat cramped on top of all our kit in one long-wheel-based Land Rover. We pulled out of our Welsh barracks and headed north into the unknown.

When we arrived at our destination, we were all ushered into a large, stark briefing-room full of hardened, weathered-looking soldiers.

The 22 SAS chief instructor, in his broad Yorkshire accent, told us simply that Selection's Grim Reaper would likely claim the vast majority of us over the next six days. But that if we wanted it badly enough, then it was there for the taking.

"You've got to want it in here, though, lads," he continued, thumping his chest. "It's all in here."

"Okay. First parade is at 0500 tomorrow morning. Further instructions will be posted on the noticeboard each evening. Good luck."

With that he turned and left us to settle in.

CHAPTER 52

I carefully packed my kit into the locker. I set my alarm and tried to sleep.

In truth, I had never felt so nervous.

The whole billet was up early, long before dawn.

Every soldier was here for one purpose: to prove that they could do the distances and do the times. Everything that we had gone through so far was purely preparation for these next six days.

There would be no battle PT, no beastings, no bullshit barrack cleaning or shouting. It wasn't needed. The weights, the distances, and the clock would dictate whether we passed or failed.

At the end of Test Week, the SAS would have a small group of self-motivated, capable, fit soldiers. They would be the raw material that the SAS would then take and mold.

The SAS would teach these few how to soldier in a whole new way. Unconventional. Highly specialized and highly trained.

I went to the cookhouse and ate as much breakfast as I could get down me. I would need every ounce of that energy today.

The noticeboard had told us the weights that our packs needed to be that day. We were expected to weigh our packs ourselves and then be ready on parade at the correct time. Again, no one was treated like a kid here. It was all about self-discipline.

At 0455, I glanced down the line of us on parade. Almost every soldier was dressed slightly differently. Basic kit was the same, but boots and hats were down to the individual.

The SAS want individuals, and they never try to discourage that spirit.

Every soldier had worked hard to be there, and they had earned the right to choose their boots. We each knew the kit we liked, and we each had our own personal take on what worked best. Myself included.

We all stood quietly at ease, our big green packs leaning against us, like a ball and chain around a prisoner's ankles.

The DS quietly checked and weighed our packs in turn, before sending us to the armory to draw out our "weapons."

These were old standard-issue SLRs, but with a twist. Instead of having bolt actions and working parts inside them, they were welded shut with steel.

Nice touch, I thought.

We were then loaded into the four-ton trucks, which rumbled out of the barracks toward the mountains.

It was still dark.

I had no idea where we were going. I just sat in nervous anticipation.

Eventually the truck rumbled off the road and ground to a halt with a hiss of air from the brakes. I looked out.

I knew enough by now to recognize that we were in that horrible moon-grass region.

I should have guessed.

An hour and a half of fumes and nerves, though, had taken its toll, and I felt pretty sick.

I got off the truck and suddenly vomited all over the ground. All I could think about was all that valuable energy, that I'd desperately need all day, being wasted.

My confidence was at rock bottom at this point, as I sat waiting to be called forward and given my first map grid reference.

All those old doubts came flooding back.

I just felt suddenly way out of my depth.

I wasn't a marine or a hardened soldier of any sort. I was pretty damn wet behind the ears in every respect—and I knew it.

I breathed deeply as I stood in line. Calm.

I just needed to start this and get going.

CHAPTER 53

Soon I was off and moving.

Up the first peak and across the next valley, then crossing a river before mounting up toward the next summit.

A few hours on, I passed Trucker, climbing up toward me. He nodded and smiled. He looked like he was going strong.

I set off up the next steep face, scrambling on hands and knees in the wet, boggy terrain.

I was soon on what I hoped would be the last leg back. It was only six miles, but I then made a bad decision and chose a route that led me into a quagmire of marsh and high grass.

I was forced to crisscross endless thirty-foot-deep gorges with rocky, white-water streams pounding through them, and I had to lose vital ground and height to make any sort of progress.

I was determined not to lose my hard-earned time, and I pushed on aggressively through the moon grass. I soon saw the trucks waiting at the bottom of the valley below.

I just made it in within the time, heaved the weight of the "green monkey" pack off my aching back, and collapsed in the back, pleased but dog-tired.

Everyone had gone through similar struggles that day, I found out. The route was designed like that. But I had survived.

The next day was once again in moon-grass terrain. And once more the noticeboard had increased the required weight of our packs. We were also now in a part of the mountains I had never been in before.

I tapped another recruit on the shoulder as we queued up in the cold winter dawn, waiting to be set off individually at two-minute intervals. I asked him about the terrain, and he seemed to know the area well.

In about thirty seconds he briefed me on the pitfalls and short-cuts he had learned.

Good lad. It was invaluable intel.

Selection was good like that. It wasn't a competition. If the training major could be proved wrong, and all of us passed, he would have been the first to celebrate. The SAS aren't restricted on how many recruits they can pass. They are only restricted by their standards.

I set off fast. By now I had walked so many miles of this moon grass that I was actually growing strangely accustomed to the harsh terrain.

That day I finished well, despite the torrential rain that had beaten down on us unceasingly. I stretched off in the back of the trucks and chatted to the other lads on the journey back.

I was gaining in stature and confidence.

By the morning of the next day I noticed a few less trucks. I had heard that quite a lot of recruits had already been binned. They had either got lost, been beaten by the weight of their pack, or failed to make the time.

It was hard to keep track of, but the noticeboard listed the recruits left on the course each evening, and so far my name was still on there.

I wanted to stay the gray man—no dramas, no fuss.

Just do the job, keep within the time, and stay on the list.

CHAPTER 54

Our slowly diminishing group of recruits clambered once more into the back of the big metal lorries, heading yet again to the moon-grass hellhole.

That day we would be covering a lot of the same area that I had been in when I had failed six months earlier. It was time to put those demons to bed.

I was careful not to make the same mistakes: I nibbled on the snacks that I had stuffed in my pocket from breakfast and I drank regularly to keep hydrated.

But just when I was gaining confidence that I had this one under control, I made a careless mistake.

I dropped off the high ground too early, and soon found myself floundering again in the worst of the boggy marsh. Burning up valuable energy and precious time. I could feel my tired limbs leaking energy, and the weight of the pack was pushing my sinking legs further and further into the boggy ground with each step.

To make matters worse, I could see distant figures on the skyline above steaming past me.

I was soon so exhausted that I just had to stop and rest. Just for a minute, to get the weight off my shoulders. I needed to take stock. I downed all the nibbles I could find in my pockets. Rationing was now out. I needed energy.

I reassessed the map and my timing. I had to come up with a plan to get myself out of this mess, and fast.

I turned 90 degrees and started to climb back up onto the high ground that I had just come off. This was way off-route, I should be heading down, but I just knew that the high ground would be better than fighting a losing battle in the bog. I had done that before—and lost.

The wind was blowing hard now, down from the plateau, as if trying to deter me. I put my head down, ignored the shoulder straps that pulled and heaved against my lower neck muscles, and went for it. I had to take control.

I was refusing to fail Selection again in this godforsaken armpit of a place.

Once on the ridge, I started to run. And running anywhere in that moon grass, with the weight of a small person on your back, was a task. But I was on fire. I kept running. And I kept clawing back the time and miles.

I ran all the way into the last checkpoint and then collapsed. The DS looked at me strangely and chuckled to himself.

"Good effort," he commented, having watched me cover the last mile or so of rough ground. I had made it within time.

Demons dead. Adrenaline firing.

⚜

There were only three more marches to complete on Test Week. But they were monster ones.

The first march was back in the Brecon Beacons. It was some

twenty miles long, between the three highest summits—but with three RVs cruelly placed all the way back down at the floor of each valley.

The weight of our packs had also been increased substantially. I had had to take a second look at the noticeboard the night before just to confirm it.

Each morning, as we waited in line to start the march, it was a struggle just to heave the weight of the pack onto my back. Often the easiest way was to squat on the ground, slip your arms into the shoulder straps and then get a buddy to haul you up to your feet.

Once up, you had to stay up.

The weight of the pack was always worse at the start and end of each march, and the first couple of hours invariably felt the most painful.

Any blisters on your shoulder blades would weep painfully, as the weight of the pack went back on. Then somehow your mind would shut out the pain for a while. Until, by the end of the march, your shoulders would start to wilt and cramp up as if they were on fire.

The bloodied, taped-up, and blistered lower backs and shoulders of so many of the recruits told that story best, and the shower block always looked like a field hospital.

Blistered backs and feet being agonizingly stripped and redressed with zinc tape. Soldiers silently going about their business.

In fact much of our time in the evenings was spent redressing and retaping the inevitable blisters that every recruit had to endure.

That morning, I was sick again while we stood around waiting. I hated the waiting. Being sick was pure nerves.

I looked at my day's source of energy on the ground at my feet. Bad start.

On setting off, the snow started to fall thickly, and on top of the first summit I found that my energy was starting to wane fast. Again. My body was simply getting drained of its reserves, day after day.

And it was impossible to replenish those reserves in only a snatched few hours' sleep each night.

I hated this faint, dizzy feeling I was getting.

Why am I getting this now? I need energy.

But the vomiting, lack of sleep, and hour after hour of hard route marches through mountainous bogs, day after day, was systematically taking its clear toll on me.

By halfway I was behind time, and I knew that I needed to up the gear, regardless of how I was feeling. I knuckled down, pushed harder, and sure enough I found that the harder I pushed myself, the more my strength returned.

Finally, I completed the day within the time. I was fired up and still running on adrenaline as I threw my kit in the back of the wagon.

Good job, Bear.

What I didn't realize was that the price of digging so deep, day after day, was that my reserves and endurance levels were getting weaker and weaker.

And you can't run on empty forever.

CHAPTER 55

The next day was a much shorter distance, but the weight was increased again—significantly.

Short and sharp, I thought. *Work hard, Bear, once more.*

The driving, horizontal rain made navigation really hard. And, within minutes of starting out, all my kit was drenched through. I looked like I had just done a deep-river crossing.

Despite being soaked through, I wasn't cold. I was working hard for that.

I pulled the hood of my jacket down lower over my head, and pushed on into the wind.

Six hours later, I saw the end trucks ahead. I heaved the huge pack onto the back and changed into dry kit for the slow, rumbling journey back to camp. Then it was back into the long, laborious process of cleaning my kit, repatching my feet, and prepping for the next day.

Those of us who remained knew all too well what the final twenty-four hours held in store for us.

One march, one last push. But it was a monster.

Endurance is the route march that has made the Selection famous—it is also a march on which a soldier had died some years earlier from fatigue. It is a true leveler—and unifier to all who pass.

The march would take us across the whole Brecon Beacons mountain range . . . and then back again. To drive the magnitude of the task home to us, we realized that we would need two 1:50,000 map sheets just to cover the route.

Symbolically, it was also the last test of the mountain phase of Selection.

Pass this in under twenty-four hours and you were through to the continuation phase of SAS(R) Selection.

❧

At 2:00 A.M. I woke to the sound of my alarm clock. I hated that noise.

Slowly I sat up.

The lights were already on, and everyone was busy taping up their feet or covering the blisters on their backs. The guy next to me looked pale and haggard as he silently taped his toes, like a boxer carefully wrapping his hands before a fight.

I had somehow avoided ever using too much blister tape. I had persevered in the early days to get my back and feet accustomed to the weight, and looking at the backs and ankles around me strapped and taped up tight, I was grateful for that, at least.

I had survived thus far with only a few annoying blisters, and that can make a critical difference.

My body, though, felt utterly exhausted, and my ankles and feet were both badly swollen.

The best I could do was literally to hobble slowly the hundred yards to the cookhouse.

Halfway I stopped to rest—and think.

Look at yourself, Bear, I thought. *Today is Endurance. Yet you can hardly walk to the cookhouse.*

I tried to put the thought aside.

The parade that night in the dark was deathly quiet. No one spoke. We were now but a tiny fraction of those who had started out only a week ago. Trucker was still there. He had been stubbornly, quietly, doing the distances, making the time. No fuss. Good lad.

"We can do this, buddy," I muttered to him as we stood waiting. "Just one more march and we can nail this, Trux."

He smiled wearily back.

He looked like the walking wounded. We all did. Strong men, shuffling on hurting feet.

Just let me get moving, I thought, *and the pumping blood will shake the stiffness and pain from my back and feet.*

No one talked on that last truck journey out to the mountains. We all sat huddled, heads covered by hats or hands, in our own worlds.

It was freezing cold in the middle of that February night.

The hiss of brakes and the jolt of the dying engine shook us into life. I looked outside.

It was dark, and the snow was thick on the ground. Time to dismount.

Our packs now weighed 55 lbs plus belt kit, water, food, and weapon. Too bloody heavy.

They weighed our packs on the old meat-hook scales slung roughly off the back of one of the trucks.

The scale read that Trucker's pack was underweight by a pound.

The DS tossed a ten-pound rock at him to add to his pack. Endurance was Endurance. None of us could expect any favors here.

Trux and I helped each other saddle up and heave the packs onto our backs, then, one by one we lined up, waiting to be set off at the customary two-minute intervals.

It was bitingly cold, and the wind was quite strong even down here at the foot of the mountains. We all turned our backs to the wind as we waited in line.

Finally—my name.

"Grylls. The clock's ticking. Go."

CHAPTER 56

I headed off across the track into the darkness.

I set my bearing to the first trig point on the summit ridge, put my head down and started to move as fast as my feet would carry me.

The first checkpoint was some two thousand feet above, and I reckoned I could cut the corner off by heading up the bowl of the valley instead of following the ridgeline.

I knew early on that this was a mistake.

I had grossly underestimated how deep the snow pack would be, but by then I was committed to this route and couldn't afford to go back.

The snow pile in the bowl was this horrible waist-deep drift snow. I was reduced to a snail's pace.

I could see this trail of figures above me, silhouetted against the full moon skyline. It was all the other recruits moving steadily up.

Meanwhile I was floundering in this hellhole of deep snow, going nowhere.

I had hardly even started Endurance.

I cursed myself.

What a crap decision, Bear.

I was pouring with sweat already.

It took me over an hour to clear the ridgeline, and by then there was no sign of any other recruits. I was on my own and behind.

The wind was horrendous as I crested the ridge, and it was truly a case of moving two paces forward, then stumbling back one.

I worked my way cautiously along the ridge's narrow sheep track, with a sheer drop of some eight hundred feet just yards to my right.

Suddenly a small icy pool under me cracked, and I dropped up to my thighs in freezing cold, black, oozing mud.

I was now wet, and covered in this heavy, black clay that clung like glue to my legs.

Cracking start.

I just put my head down and carried on.

As the first flicker of dawn began to rise, I ascended, for one last symbolic time, the east ridge of that one high peak we had got to know so well.

I had been strong on this mountain so many times, but this time, I was reduced to a slow plod up its steep face—head bowed, legs straining under the weight, breathing hard.

It felt like a final submission to the mountain's enduring ability to make mere humans buckle.

As we descended and then started to climb up into the next valley, I found myself ascending toward a spectacular winter sunrise, peeping over the distant skyline.

We would walk all through this day, and wouldn't finish until after midnight the next day—that was if we completed Endurance at all.

I just kept plodding and plodding, and then plodded some more.

Keep the pace; control your breathing; keep pushing.

The hours blurred into themselves. It was a war of attrition with my mind and body—all the time trying to ignore the growing swelling of bruised feet inside wet, cracked boots.

I descended yet another steep, snow-covered mountain down toward a reservoir: our halfway mark. Exhausted, I dropped my pack down and rummaged for some food. I needed energy.

The other recruits I could see were all eating madly as they shuffled out of the RV. Dark, wet, hunched figures, moving fast across the moorland leading back up into the mountains, chewing on oatmeal ration biscuits or army chocolate bars.

I had been stationary for more than five minutes now at the checkpoint, waiting in turn. I knew I had to start moving soon or my legs would start to seize up. Stops any longer than a few minutes were always more painful to get going from again.

I saddled up and started back up the same face I had just descended. I was soon slowed by more of the incessant moon grass and marshy bog. I tried to push through it as fast my body would take me.

Ten miles later, I caught up with Trucker and we moved on together—two lone figures trying to keep the pace, fighting this creeping exhaustion.

At the next checkpoint, I took my boots off, which were filled to the brim with mud and water from the marshy terrain. I put fresh socks on and drained my boots. In wet boots, fresh socks didn't really make much difference, but they did mentally. We now only had eighteen miles to go—and I had new socks.

Psychologically, it was a fresh start.

Get on, Bear, get up, and get moving. Finish this.

CHAPTER 57

VW Valley is one of the final mountains one climbs on Selection—but it's among the worst.

VW stands for Voluntary Withdrawal, and when you see the mountain you can understand why people have often quit here.

Steep, windswept, and boggy—and at mile thirty it is the point where many recruits quit and remove themselves from the course—broken by the sheer distance, weight, and speed.

But not me. Not now.

On my backside, I slid down the first steep reentrant leading into the bowl of the valley. I was using the butt of my weapon to steer me as I glissaded down the snow, and I finally slowed at the bottom, near an iced-over stream.

I crossed it and started straight up the face with Trucker behind me.

On and on and on—until finally at the crest I collapsed and waited for him.

Trux's feet were both badly swollen. Later on he discovered that he'd broken both of his big toes somewhere around this point. It was purely from the incessant pounding his feet were taking. He was in agony.

I heard him muttering under his breath. He was mumbling Bible verses to himself.

We had often both quietly prayed together before the big marches. Now we needed that help more than ever.

"I am holding you by your right hand . . . Do not be afraid. I am here to help you." Isaiah, 41:13.

If ever I needed to hear such words it was now.

It is easy to be cynical and to think you do not need help when all is going your way; but if Selection taught me anything it is that we all have our limits. To push beyond those limits sometimes requires something beyond just ourselves.

That is what my faith has given me—a secret strength and help when I have needed it most.

I needed it now.

As we cleared the summit, the mist descended and darkness began to fall again. We soon began to get very cold. We were exhausted, staggering through this boggy plateau in the failing light, and gradually we realized we had become disoriented out of sheer fatigue.

We were descending slowly when we should have been still on the plateau.

"Where the hell are we?" I mumbled to myself, shivering, as I restudied the map.

We both searched in circles for the small cliff-edge path that would take us down to our next checkpoint.

It was soon pitch-black and the mist was thick on the mountaintops, reducing visibility to almost zero.

I was in front when suddenly I slipped and started to slide fast down this muddy, icy gulley. Trucker was right behind me, falling, too.

As we slowed in the snowy gravel slush, I turned to climb back up where we had fallen, when suddenly we saw a light just below us.

I realized that this was the checkpoint we had been looking for in vain. What an answer to our desperate, quiet prayers!

We checked in and headed out for the last RV.

Suddenly the going got almost impossible. I went up to my waist in bog three times. The terrain was also littered with endless cut tree trunks, half-submerged in the peaty ground.

I was freezing cold and badly dehydrated now. This march was beginning to beat me.

I had nothing more to give. Slowly but surely, from sheer exhaustion, I was beginning to shut down.

Matt, one of the other recruits from our squadron, was with us now as well. He could see I was at my limit. He pulled me aside and made me put on an extra layer of clothing. He shared his water bottle with me and helped me stand.

He did more for me in that hour than I can ever thank him for. Then, together, the three of us pressed on.

Soon we spotted a dirt track down below us. It was a way out from these cursed tree stumps. We knew the consequences of being caught using a track: RTU'd at once.

But we were getting nowhere in this godforsaken terrain, and we needed to make up time if we were to pass this final march.

It was do or die.

We picked our way through the maze of dense tree stumps and stumbled out onto the track.

Cautiously, we began to follow it.

Suddenly we saw headlights ahead, and we dived over a barbed-wire fence. We had nowhere to hide—so just hit the dirt. We lay there, faces pressed into the mud, and didn't move.

I prayed that the headlight beam wouldn't pick us out.

The Land Rover, with the DS inside, rumbled slowly past without stopping. They hadn't spotted us.

We risked the track for another thirty minutes, then cut east back into the woods and then onto open moorland again.

The end was now only eight miles away.

But the end just never seemed to come. We were like the walking dead.

Matt, Trucker, and I had to stop and sit down every five hundred meters for a rest, but then we'd fall into a daze in a matter of seconds as the weight came off our shoulders and legs.

Two minutes sitting, slumped in the snow and mud, then I'd have to kick Matt and get him moving again. It was my turn to help him.

"Get up, Matt, we've got to finish this."

Eventually, across the reservoir, we spotted what we'd been looking for.

Headlights glistening on the water.

They were coming from the four-ton trucks that stood waiting for us at the end. We could hear the distant low rumble of their diesel engines turned on to fire the heaters inside the cabs.

It was only half a mile as the crow flies across the reservoir, but probably three miles to march all the way around.

Renewed energy soared to my muscles. I picked up the pace and started to march as fast as I could. It was pure adrenaline, driving me to finish this hell.

Finally, after twenty-one hours, Matt, Trucker, and myself were the first of the twenty-one SAS recruits to finish Endurance.

I had never felt so exhausted, relieved, proud, and broken in all my life.

But all I cared about was that I was through the mountain phase of SAS Selection.

Continuation training, though, would prove to be a very different and much tougher beast altogether.

CHAPTER 58

At the end of the hill phase, only a handful of recruits from our squadron remained.

It took me nearly six days to get any real feeling back into my swollen feet and blistered back, but I had proven myself fit and resilient in the mountains.

Now would come the time to be trained.

First we had to learn what they called "green army" skills (which are the regular, basic soldiering skills), and then, when these were mastered, we would move on to learn the SF skills.

It would be on these specialist skills that the bulk of our time would be spent. After all, it was now time for the DS to take the raw materials and shape us into the highly trained, resourceful, specialist soldiers that the SAS are famed for.

This process would teach us to carry out intricate skills accurately, swiftly, and, most important, intuitively. The learning curve to reach this standard would be intense. We were told that any mistakes or slipups would be excused once only. After that you had to get the drills right, every time—if you didn't, you were out.

More than anything, I wanted to be capable of the standard the SAS required, to make the grade and learn the skills. I was determined not to mess up this opportunity that I had worked so hard to get.

We had ahead of us many long weekends to learn these specialist skills. Then would come a long, intensive battle camp lasting several weeks, where our skills and character would be put to the test under exhausting and pressured conditions to see if ultimately we were up to becoming SAS soldiers.

At the end of this would come the most grueling of phases, designed to initiate combat troops to be prepared for capture. If we successfully came through that (and we were told that this phase always claimed a few scalps), then, and only then, would the WHO DARES WINS cap-badge and SAS beret be earned.

❦

On our first weekend training at SAS HQ, the pace started hard. But now it wasn't all about the physical. This was about learning the skills—and then combining those skills with the physical strength we had developed.

We were summoned before dawn into an underground bunker. This was where all the lectures and information would now be thrown at us—thick and fast.

"Explanation. Demonstration. Imitation." That was the mantra. We would have a drill explained to us, be shown it, then be expected to perform it. Again and again until we got it perfect.

We would cover a huge amount of ground in these days, getting familiar with any of the SOPs (standard operating procedures) that UK Special Forces use.

What I noticed, though, was that the atmosphere now was very different—we were no longer treated as recruits, as numbers—but were treated more like potential SAS soldiers—soldiers the DS might well have to fight alongside in the near future.

So those DS now had a vested interest in making sure we learned the drills properly and that any weak links among us were weeded out.

In many ways this next phase was less forgiving than the mountains. If that was possible. It was more subjective—if the DS didn't think you were up to the job, or you weren't picking things up fast enough—or if they simply reckoned your face didn't quite fit, then you were gone. No questions asked.

What the DS cared about now was this: Are you quick to learn? Can you react, adapt, and improvise? Can you remain calm under pressure? Can you work well in a small team, as well as alone? Are you self-disciplined, organized, yet able to show controlled aggression when needed?

I could also now understand why the physical levels demanded had been so high. That fitness was now being put into practice—it had a purpose.

"You have a heli extraction due in five hours—the location is fifteen miles away. You also have one casualty and an enemy force on your tail. If the mission is to be successful you have to make that heli RV—so get moving."

And I was loving it.

CHAPTER 59

There was no doubting we now felt more part of the SAS fold, and it felt good.

As we rehearsed the enemy contact drills over and over again, the adrenaline flowed nonstop. We were either fighting our way out of snap ambushes, lugging ammunition and radios up mountains, or preparing for dawn raids on disused farm buildings.

In between it all we would still be doing endless runs and PT sessions, and of course the inevitable battle PT and pack run.

Just when we were getting the hang of one set of drills, they would throw a whole load more at us. It was a relentless pace, mentally, to keep up with, and it is why the SAS are considered to be the ultimate "thinking-man's soldier."

That ability to think clearly and act decisively when all about you is chaos. Oh, and to learn ultrafast.

Camouflage, tracking, caching, or CTRs (close target recces). Weapon drills: in the mud, underwater, in the dark. Training on all the many different foreign weapons; learning how to assemble and fire them quickly and accurately. Live-firing during four-man contact drills, while ducking and weaving up "jungle" target lanes, expending hundreds and hundreds of rounds.

And through it all, we were learning how to work as the ultimate team: to know instinctively how each of us reacted under pressure, and where our individual strengths lay.

The idea was that when we needed him, we would just know our wingman would be there.

Tension was always high, as the consequences of mistakes began to get more serious. We were in this together, and errors would cost us collectively. At best, it might be a night of push-ups, and at worst one of our lives. (Real bullets, being fired at targets in the dark, while diving and scraping through ditches, are always unforgiving in such close proximity to one another.)

Our final battle camp was fast approaching, and the DS's discussions over our individual suitability for SAS service were becoming more frequent now.

They also continued to increase the physical pressure, as time and time again the DS would have us running up and down mountainsides with heavy machine guns and boxes of ammunition.

"Good—now do it all again—but this time strip and reassemble a rifle as you climb."

And through it all, we knew that, by the end, not all of us would pass.

⚜

The journey up to battle camp started badly.

"If you can't even load a bloody truck with all your kit properly, then you've got no bloody chance of passing what's ahead of you, I can assure you of that!" Taff, our squadron DS, barked at us in the barracks before leaving.

I, for one, was more on edge than I had ever felt so far on Selection.

I was carsick on the journey north, and I hadn't felt that since I'd been a kid heading back to school. It was nerves.

We also quizzed Taff for advice on what to expect and how to survive the "capture-initiation" phase.

His advice to Trucker and me was simple: "You two toffs just keep your mouths shut—23 DS tend to hate recruits who've been to private school."

The 23 SAS were running the battle camp (it generally alternated between 21 and 23 SAS), and 23 were always regarded as tough, straight-talking, hard-drinking, fit-as-hell soldiers. We had last been with them at Test Week all those months earlier, and rumor was that "the 23 DS are going to make sure that any 21 recruits get it the worst."

Trucker and I hoped simply to try and stay "gray men" and not be noticed. To put our heads down and get on and quietly do the work.

This didn't exactly go according to plan.

"Where are the lads who speak like Prince Charles?" The 23 DS shouted on the first parade when we arrived.

"Would you both like newspapers with your morning tea, gents?" the DS sarcastically enquired.

Part of me was tempted to answer how nice that would be, but I resisted.

The DS continued: "I've got my eye on you two. Do I want to have to put my life one day in your posh, soft hands? Like fuck I do. If you are going to pass this course you are going to have to earn it and prove yourself the hard way. You both better be damned good."

Oh, great, I thought.

I could tell the next fortnight was going to be a ball-buster.

CHAPTER 60

The first five days were a blur of limited sleep, endless tests, and more PT than we had ever done before.

Each morning began with one of these hour-long, killer PT sessions, held at 0500, before the day's program had even begun.

Meals were often eaten standing up, and I wasn't quite sure why they had bothered to issue us with beds, we got to see them so little.

We'd go from stripping foreign weapons blindfolded, and against the clock, to a ballistics lecture; then into a practical signaling exercise; then from a lake crossing into another pack run; followed by live contact drills, helicopter rehearsals, a field medics lecture, and a practical assessment.

The pace was intense, and the DS wanted to test our individual mental and physical abilities to stay alert and switched on and working well as a team, even when our heads were bursting with new information and we were physically shattered.

We were up each night until 3:00 or 4:00 A.M., often doing mock ambushes and live attacks.

The hardest times were when we were just lying there in some ditch in the pouring rain, so tired that it was near impossible not to nod off for a few seconds. Cold, hungry, and drained of adrenaline—waiting for the DS to pass through our "ambush" site high up on the boggy Yorkshire moorland that surrounded the barracks.

Often they never showed, and we would finally haul ourselves, and all our kit and weaponry, back to camp in the early hours, where we'd have to clean everything like new.

Only then could we collapse into our billets for a precious couple of hours' sleep.

I learned to dread the alarm that roused us each morning for PT, after only having had such a small amount of sleep.

My body felt like the walking dead—tired, bruised, stiff. Yet the skill level we were required to operate at increased every day.

That was the real test of this phase: Can you maintain the skills when you are beat?

I remember one early-morning PT session in particular. We were doing our usual series of long shuttle sprints and fireman's lifts, which had us all on the point of vomiting. Just when I thought I could run no longer with the weight on my shoulders, there was a loud thud and cry of pain from behind me.

I glanced behind me to see a recruit lying sprawled out on the concrete, oozing blood.

Apparently, the guy carrying this poor recruit on his shoulders had sprinted too close to a lamp post on the road and, as he passed it, he had thwacked the guy's head so hard he had been knocked clean out.

The silver lining was that the medics moved in, and we were all dismissed half an hour early. Perfect. But this didn't happen that often. In fact, that was about the only tiny letup we got for two weeks.

This general lack of sleep really got to me. And little can prepare people for how they will react when deprived of it—over multiple days. Everything suffers: concentration, motivation, and performance. All key elements for what we were doing. But it is designed that way. Break you down and find out what you are really made of. Underneath the fluff.

I remember during one particular lecture (on the excruciatingly boring topic of the different penetration abilities of different bullets or rounds), looking over to my left and noticing Trucker jabbing his arm with a safety pin every few minutes in an attempt to keep himself awake.

The sight cheered me up no end.

What became so draining was that nothing that any of us did went unnoticed. Again, it was carefully planned that way: they wanted to see us work under the maximum amount of fatigue and pressure.

Soon I was just longing for the final four-day exercise, where at least we could get out on the ground, in our patrols, away from this intense scrutiny and hell.

The day of the final exercise started in the cold predawn (as usual), but with no PT (unusual), and we were moved into our small four-man patrols.

We could no longer have any interaction with anyone outside of our own small team or cell. (This is a standard operational security measure to ensure that if you are captured then you have no knowledge of any other patrol's particular mission.) It effectively acts to keep you 100 percent mission-focused.

Orders were issued and individual patrols briefed on their mission-specific details.

The day was then a flurry of mission preparations: stripping down our individual kit to the bare minimum so we could carry enough ammunition between us. Filling magazines with rounds and tracer rounds, cleaning weapons, studying maps, rehearsing drills, memorizing emergency heli RVs, going over E&E (escape and evasion) procedures, and testing radio comms.

I was fired up, and chomping to get going.

The four of us then ate, went over the mission once more, and then rechecked our kit once again.

The helicopter was due at dusk.

Above: 7:22 A.M., May 26, 1998. Neil and me with the regimental flag on the summit of Everest.

Left: Celebrating, finally, at the end of the Everest ascent. Drained but so happy.

Crevasse crossing in the Khumbu Icefall on Everest.

Above: Geoffrey, Mick, me, and Neil—celebrating British success the British way in the relative warmth of base camp.

Left: Returning to Everest almost ten years later to fly the first powered paraglider above the summit of the mountain. Another high-risk mission!

Above: Shara and me just before we got married.

Right: Shara on the deck of our houseboat in London for Jesse's christening.

Above: One of my favorite times of day: reading to the boys. Our best-loved book: *The Bear Scouts' Adventure*!

Left: On our little island in North Wales—living life to the full.

Top: Jesse, Huckleberry, and Marmaduke—our three beautiful boys.

Left: Shara and Marmaduke—one of my favorite pictures in the world. Shara is so happy.

Right: As a family we do a lot of this sort of thing. Simple pleasures.

Above: Life doesn't get much better than this: climbing with Jesse along the cliff tops of our Welsh island home.

Left: Keeping fit has always been an important part of my job—and I love it when the family joins in as well!

CHAPTER 61

It was a bright night as we watched the chopper swoop in low over the camp, silhouetted against the moon. We threw our packs on board and climbed inside.

It was my first time in a military helicopter flying at low level through the mountains to a remote landing zone (LZ) at night. As part of the team, as fit and as trained as I could have ever hoped to be, I felt invincible.

The chopper soon came to a hover, barely five feet off the ground on the top of a bleak mountain. We silently piled off and took up our all-round-defense positions as the heli disappeared down off the peak, into the night sky.

Soon it was all silent, save for the noise of the wind steadily blowing across the back of our packs as we lay quietly and waited. We needed to tune our senses in before we started to move.

We then patrolled off. Our first contact was seven miles away.

We were to be met by a nondescript person in a nondescript vehicle, who would relocate us closer to our target and provide updated intelligence on our mission.

We arrived, took up split positions, waited, and listened.

Slowly, though, the tiredness of the night began to creep in, as the adrenaline of the previous hours began to wear off.

Stay awake. Come on, Bear. Get a grip.

Those hours waiting, immobile, cold and stiff, were a fight to stay awake through.

Every few minutes I'd nod off and then wake with a start, trying to shake the fatigue from my head. I even tried resting my chin on my rifle's foresight, which was sharp and pointed, in an attempt to keep myself awake.

Finally, the agent pulled up in the clearing.

Quickly and silently, we piled into the back of his transit van. For half an hour the agent drove us through narrow lanes as we pored over the sketch map we had just been given in the back. The red light of our torches flickered crazily.

Soon we were dropped off in a turnout on a small deserted road, and the vehicle disappeared into the night.

We set off cross-country and patrolled to our prearranged operating procedure (OP) point, where we would set eyes on our primary target for the first time.

❧

The scenario for the exercise was simple.

Our target was the suspected hideout of a kidnap-hostage sting. On confirmation of this intel, we would have twenty-four hours to regroup with two further patrols, brief them, form a plan to rescue the hostage, and then execute the mission. We would then have to extract ourselves to our final RV.

From here, all patrols, plus the hostage, would be extracted.

At the end of all of this, we would be compromised. We would be intentionally caught and would then begin the final phase of capture-initiation.

Through everything that would happen during this final test, we of course would know it was all simulation. Yet we had

learned over the months of continuation training to treat everything we did as real.

That was the key to preparing troops for combat: train hard,
fight easy. Make the training as real as possible and when it then
happens for real, there are fewer surprises.

And one thing the SAS have become very good at over the years
is making that training simulation feel utterly real.

Trust me.

CHAPTER 62

We located a good OP position overlooking a deserted house—which was our target. We camouflaged ourselves and set about our OP rota. This would consist of working in pairs on two-hour shifts, observing the target and taking notes on any enemy movements, and eating and resting.

It was a welcome relief finally to be able to close my eyes, even if only briefly.

It was summer, and the sun shone all day on our well-hidden camouflaged position, which made a change from the incessant summer showers we had endured for the previous ten days. And quietly, undetected, we lived and watched, only three hundred yards from the target location.

Our task the next night was to guide two further patrols into our location from a few miles out. Matt and I were to meet and bring the other patrols in, while the other two in our patrol maintained the OP rota.

The meeting was set for between 0300 and 0500 hours.

Matt and I reached the RV early and sat and waited.

Deep in a thorny thicket, the wind and rain having returned now, I pulled my hood over my head to try and keep warm.

We waited in alternate shifts to keep awake. But Matt, like me, was dead tired, and soon, unable to stay awake any longer, we both fell asleep on watch. Bad skills. I woke just as I heard the rustling of the other patrols approaching.

One of the 23 DS was in the first patrol, and I quickly crawled forward, tapped him on the shoulder, and began to guide him back to where we had been waiting.

The DS gave me a thumbs-up, as if to say "well done," and by the time I had returned to where Matt was, he had shaken himself awake and looked like a coiled spring who had been covering all his fields of fire vigilantly all night long.

Little did the DS know that five minutes earlier, Matt and I had both been fast asleep, hats pulled over our eyes, snoozing like babies in a pram. If we had been caught we would have been binned instantly.

(I challenge you, though, to find any SAS soldier who didn't have at least one such narrow escape at some point during his journey through Selection.)

No one is perfect.

❧

By first light we had guided the other patrols into our main OP location, a few hundred yards back from the main target. We rested up in our position and continued to observe. By late afternoon, still no activity had been reported.

Then, suddenly, that all changed.

We observed a van race up the track at high speed, approaching the house. Two men dressed in blood-red balaclavas exited the van, threw open the rear doors, and dragged a girl out by her hair, screaming.

They went into the house and slammed the door shut.

We relayed the intel, and were immediately tasked by radio with forming a rapid plan of recovery and extraction.

That was all we needed.

Minutes later, with dusk falling, we were ready to carry out the hostage rescue.

One group was to hit the terrorists, and recover the hostage—and the other patrols would cover them and take out any QRF (quick reaction force) that the terrorists might have in place to reinforce them.

The plan went like clockwork. It seemed that all the training had paid off. We stormed the building, "shot" the terrorists, and extracted the hostage.

The details are not for sharing. But it all happened very fast. Soon we were all huddled in the stripped-out rear of a transit van, speeding down the country lanes. Out of there.

Job done.

As arranged, our contact had met us as soon as the sting had gone down. Another vehicle had taken the "hostage" away for debrief.

I felt electric and was still buzzing with the adrenaline that coursed through my body.

The first part of the exercise was done, the finish goal within reach, and we were now barely one day away from getting badged.

But the final day and night of hell would be make-or-break.

CHAPTER 63

Some things are near impossible to prepare for. I was nervous as hell.

We were squashed in the back of the transit van: four sweaty, muddy men, all our belt kit, our rifles, and packs all crammed on top of each other; and the low light on the inside roof of the cargo area flickered faintly as we careered around the lanes.

My compass told me that we were not heading south. I knew instinctively that something was wrong.

Suddenly the van pulled over, the brakes were slammed on, and we stopped very sharply.

At first there was silence, then it started.

Bang, bang, bang, on the metal panels of the van.

It had begun.

⚜

What followed, and then went on until the following day, was a blur of mental and physical stress and trauma, intended to re-create and simulate the duress of captivity. It is truly unpleasant and truly terrifying—but as for the details, I am not at liberty to disclose what actually happens.

The day before our final exercise had begun, the DS had made the briefing crystal clear.

"Don't give them anything or they will exploit it. Be smart. Stay focused despite the pain and fatigue. Slip up for a second and you fail. And no one is your friend, until you see me walk in wearing a white cross on my sleeve. Only then is the exercise over."

"The Red CROSS is not my white cross; a vicar's CROSS is not my white cross . . . the offer of a hot-CROSS bun and a sip of tea is not my white cross. Do you understand?"

He reiterated. "Don't get caught out—not at this stage of Selection."

Their tactics were brutal but effective. But no one was going to rob me of this opportunity now. I was so close to finishing SAS Selection. I wasn't going to give them anything.

My mind was racing, but deep down I knew that despite it all, I was holding my control. I would not give in to these bastards. I sang hymns in my head and prayed continually. *Keep me strong.*

I'd never felt this battered and tired.

My head ached uncontrollably and the muscles in my back screamed from cramp. I collapsed again, and again. I was exhausted, hungry, thirsty, and shivering uncontrollably in the cold underground air.

The minutes blurred into hours, and the hours seemed to never end.

Was it day or was it night?

I no longer had any idea.

Finally, finally, I was thrown into this tiny, dark cell. It all went quiet. But I instantly noticed the warmth. And I could just make out the shape of the room under the crack in my blindfold.

I waited.

I was half-naked with my camouflage jacket pulled back

halfway down my back, and I was huddled over shivering. I must have looked a mess.

I could taste the snot smeared down my face.

A hand pulled my blindfold off and a light went on.

"Recognize this, Bear?" a voice said softly.

I squinted. The DS was pointing at a white cross on his arm. I didn't react. I needed to double-check in my mind.

"This means the end of the exercise—Endex. Remember?"

I did, but still I didn't react yet. I needed to check once more in my mind. Then, finally, I nodded weakly at him. And he smiled back.

It was the end.

"Well done, buddy. Now take a seat, take five, and get this brew down you. The quack will be in to see you in a few minutes."

The DS put a blanket around my shoulders. A smile spread across my face and I felt a tear of relief trickle down my cheek.

For an hour a psychiatrist then debriefed me. He told me that I had done well and had resisted effectively. I felt just so relieved. I loved that psychiatrist.

The real lesson of this was twofold: Control your mind; and Don't get caught.

As the DS said, "Remember, at the end of the day, these guys are on your side. They are British, they aren't a real enemy. If they were, then that'd be when things would get messy. So remember: do not get captured!"

It is a lesson I have never forgotten, and is probably why I have, over the years, become very, very good at getting out of all sorts of scrapes.

⚜

Back in the barracks, those of us still left were white-faced and very shaky, but we were so relieved that the ordeal was finally over.

Trucker looked particularly bad, but had this huge grin. I sat on his bed and chatted as he pottered around sorting his kit out. He kept shaking his head and chuckling to himself.

It was his way of processing everything. It made me smile.

Special man, I thought to myself.

We all changed into some of the spare kit we had left over from the final exercise and sat on our beds, waiting nervously.

We might have all finished—but—had we all passed?

"Parade in five minutes, lads, for the good and the bad news. Good news is that some of you have passed. Bad news . . . you can guess."

With that the DS left.

I had this utter dread that I would be one of the ones to fail at this final hurdle. I tried to fight the feeling.

Not at this stage. Not this close.

The DS reappeared—he rapidly called out a short list of names and told them to follow him. I wasn't in that group. The few of us remaining, including Trucker, looked at one another nervously and waited.

The minutes went by agonizingly slowly. No one spoke a word.

Then the door opened and the other guys reappeared, heads down, stern-faced, and walked past us to their kit. They started packing.

I knew that look and I knew that feeling.

Matt was among them. The guy who had helped me so much on that final Endurance march. He had been failed for cracking under duress. Switch off for a minute, and it is all too easy to fall for one of the DS's many tricks and tactics.

Rule 1: SAS soldiers have to be able to remain sharp and focused under duress.

Matt turned, looked at me, smiled, and walked out.

I never saw him again.

CHAPTER 64

So that is how we came to be standing in a sparse room, in a nondescript building in the barracks at SAS HQ—just a handful out of all those who had started out so many months earlier.

We shuffled around impatiently. We were ready.

Ready, finally, to get badged as SAS soldiers.

The colonel of the regiment walked in, dressed casually in lightweight camo trousers, shirt, beret, and blue SAS belt.

He smiled at us.

"Well done, lads. Hard work, isn't it?"

We smiled back.

"You should be proud today. But remember: this is only the beginning. The real hard work starts now, when you return to your squadron. Many are called, few are chosen. Live up to that." He paused.

"And from now on for the rest of your life remember this: you are part of the SAS family. You've earned that. And it is the finest family in the world. But what makes our work here extraordinary is that everyone here goes that little bit extra. When everyone else gives up, we give more. That is what sets us apart."

It is a speech I have never forgotten.

I stood there, my boots worn, cracked, and muddy, my trousers ripped, and wearing a sweaty black T-shirt.

I felt prouder than I had ever felt in my life.

We all came to attention—no pomp and ceremony. We each shook the colonel's hand and were handed the coveted SAS sandy beret.

Along the way, I had come to learn that it was never about the beret—it was about what it stood for: camaraderie, sweat, skill, humility, endurance, and character.

I molded the beret carefully onto my head as he finished down the line. Then he turned and said: "Welcome to the SAS. My door is always open if you need anything—that's how things work around here. Now go and have a beer or two on me."

Trucker and I had done it, together, against all the odds.

So that was SAS Selection. And as the colonel had said, really it was just the beginning.

Since I did Selection all those years ago, not much has really changed.

The MOD (Ministry of Defence) website still states that 21 SAS soldiers need the following character traits: "Physically and mentally robust. Self-confident. Self-disciplined. Able to work alone. Able to assimilate information and new skills."

It makes me smile now to read those words. As Selection had progressed, those traits had been stamped into my being, and then during the three years I served with my squadron they became molded into my psyche.

They are the same qualities I still value today.

The details of the jobs I did once I passed Selection aren't for sharing publicly, but they included some of the most extraordinary training that any man can be lucky enough to receive.

I went on to be trained in demolitions, air and maritime insertions, foreign weapons, jungle survival, trauma medicine, Arabic, signals, high-speed and evasive driving, winter warfare, as well as "escape and evasion" survival for behind enemy lines.

I went through an even more in-depth capture initiation program as part of becoming a combat-survival instructor, which was much longer and more intense than the hell we endured on Selection.

We became proficient in covert night parachuting and unarmed combat, among many other skills—and along the way we had a whole host of misadventures.

But what do I remember and value most?

For me, it is the camaraderie, and the friendships—and of course Trucker, who is still one of my best friends on the planet.

Some bonds are unbreakable.

I will never forget the long yomps, the specialist training, and of course a particular mountain in the Brecon Beacons.

But above all, I feel a quiet pride that for the rest of my days I can look myself in the mirror and know that once upon a time I was good enough.

Good enough to call myself a member of the SAS.

Some things don't have a price tag.

CHAPTER 65

Meanwhile, Trucker and I, through all of this, had been renting that cottage together, on a country estate six miles outside of Bristol. We were paying a tiny rent, as the place was so rundown, with no heating or modern conveniences. But I loved it.

The cottage overlooked a huge green valley on one side and had beautiful woodland on the other. We had friends around most nights, held live music parties, and burned wood from the dilapidated shed as heating for the solid-fuel stove.

Our newly found army pay was spent on a bar tab in the local pub.

We were probably the tenants from hell, as we let the garden fall into disrepair, and burned our way steadily through the wood of the various rotting sheds in the garden. But heh, the landlord was a miserable old sod with a terrible reputation, anyway!

When the grass got too long we tried strimming it—but broke both our string trimmers. Instead we torched the garden. This worked a little too well, and we narrowly avoided burning down the whole cottage as the fire spread wildly.

What was great about the place was that we could get in and out of Bristol on our 100 cc motorbikes, riding almost all the way on little footpaths through the woods—without ever having to go on any roads.

I remember one night, after a fun evening out in town, Trucker and I were riding our motorbikes back home. My exhaust started to malfunction—glowing red, then white hot—before letting out one massive backfire and grinding to a halt. We found some old fence wire in the dark and Trucker towed me all the way home, both of us crying with laughter.

From then on my bike would only start by rolling it down the farm track that ran down the steep valley next to our house. If the motorbike hadn't jump-started by the bottom I would have to push the damn thing two hundred yards up the hill and try again.

It was ridiculous, but kept me fit—and Trucker amused.

Fun days.

We lived the life of our many student buddies out and about the town, yet would also then suddenly disappear for three weeks with our squadron, returning as soon as we could with a nice suntan—back to the pretty girls of Bristol.

It was a perfect existence, and only a handful of our close buddies ever knew that we weren't just normal students—albeit students who didn't go to lectures. (Although few of our buddies seemed to go to many of those, either!)

It was a perfect "work hard, play hard" lifestyle. We were fit, doing a job we both loved, yet, when we were not with our squadron, we were having a great time in a university town.

Two years passed like this, and as a young man I was living my dream.

I mean, find me a young man who isn't going to love being trained in how to blow stuff up, climb cliffs, skydive at night, and practice evasive high-speed driving!

But it had taken a lot of hard work to reach that point.

Along the way, Trucker and I encouraged several close friends to try for Selection as well, but sadly none of them ever got very far down the road. Some people suited the life, others simply didn't.

One of those friends once asked me to sum up the qualities needed for life in the SAS.

I would say that what matters is the following: to be self-motivated and resilient; to be calm, yet have the ability to smile when it is grim. To be unflappable, able to react fast, and to have an "improvise-adapt-and-overcome" mentality.

Oh, and good tunnel vision when it comes to crunch time.

Looking forward, these are also many of the same qualities that I have relied on so heavily in subsequent adventures, from big expeditions like Everest to filming the likes of *Escape to the Legion*, *Man vs. Wild*, and *Worst-Case Scenario*.

It's not rocket science; it's just about showing heart in the big moments. I have always liked that.

But, and this was the big but . . . little did I know quite how much I was going to need some of those qualities when my accident happened. And like Selection, some things are hard to prepare for.

That cool evening, high in the sky above the desert plains of Africa, was one such life-changing, life-defining moment.

PART 3

✣

ADVERSITY

There is no education like adversity.
—Benjamin Disraeli

CHAPTER 66

In the summer of 1996 I was helping out for a month on a game farm in the northern Transvaal in South Africa, culling deer and advising on how to keep poachers at bay. I was working alongside the black workers every day and being paid for the privilege.

I decided to head north to Zimbabwe for some downtime and some fun, to spend some of my wages, before heading home to the UK.

Fun, for me, meant skydiving with good friends, with cool drinks in the evening.

Life was all good.

⚜

The sky was beginning to fade and the brilliance of the African sun was being replaced by the warm glow of dusk.

We huddled together in the small plane, and my feet began to get cramp. I tried to tense them and get the blood flowing again.

As is often the case, there was no eye contact with the others as we climbed up to nearly sixteen thousand feet. People were engaged in their own little worlds.

The plane leveled out. The guys became alert again, checking and rechecking equipment. Someone reached for the door.

As it slid back on its rails, the ferocious noise of the engine and 70 mph slipstream broke the silence.

"Red On."

All seemed strangely serene as we stared at the bulb flashing at us.

It flicked to green.

"Go."

One by one, the guys dropped from the door and quickly fell away. Soon I was alone in the cargo area of the plane. I looked down, took that familiar deep breath, then slid off the step.

As the wind molded my body into an arch I could feel it respond to my movements. As I dropped a shoulder the wind began to spin me, and the horizon moved before my eyes.

This feeling is known simply as "the freedom of the sky."

I could just make out the small dots of the others in free fall below me, then I lost them in the clouds. Seconds later I was falling through the clouds as well. They felt damp on my face. How I loved that feeling of falling through whiteout!

Three thousand feet. Time to pull.

I reached to my right hip and gripped the rip cord. I pulled strongly. Initially it responded as normal.

The canopy opened with a crack that interrupted the noise of the 130 mph free fall. My descent rate slowed to 25 mph.

Then I looked up and realized something was wrong—very wrong.

Instead of a smooth rectangular shape above me, I had a very deformed-looking tangle of chute, which meant the whole parachute would be a nightmare to try to control.

I pulled hard on both steering toggles to see if that would help me.

It didn't.

I started to panic.

I watched the desert floor becoming closer, and objects becoming more distinct. My descent was fast—far too fast.

I'd have to try and land it like this.

Before I knew it, I was too low to use my reserve chute. I was getting close to the ground now, and was coming in at speed. I flared the chute too high and too hard out of fear. This jerked my body up horizontally—then I dropped away and smashed into the desert floor.

My body bounced like a rag doll. I landed in a cloud of dust and dirt, and just lay there, groaning.

I had landed directly on my back, right on top of the tightly packed reserve chute that formed a rock-hard square shape in the middle of the pack. The impact felt as if that rock-hard chute had been driven clean through the central part of my spine.

I couldn't stand up; I could only roll over and moan in agony into the dusty ground.

I was crying as I lay there in the dust, waiting for my buddies to come and help—I just knew that I had blown it.

We get one shot at life, and in those agonizing moments I realized I had messed this up big-time.

I had this pit-of-my-stomach fear that life would never be the same again.

CHAPTER 67

I lay there, delirious, drifting in and out of consciousness.

As the guys I was with began to help lift me, I was still moaning in pain. Eyes squeezed tight, writhing in this slow, contorted agony.

I could hear one of them say that my canopy had a big tear in it. That would explain why the chute had been so wild to handle.

But the rules are simple, and I knew them: If your canopy is uncontrollable, then you have to cut the chute away and release yourself from it. Then go back into free fall and pull your reserve.

I hadn't done that. I had thought that I could control it.

I'd been wrong.

I then remember being slumped in an old Land Rover and driven frantically to the nearest hospital. I was carried inside and sat carefully down in a wheelchair.

Two nurses then wheeled me down a corridor, where a doctor did a rough assessment. Every time he tried to examine me, I winced in agony. I remember apologizing to the doctor, over and over.

Then I remember him wielding a long syringe and jamming it into me.

The pain went instantly, and, in a haze, I tried to stand up and walk. The nurses grabbed me and laid me back down.

I remember this Scottish doctor's voice (which seemed strange as we were in the middle of southern Africa), saying to me that it would be some time before I would be doing any walking again. And after that I don't remember much more.

When I woke up a man in a green beret with a big feather poking out of it was leaning over me. *I must be hallucinating,* I thought.

I blinked again but he didn't go away.

Then this immaculate, clipped British accent addressed me.

"How are you feeling, soldier?"

It was the colonel in charge of British Military Advisory Team (BMAT) in southern Africa. He was here to check on my progress.

"We'll be flying you back to the UK soon," he said, smiling. "Hang on in there, trooper."

The colonel was exceptionally kind, and I have never forgotten that. He went beyond the call of duty to look out for me and get me repatriated as soon as possible—after all, we were in a country not known for its hospital niceties.

The flight to the UK was a bit of a blur, spent sprawled across three seats in the back of a plane. I had been stretchered across the tarmac in the heat of the African sun, feeling desperate and alone.

I couldn't stop crying whenever no one was looking.

Look at yourself, Bear. Look at yourself. Yep, you are screwed. And then I zonked out.

An ambulance met me at Heathrow, and eventually, at my parents' insistence, I was driven home. I had nowhere else to go. Both my mum and dad looked exhausted from worry; and on top of my physical pain I also felt gut-wrenchingly guilty for causing such grief to them.

None of this was in the game plan for my life.

I had been hit hard, broadside and from left field, in a way I could never have imagined.

Things like this just didn't happen to me. I was always the lucky kid.

But rogue balls from left field can often be the making of us.

CHAPTER 68

I was in and out of the hospital almost daily from then on.

They X-rayed, poked, and prodded me, and then they did it again for good measure.

T8, T10, and T12 vertebrae were fractured. It was as clear as day to see.

You can't hide from an X-ray.

Those are the main vertebrae in the middle of my back. And they are the ones that are hardest to break.

"Will I walk again properly?" was all I kept asking the doctors.

Yet no one would give me an answer. And that not knowing was the worst.

The doctors decided it would actually be best not to operate immediately. They deduced (and they were right), that as I was young and fit, my best chance of any sort of recovery was to wait and see how the injury responded naturally.

The one thing they did all keep saying was that I was "above-average lucky."

I knew that I had come within a whisker of severing my spinal cord and never moving again.

I became affectionately known as the "miracle kid."

Miracle or not, what I did know was that whenever I tried to move just a few inches to the left or right, I felt sick with the agony. I could hardly shift at all without excruciating pain.

Whenever I got out of bed I had to wear a big metal brace that was strapped around me.

I felt like an invalid. I was an invalid. This was crazy.

I'm screwed.

You stupid, stupid idiot, Bear. You could have landed that canopy if you hadn't panicked, or you should have cut it away and pulled that reserve early.

As it was, I had done the worst of both worlds: I had neither gone for the reserve straight away nor had I managed to land the canopy with any degree of skill.

I felt I could have avoided this accident if I had been smarter, faster, clearer-headed. I had messed up, and I knew it.

I vowed that I would never fall short in those areas again.

I would learn from this, and go on to become the fastest, clearest-thinking dude on the planet.

But for now, the tears kept coming.

⚜

I woke in bed, sweating and breathing heavily. It was the third time I'd had this nightmare: reliving that horrible feeling of falling, out of control, toward the ground.

I was now on month two of just lying there prone, supposedly recovering. But I wasn't getting any better.

In fact, if anything, my back felt worse.

I couldn't move and was getting angrier and angrier inside. Angry at myself; angry at everything.

I was angry because I was shit-scared.

My plans, my dreams for the future hung in shreds. Nothing

was certain any more. I didn't know if I'd be able to stay with the SAS. I didn't even know if I'd recover at all.

Lying unable to move, sweating with frustration, my way of escaping was in my mind.

I still had so much that I dreamt of doing.

I looked around my bedroom, and the old picture I had of Mount Everest seemed to peer down.

Dad's and my crazy dream.

It had become what so many dreams become—just that—nothing more, nothing less.

Covered in dust. Never a reality.

And Everest felt further beyond the realms of possibility than ever.

Weeks later, and still in my brace, I struggled over to the picture and took it down.

People often say to me that I must have been so positive to recover from a broken back, but that would be a lie. It was the darkest, most horrible time I can remember.

I had lost my sparkle and spirit, and that is so much of who I am.

And once you lose that spirit, it is hard to recover.

I didn't even know whether I would be strong enough to walk again—let alone climb or soldier again.

And as to the big question of the rest of my life? That was looking messy from where I was.

Instead, all my bottomless, young confidence was gone.

I had no idea how much I was going to be able to do physically—and that was so hard.

So much of my identity was in the physical.

Now I just felt exposed and vulnerable.

Not being able to bend down to tie your shoelaces or twist to clean your backside without acute and severe pain leaves you feeling hopeless.

In the SAS I had both purpose and comrades. Alone in my room at home, I felt like I had neither. That can be the hardest battle we ever fight. It is more commonly called despair.

That recovery was going to be just as big a mountain to climb as the physical one.

What I didn't realize was that it would be a mountain, *the* mountain, that would be at the heart of my recovery.

Everest: the biggest, baddest mountain in the world.

CHAPTER 69

Sometimes it takes a knock in life to make us sit up and grab life. And I had just undergone the mother of all knocks.

But out of that despair, fear, and struggle came a silver lining—and I didn't even know it yet.

What I did know was that I needed something to give me back my hope. My sparkle. My life. I found that something in my Christian faith, in my family, and also in my dreams of adventure.

My Christian faith says that I have nothing ever to fear or worry about. All is well.

At that time, in and out of hospital, it reminded me that, despite the pain and despair, I was held and loved and blessed—my life was secure through Jesus Christ.

That gift of grace has been so powerful to me ever since.

My family said something very similar: "Bear, you are an idiot, but we love you anyway, forever and always."

That meant the world to me and gave me back some of the confidence that I was struggling to find again.

Finally, I had my not insubstantial dreams of adventure. And those dreams were beginning to burn bright once more.

You see, I figure that life is a gift. I was learning that more than anyone.

My mum always taught me to be grateful for gifts. And as I slowly began to recover my strength and confidence, I realized that what mattered was doing something bold with that present.

A gift buried under a tree is wasted.

Alone one night in bed, I made a verbal, out-loud, conscious decision, that if I recovered well enough to be able to climb again, then I would get out there and follow those dreams to the max.

Cliché? To me it was my only hope.

I was choosing to live life with both arms open—I would grab life by the horns and ride it for all it was worth.

Life doesn't often give us second chances. But if it does, be bloody grateful.

I vowed I would always be thankful to my father in heaven for having somehow helped me along this rocky road.

⚜

After three months in bed at home, I was posted to the UK's Military Rehabilitation Centre at Headley Court, just outside of London. I could walk around a little now, but still the pain hounded me.

Headley Court and all the staff there were truly amazing. They gave me focus and structure; they gave me clear goals and helped me rediscover my hope again.

The treatment was intense. I often did up to ten hours of "work" a day. An hour stretching on a mat, an hour in a hydra-pool, an hour's counseling, an hour physio (with the pretty nurses!), an hour of movement classes, then lunch, and so on.

Slowly my movement returned and the pain lessened, until, by the time I left the center some eight months after the accident, I really was on the mend.

I knew I was getting better when I sneaked out one night,

caught a train home, collected my 1200 cc motorbike, and, still strapped up in my metal back brace, rode the bike back to Headley Court before dawn.

The nurses would have gone nuts if they could have seen me, but my motorbike was my independence—and the risky-but-successful mission also meant my spirit was returning.

I was smiling again.

CHAPTER 70

Just before my accident, I had met a great girl who was a student at Cambridge.

With my newly found wheels, I used to ride like a lunatic up the motorway to see her after our final evening parade at the rehab center. I would take her out for dinner, sleep over, and then get up at 4:00 A.M. to race the two hours back down to Headley Court and morning parade.

The staff had no idea. No one, they imagined, could be that stupid.

It was often so cold in the middle of winter that I remember riding along, back brace on over my leathers, and one hand at a time resting on the engine to keep warm. Talk about reckless, bad driving. But it was great fun.

The relationship petered out soon after, though—the Cambridge girl was way too clever for me. And I am not sure I was the most stable of boyfriends.

⚜

So much of my focus during my recovery was centered around Everest. It gave me something to aim for—a goal—however far away that goal may have been.

No one in my family really took it seriously. I mean, I could still hardly walk properly. But I was deadly serious.

Interestingly, none of the nurses mocked me. They all understood that recovery is all about focus and goals. But I also sensed that few of them really thought it would be possible.

Out of the many British military attempts, only one had ever reached the summit of Everest. It was achieved by two of the fittest, strongest, most experienced mountaineers in the country.

Both were also SAS soldiers, at the peak of their physical condition. They had achieved it, just, by the skin of their teeth, narrowly escaping with their lives, having suffered horrendous frostbite and lost limbs.

For the time being, that was a bit academic. What mattered was that I had something to get stronger for. However crazy and far away from reality it might have seemed.

Life has taught me to be very cautious of a man with a dream, especially a man who has teetered on the edge of life. It gives a fire and recklessness inside that is hard to quantify.

It can also make them fun to be around.

⚜

I was soon discharged from the rehab center and sent back to the SAS. But the doctor's professional opinion was that I shouldn't military parachute again. It was too risky. One dodgy landing, at night, in full kit, and my patched-up spine could crumple.

He didn't even mention the long route marches carrying huge weights on our backs.

Every SF soldier knows that a weak back is not a good opener for life in an SAS squadron.

It is also a cliché just how many SAS soldiers' backs and knees are plated and pinned together, after years of marches and jumps.

Deep down I knew the odds weren't looking great for me in the squadron, and that was a very hard pill to swallow.

But it was a decision that, sooner or later, I would have to face up to. The doctors could give me their strong recommendations, but ultimately I had to make the call.

A familiar story. Life is all about our decisions. And big decisions can often be hard to make.

So I thought I would buy myself some time before I made it.

In the meantime, at the squadron, I took on the role of teaching survival to other units. I also helped the intelligence guys while my old team were out on the ground training.

But it was agony for me. Not physically, but mentally: watching the guys go out, fired up, tight, together, doing the job and getting back excited and exhausted. That was what I should have been doing.

I hated sitting in an ops room making tea for intelligence officers.

I tried to embrace it, but deep down I knew this was not what I had signed up for.

I had spent an amazing few years with the SAS, I had trained with the best, and been trained by the best, but if I couldn't do the job fully, I didn't want to do it at all.

The regiment is like that. To keep its edge, it has to keep focused on where it is strongest. Unable to parachute and carry the huge weights for long distances, I was dead weight. That hurt.

That is not how I had vowed to live my life, after my accident. I had vowed to be bold and follow my dreams, wherever that road should lead.

So I went to see the colonel of the regiment and told him my decision. He understood, and true to his word, he assured me that the SAS family would always be there when I needed it.

My squadron gave me a great piss-up, and a little bronze statue of service. (It sits on my mantelpiece, and my boys play soldiers with it nowadays.) And I packed my kit and left 21 SAS forever.

I fully admit to getting very drunk that night.

CHAPTER 71

Whatever doesn't kill you only serves to make you stronger. And in the grand scheme of life, I had survived and grown stronger, at least mentally, if not physically.

I had come within an inch of losing all my movement and, by the grace of God, still lived to tell the tale. I had learned so much, but above all, I had gained an understanding of the cards I had been playing with.

The problem now was that I had no job and no income.

Earning a living and following your heart can so often pull you in different directions, and I knew I wasn't the first person to feel that strain.

My decision to climb Everest was a bit of a "do or die" mission.

If I climbed it and became one of the youngest climbers ever to have reached the summit, then I had at least a sporting chance of getting some sort of job in the expedition world afterward—either doing talks or leading treks.

I would be able to use it as a springboard to raise sponsorship to do some other expeditions.

But on the other hand, if I failed, I would either be dead on the mountain or back home and broke—with no job and no qualifications.

The reality was that it wasn't a hard decision for me to make. Deep down in my bones, I just knew it was the right thing to do: to go for it.

Plus I have never been one to be too scared of that old impostor: failure.

I had never climbed for people's admiration; I had always climbed because I was half-decent at it—and now I had an avenue, through Everest, to explore that talent further.

I also figured that if I failed, well at least I would fail while attempting something big and bold. I liked that.

What's more, if I could start a part-time university degree course at the same time (to be done by e-mail from Everest), then whatever the outcome on the mountain, at least I had an opening back at MI5. (It's sometimes good to not entirely burn all your bridges.)

❋

Life is funny.

You get focused, start pumping out certain vibes into the universe, and things often begin to collude in your favor. I have noticed that on many occasions.

Within a month of starting to write sponsorship letters to companies about Everest (with no idea of how I was ever going to get onto an Everest expedition), I heard of an old military buddy planning to get together a new British team to try to climb the mountain's southeast ridge.

I had crossed paths with Captain Neil Laughton on several occasions, but didn't know him well. He was an ex–Royal Marines commando, robust, determined, and—as I came to learn later—one of the most driven men I have ever met.

Neil had got very close to Everest's summit two years earlier—

the same year that a storm hit high on the mountain, claiming eight climbers' lives in twenty-four hours. Yet despite the very real risks, and the fatalities that he had witnessed firsthand on the mountain, he was 100 percent focused on trying again.

Many people find it hard to understand what it is about a mountain that draws men and women to risk their lives on her freezing, icy faces—all for a chance at that single, solitary moment on the top. It can be hard to explain. But I also relate to the quote that says: "If you have to ask, you will never understand."

I just felt that maybe this was it: my first real, and possibly only, chance to follow that dream of one day standing on the summit of Mount Everest.

Deep down, I knew that I should take it.

Neil agreed to my joining his Everest team on the basis of how I'd perform on an expedition that October to the Himalayas. As I got off the phone from speaking to Neil, I had a sinking feeling that I had just made a commitment that was going to change my life forever—either for the better or for the worse.

But I had wanted a fresh start—this was it, and I felt alive.

A few days later I announced the news to my family. My parents—and especially my sister, Lara—called me selfish, unkind, and then stupid.

Their eventual acceptance of the idea came with the condition that if I died then my mother would divorce my father, as he had been the man who had planted the "stupid idea" in my head in the first place, all those years earlier.

Dad just smiled.

Time eventually won through, even with my sister, and all their initial resistance then turned into a determination to help me— predominantly motivated by the goal of trying to keep me alive.

As for me, all I had to ensure was that I kept my promise to be okay.

As it happened, four people tragically died on Everest while we were there: four talented, strong climbers.

It wasn't within my capability to make these promises to my family.

My father knew that.

CHAPTER 72

The Himalayas stretch without interruption for one thousand seven hundred miles across the top of India. It's hard to visualize the vast scale of this mountain range, but if you were to stretch it across Europe it would run the entire distance from London to Moscow.

The Himalayas boast ninety-one summits over twenty-four thousand feet, all of them higher than any other mountain on any other continent. And at the heart is Everest, the crowning glory of the physical world.

It was not until May 9, 1953, that her summit was eventually reached for the first time, by Edmund Hillary and Sherpa Tenzing Norgay. Many had tried before, and many had died—in pursuit of what was beginning to be deemed the impossible.

By the 1990s, Everest saw the emergence of commercial expeditions attempting to climb the mountain.

Climbers could now pay up to $60,000 for the chance just to be part of an Everest attempt. But this also opened the climb up to clients who lacked essential mountain skills.

The pressure upon expedition leaders to justify the cost often meant that these people found themselves too high on the mountain, without the necessary experience, dangerously tempting disaster.

Then, in 1996, the combination of a freak storm and climbers' inexperience resulted in a fateful tragedy. On top of the eight lives lost in one night, the mountain took a further three lives the next week.

But it wasn't only novices who died up there.

Among the dead was Rob Hall, one of the most highly acclaimed mountaineers in the world. He ran out of oxygen attempting to rescue a stricken climber. He collapsed from a lethal combination of exhaustion, oxygen deprivation, and the cold.

Somehow, as night fell and the thermometer plummeted, he managed to hold on.

Rob endured a night at 28,700 feet with temperatures as low as minus fifty degrees centigrade. Then at dawn he spoke to his wife, Jan, from his radio, patched through to a satellite phone at base camp.

She was pregnant with their first child, and those on the mountain sat motionless as he spoke to her. "I love you. Sleep well, my sweetheart. Please don't worry too much."

They were his last ever words.

The lessons were clear: Respect the mountain—and understand what altitude and bad weather can do to even the strongest of climbers. In addition, never tempt the wild, and know that money guarantees you nothing—least of all safety—when you climb a mountain as big as Everest.

⚜

Since we were on Everest, many other climbers have succeeded on the "big one" as well. She has now been scaled by a blind man, a guy with prosthetic legs, and even by a young Nepalese teenager.

Don't be fooled, though. I never belittle the mountain. She is still just as high and just as dangerous. Instead, I admire those mountaineers—however they have climbed her. I know what it is really like up there.

Humans learn how to dominate and conquer. It is what we do. But the mountain remains the same—and sometimes she turns and bites so damn hard that we all recoil in terror.

For a while.

Then we return. Like vultures. But we are never in charge.

It is why, within Nepal, Everest is known as the mother goddess of the sky—lest we forget.

This name reflects the respect the Nepalese have for the mountain, and this respect is the greatest lesson you can learn as a climber. You climb only because the mountain allows it.

If the peak hints at you to wait, then you must wait; and when she begins to beckon you to go then you must struggle and strain in the thin air with all your might.

The weather can change in minutes, as storm clouds envelop the peak—and the summit itself stubbornly pokes into the fierce band of jet-stream winds that circle the earth above twenty-five thousand feet. These 150+ mph winds cause the majestic plume of snow that pours off Everest's peak.

A constant reminder that you have got to respect the mountain.

Or you die.

CHAPTER 73

At this stage though, with the greatest will in the world, I wasn't going to be climbing anything, not unless I could raise the sponsorship.

And little did I know quite how hard that could be.

I had no idea how to put a proposal for sponsorship together; I had no idea how to turn my dream into one company's opportunity; and I certainly didn't know how to open the doors of a big corporation just to get heard.

On top of that, I had no suit, no track record, and certainly no promise of any media coverage.

I was, in effect, taking on Goliath with a plastic fork. And I was about to get a crash course in dealing with rejection.

This is summed up so well by that great Churchill quote: "Success is the ability to go from one failure to another with no loss of enthusiasm."

It was time to get out there with all of my enthusiasm, and commit to fail . . . until I succeeded.

⚜

In every potential sponsor's eyes, I was a nobody. And soon I had notched up more rejection letters than is healthy for any one man to receive.

I tried to think of an entrepreneur and adventurer that I admired, and I kept coming back to Sir Richard Branson, the founder of Virgin.

I wrote to him once, then I wrote once more. In all, I sent twenty-three letters.

No response.

Right, I thought, *I'll find out where he lives and take my proposal there myself.*

So I did precisely that, and at 8:00 P.M. one cold evening, I rang his very large doorbell. A voice answered the intercom, and I mumbled my pitch into the speakerphone.

A housekeeper's voice told me to leave the proposal—and get lost.

It's not clear quite what happened next: I assume that whoever had answered the intercom meant just to switch it off, but instead they pressed the switch that opened the front door.

The buzzing sound seemed to last forever—but it was probably only a second or two.

In that time I didn't have time to think, I just reacted . . . and instinctively nudged the door open.

Suddenly I found myself standing in the middle of Sir Richard Branson's substantial, marble-floored entrance hall.

"Uh, hello!" I hollered into the empty hall. "Sorry, but you seem to have buzzed the door open," I apologized to the emptiness.

The next thing I knew, the housekeeper came flying down the stairs, shouting at me to leave.

I duly dropped the proposal and scarpered.

The next day, I sent around some flowers, apologizing for the intrusion and asking the great man to take a look at my proposal. I added that I was sure, in his own early days, he would probably have done the same thing.

I never got a reply to that one, either.

Later that week, I was bicycling down a pavement in the City of London when I passed a company called DLE, which stands for Davis Langdon & Everest.

Hmm, I thought, as I skidded to a halt.

I took a deep breath and then confidently walked into their ultraclean, ultrasmart reception, and asked to be put through to the CEO's office, saying it was both urgent and confidential.

Once I had the CEO's secretary on the line, I pleaded with her to help me get just two minutes of her boss's time.

Eventually after three attempts, due to a combination of pity and intrigue, she agreed to ask the CEO to see me for "literally two minutes."

Bingo.

I was escorted into a lift and then ushered into the calm of the CEO's top-floor office. I was very nervous.

The two head guys, Paul Morrell and Alastair Collins, came in, looking suspiciously at this scruffy youngster holding a pamphlet. (They later described it as one of the worst-laid-out proposals they had ever seen.)

But they both had the grace to listen.

By some miracle, they caught the dream and my enthusiasm, and for the sake of £10,000 (which to me was the world, but to them was a marketing punt), they agreed to back my attempt to put the DLE flag on top of the world.

I promised an awesome photograph for their boardroom.

We stood up, shook hands, and we have remained great friends ever since.

I love deals like that.

CHAPTER 74

So I got lucky. But then again, it took me many hundreds of rejections to manage to find that luck.

I am sure there is a lesson in that somewhere.

Someone had taken a punt and had faith in me. I wouldn't let them down, and I would be eternally grateful to them for giving me that chance to shine.

Once DLE were on board, a few other companies joined them. It's funny how, once one person backs you, somehow other people feel more comfortable doing the same.

I guess most people don't like to trailblaze.

So before I knew it, suddenly, from nothing, I had the required funds for a place on the team. (In fact I was about £600 short, but Dad helped me out on that one, and refused to hear anything about ever being paid back. Great man.)

The dream of an attempt on Everest was now about to become a reality.

So many people over the years have asked me how to get sponsorship, but there is only one magic ingredient. Action. You just have to keep going.

Then keep going some more.

Our dreams are just wishes, if we never follow them through

with action. And in life, you have got to be able to light your own fire.

The reality of planning big expeditions is often tedious and frustrating. There is no glamour in yet another potential sponsor's rejection letter, and I have often felt my own internal fire flickering close to snuff point.

Action is what keeps it alight.

⚜

Funds secured, I then planned to head off for six weeks to join the British Ama Dablam Expedition, in the Himalayas.

This was a dream climb for me, and I was offered a very cheap place on the team by Henry Todd, a well-known Scottish mountaineer, who would be organizing logistics for us on Everest.

I knew that this was my chance to show both Henry and Neil that I was able to look after myself and climb well at high altitude.

After all, talk is cheap when you are safely tucked up back in London.

It was time to train hard and show my mettle again.

Ama Dablam is one of the most spectacular peaks on earth. A mountain that was once described by Sir Edmund Hillary as being "unclimbable," due to her imposing sheer faces that rise out among the many Himalayan summits.

Like so many mountains, it is not until you rub noses with her that you realize that a route up is possible. It just needs a bit of balls and careful planning.

Ama Dablam is considered by the world-renowned Jagged Globe expedition company to be their most difficult ascent. She is graded 5D, which reflects the technical nature of the route: "Very steep ice or rock. Suitable for competent mountaineers who have climbed consistently at these standards. Climbs of this grade are exceptionally strenuous and some weight loss is inevitable."

Ha. That's the Himalayas for you.

I look back so fondly on those four weeks spent climbing Ama Dablam.

We had a great international team, including the very brilliant Ginette Harrison, who was tragically killed a couple of years later on another big Himalayan peak. (I have always counted it such a privilege to have climbed with Ginette—so shining, strong, beautiful, and talented; and her subsequent death was a tragic and great loss to the climbing world.)

Also on Ama Dablam with us was Peter Habeler, one of mountaineering's greatest heroes, and the first man to scale Everest without oxygen, alongside Reinhold Messner.

So I was in intimidating company; but I thrived.

I climbed on my own for a lot of the time on the mountain, absorbed in my own world: earphones in, head down, working hard. All the time, Everest was still looming high above us, only ten miles to the north.

I took quite a few risks up there in how I climbed—and I look back now and wince a little. I showed a pretty casual regard for ropes and clipping in, preferring instead to get up early, ice axes in hand, and get on with it.

I remember at one time being on a sheer rock face, with a good four thousand feet of vertical exposure under me. I was precariously balanced on the two small front points of my crampons, humming a Gypsy Kings tune to myself, trying to stretch across to a hold that was just beyond my comfortable reach.

It took a small leap of faith to jump, grab, pray it held, and then carry on up—but it was a leap and an attitude that was typical of quite a few moments I had high up on Ama Dablam.

A kind of nonchalant recklessness that isn't always that healthy.

But I was fired up and fearless, and I felt so grateful to be able to climb like this after my accident. I was strong again for the first time—and sleeping on the hard ice was perfect for my back.

Climbing with attitude, though, is dangerous. (I try to be way safer nowadays, for the record.) But I got away with it, and was ascending fast and efficiently.

After three hard weeks, I found myself huddled on the summit of Ama Dablam.

I was beat. It had taken a lot to make that final summit pitch. I knelt there, cowering from the wind, and glanced left through my goggles.

Through the swirling clouds I watched the distant summit of Everest reveal herself.

Like a restless giant. Snow pouring off the peak.

Strong, detached, and still six thousand five hundred feet above where I was now, I realized Everest was going to be a whole different beast.

I wondered what on earth had I let myself in for.

CHAPTER 75

I made it home in one piece, aware that however fit I was, I needed to be fitter still.

Everest would demand it and reward it.

Every moment I had was spent training and climbing in the mountains: Wales, the Lake District, and the Highlands of Scotland.

That New Year I was invited to stay with one of my old school buddies, Sam Sykes, at his house on the far northwestern coast of Sutherland, in Scotland.

It is as wild and rugged a place as anywhere on earth, and I love it there.

It also happens to boast one of my favorite mountains in the world, Ben Loyal, a pinnacle of rock and steep heather that overlooks a spectacular estuary. So I did not need much encouraging to go up to Sam's and climb.

This time up there, I was to meet the lady who would change my life forever; and I was woefully ill-prepared for the occasion.

I headed up north primarily to train and climb. Sam told me he had some other friends coming up for New Year. I would like them, he assured me.

Great. As long as they don't distract me from training, I

thought to myself. I had never felt more distant from falling in love. I was a man on a mission. Everest was only two months away.

Falling in love was way off my radar.

One of Sam's friends was this young girl called Shara. As gentle as a lamb, beautiful and funny—and she seemed to look at me so warmly.

There was something about this girl. She just seemed to shine in all she did. And I was totally smitten, at once.

All I seemed to want to do was hang out with her, drink tea, chat, and go for nice walks.

I tried to fight the feeling by loading up my backpack with rocks and heavy books, then going off climbing on my own. But all I could think about was this beautiful blond girl who laughed in the most adorable way at how ridiculous it was to carry Shakespeare up a mountain.

I could sense already that this was going to be a massive distraction, but somehow, at the same time, nothing else seemed to matter. I found myself wanting to be with this girl all the time.

On the third day, I asked if she would like to climb Ben Loyal with me—with anyone else who fancied coming along. None of the guys wanted to join me and I ended up with a group of four girls, including Shara.

We spent two hours crossing the marshy moon grass to reach the foot of the mountain before starting up the steep slope toward the summit ridge. It was fairly sheer, but essentially we were still going the "easy" way.

Within two hundred feet, half of the girls were looking pretty beat.

I figured that having slogged across the marsh for so long, we should definitely do some of the climb. After all, that was the fun bit.

They all agreed and we continued up steadily.

Before the slope eases at the top, though, there is a section where the heather becomes quite exposed. It is only a short, few hundred feet, and I wrongly figured the girls would enjoy a safe, steep scramble that didn't require any ropes. Plus the views were amazing out to sea.

But things didn't quite go to plan.

The first panicked whimper seemed to set off a cacophony of cheeps, as, one by one, the girls began to voice their fears. It is funny how quickly everyone can go from being totally fine to totally not-fine, very fast, once one person starts to panic.

Then the tears started.

Nightmare.

I ended up literally having to shadow the three girls who were worst struck by this fear, one by one down the slope. I had to stand behind them, hands on top of their hands, and help them move one step at a time, planting their feet exactly where I did, to shield them from the drop.

The point of this story is that the only girl who was supercool through the whole mission was Shara, who steadily plodded up, and then just as steadily plodded down beside me, as I tried to help the others.

Now I was really smitten.

A cool head under pressure is truly irresistible to me, and if I hadn't been totally besotted before, then our mountain experience together tipped the balance.

I had a sneaking feeling that I had met the girl of my dreams.

CHAPTER 76

The next night was New Year's Eve, and I made a secret plan with Shara to meet her outside the back door on the stroke of midnight.

"Let's take a walk," I suggested.

"Sure. It's midnight, minus five degrees, and pitch black, but hey, let's walk." She paused. "But not up Loyal," she added, smiling.

And so we walked together along a moonlit track.

Twenty yards and then I will make the move to kiss her, I told myself.

But plucking up the courage with a girl this special was harder than I had thought.

Twenty yards became two hundred yards. Then two thousand.

Forty-five minutes later, she suggested that maybe we should turn around and head back to the house.

"Yes. Good idea." I replied.

Do it, Bear, you old woman. Do it now!

And so I did.

A quick kiss on the lips, then a longer lingering one, and then I had to stop. It was sensory overload.

Wow. That was worth the walk, I thought, smiling from ear to ear.

"Let's head back," I confirmed, still smiling.

I am not sure Shara was quite as impressed by the effort-to-reward ratio—long cold walk to short, hot kiss—but as far as I was concerned the sky and clouds had parted, and nothing would ever be the same again.

Over the next few days we spent every waking moment together. We made up silly dances, did puzzles in the evening, and she stood smiling on the beach waiting for me as I took my customary New Year's dip in the freezing cold North Atlantic.

I just had a sense that we were meant to be.

I even found out she lived in the next-door road along from where I was renting a room from a friend in London. What were the chances of that?

As the week drew to a close we both got ready to head back south to London. She was flying. I was driving.

"I'll beat you to London," I challenged her.

She smiled knowingly. "No, you won't." (But I love your spirit.)

She, of course, won. It took me ten hours to drive. But at 10:00 P.M. that same night I turned up at her door and knocked.

She answered in her pajamas.

"Damn, you were right," I said, laughing. "Shall we go for some supper together?"

"I'm in my pajamas, Bear."

"I know, and you look amazing. Put a coat on. Come on."

And so she did.

Our first date, and Shara in her pajamas. Now here was a cool girl.

From then on we were rarely apart. I delivered love letters to her office by day and persuaded her to take endless afternoons off.

We roller-skated in the parks, and I took her down to the Isle of Wight for the weekends.

Mum and Dad had since moved to my grandfather's old house in Dorset, and had rented out our cottage on the island. But we still had an old caravan parked down the side of the house, hidden under a load of bushes, so any of the family could sneak into it when they wanted.

The floors were rotten and the bath full of bugs, but neither Shara nor I cared.

It was heaven just to be together.

Within a week I knew she was the one for me and within a fortnight we had told each other that we loved each other, heart and soul.

Deep down I knew that this was going to make having to go away to Everest for three and a half months very hard.

But if I survived, I promised myself that I would marry this girl.

CHAPTER 77

Meanwhile, by day, the craziness of all the preparation that a three-month-long Everest expedition involves continued.

Mick Crosthwaite, my old Isle of Wight and school buddy, had joined Neil and myself as part of our British Everest team. I had grown up with Mick all through prep school, Eton, and the Isle of Wight, and climbed a lot with him over the years.

Physically and mentally, ever since I could remember, Mick had always been superhumanly strong.

Age nine, he would single-handedly carry and drive the entire rugby scrum, making our prep school team totally unbeatable. After university, he breezed through some of the toughest military courses and hardly broke into a sweat.

Mick has always been a great man to have fighting in your corner, and I was so happy to have the company of a soulmate with me now on Everest.

So the team was finalized.

Our planned departure date was February 27, 1998.

Because our team was small we arranged to link up with a larger expedition, headed by Henry Todd, who had organized logistics for the Ama Dablam team.

The plan was that we would be climbing on the Nepalese side, the southeast ridge. This was the original face that Hillary and Tenzing had climbed—and one of the most dangerous routes—a fact not missed by Mum.

At the time, out of the total 161 deaths on Everest, 101 had occurred on this face. Mick and I decided to travel out some four weeks before Neil and Geoffrey Stanford (the final member of the team). The idea was to get as much time training at altitude as we could, before the climb itself would start.

I said the first of what has proved to be many tearful good-byes to Shara at the airport, and flew out from the UK to Nepal.

For Mick and me, our strict acclimatization program was about to begin.

⚜

Acclimatization is all about allowing the body to adjust to having less oxygen to function with, and the key is being patient about how fast you ascend. Once you start getting up high, the effects of altitude sickness can kill very quickly. If you get this process wrong, swelling of the brain, loss of consciousness, and hemorrhaging from the eyes are some of the pleasant symptoms that can strike at any time. It is why playing at high altitude is just like playing with fire: unpredictable and dangerous.

From the peak of Everest, the land of Tibet lies sprawled out across the horizon to the north as far as the eye can see. To the south, the summit looks over the vast range of the Himalayas all the way down to the Nepalese plains.

No other bit of land stands above this point on the entire planet.

But what lies beneath the peak, for the ambitious climber, is a treacherous mix of thousands of feet of rock, snow, and ice that has claimed a disproportionate number of top mountaineers.

Here is why.

Under the summit, the descent off the southeast ridge is lined by faces of sheer rock and blue ice. These lead to a narrow couloir of deep powder snow, then eventually down to a col some three thousand feet beneath the peak.

This col, the site of where our camp four would be, sits beneath the two huge peaks of Lhotse to the south and Everest to the north.

It would take us the best part of six weeks' climbing just to reach this col.

Beneath the South Col, the gradient drops sharply away, down a five-thousand-foot ice wall known as the Lhotse Face. Our camp three would be carved into the ice, halfway up this.

At the foot of this wall starts the highest and most startling ice valley in the world. Halfway along this glacier would be our camp two, and at the lower end, our camp one. This vast tongue of ice is known simply as the Western Cwm—or the Valley of Silence.

From the lip of the glacier, the ice is funneled through the steep valley mouth where it begins to rupture violently, breaking up into a tumbling cascade of ice.

It is similar to when a flowing river narrows through a ravine, turning the water into frothing rapids. But here the water is frozen solid. The blocks of ice, often the size of houses, grumble as they slowly shift down the face.

This gushing frozen river, some five hundred yards wide, is called the Khumbu Icefall, and it is one of the most dangerous parts of the ascent.

Finally, at its feet lies Everest's base camp.

Mick and I spent those early weeks together climbing in the lower foothills of the Himalayas, acclimatizing ourselves and starting to get a sense of the scale of the task that lay ahead.

We hiked our way higher and higher into the heart of the mountains, until eventually we found ourselves at 17,450 feet, at the foot of the Khumbu Icefall and the start of the Everest climb in earnest.

We pitched our tents at the base of the big mountain and waited for the rest of the team to arrive in two days' time.

Sitting, waiting—staring up above—neck craned at Everest, I felt a sickness in the pit of my stomach. I just wanted whatever was going to unfold to begin. The waiting is always the hard part.

I had never felt so terrified, excited, anxious, and out of breath in all my life.

But this wasn't even the beginning. It was both before and below the beginning.

I decided to stop thinking ahead and to start this expedition the way I wanted it to go on.

I would give this mission my everything. I would commit to slogging my guts out twenty-four hours of every day until my eyes bled. I would consider anything short of this to be a bonus.

At least that should manage my expectations.

CHAPTER 78

Finally, Neil and Henry arrived over the horizon—the expedition itself had begun.

Base camp was now filling up with a whole multitude of climbers: teams from Singapore to Mexico to Russia. Maybe forty climbers in total—including a strong, cheerful Bolivian mountaineer, Bernardo Guarachi.

All were intent on risking everything for a shot at the top.

Not everyone would return alive.

⚜

The energy that a group of ambitious, highly driven climbers created was palpable. There was a purpose to everything. The camp was a hustle of tanned, wiry athletes, all busily organizing equipment and discussing strategies for the climb.

The other climbers under the logistical control of Henry Todd included Andy Lapkass, our team doctor, and Karla Wheelock, a quiet, friendly, but fiercely determined girl, trying to be the first Mexican female to the summit.

Also joining us was an Australian climber, Alan Silva. Blond and fit-looking, he didn't say much and seemed quite detached. It was clear he wasn't there for fun. He was a man on a mission, and you could tell it.

Then there was a Brit called Graham Ratcliffe, who had already climbed Everest from the north side. Straight-talking and good-humored, he was hoping to be the first Brit to climb the mountain from both sides.

Geoffrey Stanford was a military Guards officer who, like Neil, Mick, and me, was from the UK. An experienced Alpine climber, this was to be his first attempt on Everest.

And finally there was Michael Down, one of the most celebrated rock climbers in Canada. Cheerful, clearly competent, his outdoor look was complete—yet Michael already looked apprehensive.

Everest has a habit of making that happen to even the bravest of climbers.

He was a good man, though, and I sensed it within hours of meeting him.

In addition to these international climbers, we were supported by a climbing team of Nepalese Sherpas, led by their Sirdar boss, Kami.

Raised in the lower Himalayan foothills, these Sherpas know Everest better than anyone. Many had climbed on the mountain for years, assisting expeditions by carrying food, oxygen, extra tents, and supplies to stock the higher camps.

As climbers, we would each carry substantial-sized packs every day on Everest, laden with food, water, cooker, gas canisters, sleeping bag, roll mat, head torch, batteries, mittens, gloves, hat, down jacket, crampons, multitool, rope, and ice axes.

The Sherpas would then add an extra sack of rice or two oxygen tanks to that standard load.

Their strength was extraordinary, and their pride was in their ability to help transport those life-giving necessities that normal climbers could not carry for themselves.

It is why the Sherpas are, without doubt, the real heroes on Everest.

Born and brought up at around twelve thousand feet, altitude is literally in their blood. Yet up high, above twenty-five thousand feet, even the Sherpas start to slow, the way everyone, gradually and inevitably, does.

Reduced to a slow, agonizing, lung-splitting crawl. Two paces, then a rest. Two paces, then a rest.

It is known as the "Everest shuffle."

❖

They say that to climb Everest successfully you actually climb the mountain five times over. This is because of having to ascend then descend her continually in an attempt to allow your body to adjust slowly to the extreme altitude.

Each time we reached a new high point, we would have to turn around the next morning and descend toward base camp in order to let our bodies recover from the beating.

The long hours of slow ascent would be gone in a hour or two of rappelling back down the same icy faces. "Climb high, sleep low" was the principle, and it was morale-sapping.

Ten hours to climb up, one hour to rap back down.

The highest that our bodies would be able to acclimatize to would be camp three at about twenty-four and a half thousand feet.

Above that and your body is effectively dying, as you enter what is grimly known as the Death Zone. Here, you can no longer digest food effectively, and your body weakens exponentially in the thin air and lack of oxygen.

It was clear that this climb would be a systematic war of attrition between acclimatizing our bodies and keeping our spirits fired. And that is before you add into the pot illness, exhaustion, injuries, and bad weather.

Quietly we all knew that to be successful here, many factors would have to come good at the right time. It is why luck has such a part to play on Everest.

Our aim was to be acclimatized to camp three as soon as possible, hopefully around the end of April. Our fight then would be against the weather and the fierce jet-stream winds.

It is these winds that make the mountain, for the vast majority of the year, completely unclimbable. Their ferocious strength can literally blow a man off the face.

But twice a year, as the warm monsoon heads north across the Himalayas, the winds abate.

It is known as the "silent beckoning"—as the mountain goes strangely quiet for a precious few days.

When, and for how long this period lasts, is the gamble that every Everest mountaineer takes.

Get it wrong, or be unlucky, and you die.

Along with the mind-numbing cold, the endless crevasses, the daily avalanches, and the thousands of feet of exposure, it is these fierce jet-stream winds that contribute most heavily to Everest's grisly statistics.

As the statistics stood that year, for every six climbers who reached the summit, one of us would die.

One in six. Like the single bullet in a revolver used in Russian roulette.

I didn't like the analogy.

CHAPTER 79

On April 7, Mick, Nima—one of the Sherpas—and I would be climbing on Everest for the first time.

The others would remain at base camp to give their bodies more time to adapt to the altitude before they started up any higher.

We sat at the bottom of the Khumbu Icefall, among rolling crests of contorted ice, and began to put our crampons on. At last we were beginning the task that had been a dream for so long.

As we began to weave deep into the maze, our crampons bit firmly into the glassy ice. It felt good. As the ice steepened we roped up. In front of us were what looked like endless giant ice sculptures, disappearing into the distance above.

A few strong pushes and we would clamber over the next ice ledge, lying there breathing heavily in the ever-higher air.

We could soon see base camp below us, getting smaller in the distance.

Adrenaline surged around our bodies those first few hours that we climbed together in the early dawn light.

It was a familiar routine on a very unfamiliar mountain.

Soon we came to the first of the aluminium ladder systems that spanned the many yawning chasms. These had been prefixed in place by the Sherpas in elaborate webs of rope, ice screws, and stakes to form bridges across the icefall's giant crevasses.

Over the years, these lightweight ladders, fixed in place and adjusted every few days according to the moving ice, had proved the most efficient way of slicing a route through the icefall.

But they took a little nerve at first.

Crampons, thin metal rungs, and ice are a precarious cocktail. You just have to take your time, hold your nerve and focus on each rung—one at a time. And remember: don't look down into the gaping black abyss beneath your feet.

Focus on your feet, not the drop.

It is easier said than done.

Only a hundred or so feet below camp one, the route that the Sherpas had so diligently fixed through the ice had crumbled. The remains of the rope-and-ladder system hung like long strands of thread above a gaping chasm.

Mick and I assessed our options.

Nima was back down beneath us, refixing part of the route that needed additional ice screws.

We decided not to attempt to find a new route through to camp one—we had climbed high enough for the first day. So we turned and started down.

The journey back was tiring. Much more so than I would have imagined. My legs were aching, and my heart and lungs were pumping hard to suck every ounce of oxygen from the rarefied air.

I felt drained by a whole day in the ice. Adrenaline, concentration, and altitude make for a highly effective energy discharge.

It is a hard type of fatigue to describe: it simply saps you of all your strength and gives you nothing in return.

The sound of the metal karabiners clinking on my harness was becoming hypnotic. I squeezed my eyes tight shut, then opened them. I tried to breathe rhythmically.

We were eighteen thousand vertical feet above sea level, in the mouth of Everest's killer jaws. I noticed my hand was shaking as I fumbled with the ropes through thick mittens.

It was pure fatigue.

An hour later, it felt like we were still no closer to base camp, and it was starting to get late.

I glanced nervously around the icefall. We should be meeting back up with Nima somewhere around here, as arranged. I scanned around but couldn't see him.

I dug my crampons into the snow, leaned back against the face to get my breath back, and waited for Mick behind me.

He was still ten yards away, stepping carefully across the broken blocks of ice. We had been in this crevasse-ridden frozen death trap for more than nine hours, and we were both moving very laboriously.

Watching him, I knew that if the mighty Mick was moving this slowly then we were indeed on a big mountain.

I stood up and took a few more careful steps, testing the ice with each movement. I reached the end of one length of rope, unclipped, breathed hard, and grabbed the next rope.

I held it loosely in my hand, looked around, took another deep breath, then clipped my karabiner into the line.

Then all of a sudden, I felt the ground beneath me twitch.

I looked down and saw a crack in the ice shoot between my feet, with a quiet, slicing sound.

I didn't dare move.

The world seemed to stand still.

The ice cracked once more behind me, then with no warning, it just dropped away beneath me, and I was falling.

Falling down this lethal black scar in the glacier that had no visible bottom.

Suddenly I smashed against the gray wall of the crevasse.

The force threw me to the other side, crushing my shoulder and arm against the ice. Then I jerked to a halt as the thin rope that I had just clipped into held me.

I am spinning round and round in free air. The tips of my crampons catch the edge of the crevasse wall.

I can hear my screams echoing in the darkness below.

Shards of ice keep raining down on me, and one larger bit smashes into my skull, jerking my head backward. I lose consciousness for a few precious seconds.

I blink back into life to see the last of the ice falling away beneath me into the darkness.

My body gently swings around on the end of the rope, and all is suddenly eerily silent.

Adrenaline is coursing through my body, and I find myself shaking in waves of convulsions.

I scream up at Mick, and the sound echoes around the walls. I looked up to the ray of light above, then down to the abyss below.

I clutch frantically for the wall, but it is glassy smooth. I swing my ice axe at it wildly, but it doesn't hold, and my crampons just screech across the ice.

In desperation I cling to the rope above me and look up.

I am twenty-three years old and about to die.

Again.

CHAPTER 80

The rope I was dangling off wasn't designed for a long impact fall like mine.

It was lightweight, thin rope that got replaced every few days as the ice, on the move, tore it from its anchor point. The rope was more of a guide, a support; not like proper, dynamic climbing rope.

I knew that it could break at any point.

The seconds felt like eternity.

Then suddenly I felt a strong tug on the rope.

I kicked into the walls with my crampons again.

This time they bit into the ice.

Up I pulled, kicking into the walls a few feet higher, in time with each heave from above.

Near the lip I managed to smack my ice axe into the snow lip and pull myself over.

Strong arms grabbed my wind suit and hauled me from the clutches of the crevasse. I wriggled away from the edge, out of danger, and collapsed in a heaving mess.

I lay there, my face pressed to the snow, eyes closed, holding Mick's and Nima's hands, shaking with fear.

If Nima had not heard the collapse and been so close, I doubt Mick would ever have had the strength to haul me out. Nima had saved my life and I knew it.

Mick helped escort me the two hours back down the icefall. I clutched every rope, clipping in nervously.

I now crossed the ladders like a different man—gone was the confidence. My breathing was shallow and labored, and any vestiges of strength or adrenaline had long left me.

That thin line between life and death can make or break a man. And right now I was a mess.

Yet we hadn't even begun on Everest proper.

⚜

Lying in my tent alone that night I wept quietly, as all the emotion seeped out of me. For the second time in recent years, I knew I should have died.

I wrote:

March 31, midnight.
The emotions of today have been crazy. And through it all, I just can't quite fathom how the rope held my fall.

Over supper this evening, Nima spoke in rapid, dramatic gestures as he recounted the episode to the other Sherpas. I received double rations from Thengba, our hard-of-hearing cook, which I think was his way of reassuring me. Sweet man. He knows from experience how unforgiving this mountain can be.

My elbow is pretty darned sore where I smashed it against the crevasse, and I can feel small bits of bone floating around inside a swollen sack of fluid beneath it, which is slightly disconcerting.

The doctor says you can't do much about an elbow apart from medicate and let time try to heal. At least it wasn't my head!

I can't get to sleep at the moment—I just keep having this vision of the crevasse beneath me—and it's terrifying when I close my eyes.

Falling is such a horrible, helpless feeling. It caused me the same terror that I felt during my parachute accident.

I don't think I have ever felt so close to being killed as I did today. Yet I survived—again.

It leaves me with this deep gratitude for all the good and beautiful things in my life, and a conviction that I really don't want to die yet. I've got so much to live for.

I just pray with my whole heart never to go through such an experience again.

Tonight, alone, I put in words, thank you my Lord and my friend.

It's been a hell of a way to start the climb of my life.

P.S.: Today is my Shara's birthday. Bless her, wherever she is right now.

CHAPTER 81

"If you can find a path with no obstacles, it probably doesn't lead anywhere."

The dude who said this was dead right.

Life is all about getting up again, dusting yourself down again, learning from the lessons, and then pushing on.

And I did.

The next few days of early April, the conditions were perfect for climbing. Together we all pressed on, and apart from the constant reminder from my broken elbow, I forgot all about my close encounter with the Grim Reaper down the crevasse.

We cleared through the icefall and established our camp one at the lip. We spent a night there, and then descended back to base. Next time we would be pushing up into the mighty Western Cwm itself in an effort to reach camp two.

Our packs were heavier than before, laden down with additional kit we would need higher up the mountain. The great cwm lay before us as we made our way slowly along the vast, glaring white ice valley—like ants on a giant ski ramp.

⚜

We tentatively shuffled into, and then climbed up and out of, yet another of the giant, snow-filled chasms that scarred the glacier's face. As we climbed out of one particularly high lip of another false horizon we saw for the first time the face of Everest in the distance.

The mighty summit loomed over us, still some eight thousand vertical feet higher. It took my breath away.

As the sun rose over the top of Everest, its rays filtering between the wind and snow of the summit, we sat on our packs in silence. My heart rate soared with excitement and trepidation.

The summit seemed truly unconquerable, still so far away, aloof and unobtainable.

I decided not to look up too much, but instead to concentrate on my feet and commit to keep them moving.

I suspected that this would be the key to climbing this mountain.

We were getting more and more drained by the altitude and the scale of the glacier, and camp two never seemed to get any closer.

Finally we made it to camp two, but considering the effort it had taken to reach, it wasn't much to look at. Tucked into the shadow of the vast wall of Everest, it was gray, cold, and unwelcoming.

Shingly rock covered the dark-blue ice that ran into meltwater pools in the midday heat. Everything was wet, sliding, and slushy.

I tripped trying to scramble over a small ledge of ice. I was tired and needed to rest, but I was excited that another stage in the climb was reached—albeit the easy part.

On our next return to base camp, and after the best night's sleep I had had since arriving in Nepal, I decided that I would call home on the satellite phone.

At $3 a minute, I had not yet used the phone. I had enough debts already at this point. I'd originally intended to save my phone call for when and if I had a summit bid.

"Mum, it's me."

"Bear? It's BEAR!" she shouted excitedly.

It was so good just to hear the voices of those I loved.

I asked for all their news.

Then I told them about my narrow escape in the crevasse.

"You fell in what? A crevice?" Mum questioned.

"No, in a crevasse," I enunciated.

"Speak up. I can hardly hear you, darling." She tried to quiet everyone around her, and then resumed the conversation. "Now . . . what was that about your crevice?"

"Mum, it really doesn't matter," I said, laughing. "I love you."

Families are always great levelers.

CHAPTER 82

Four days later we were back up again at camp two on the moraine edge of the vast Western Cwm glacier.

It was 5:00 A.M. and eerily still in the predawn light as I sat huddled in the porch of my tent looking out across the ice.

It was cold. Very cold.

Mick had been tossing and turning all night. Altitude does that. It robs you of sleep, furnishes you with a permanent migraine, and sucks the air and your lungs of all moisture—ensuring everyone coughs and splutters twenty-four/seven.

Add the freezing cold, a constant urge to vomit, and an indescribable ability for even the most mundane physical task to become a labor of Herculean proportions—and you can see why high-altitude climbing is a limited market.

The reality of life up high, in the subzero, could not be less romantic.

But today was make-or-break for us.

We had reached camp two after a seven-hour climb up from base camp. It was the first time we had done the route all in one go without a night at camp one, and it had taken its toll.

Today we had to push on up higher—and this was where it would start to get much steeper and much more dangerous.

✣

Camp three is on the threshold of what the human body can survive, and as I had been repeatedly told by doubting journalists, the body's ability to adapt to high altitude improves as you get out of your twenties and into your thirties.

Well, at twenty-three, age wasn't in my favor, but I tried not to think about that and the doubters.

Yes, I was young, but I was hungry, and the next few weeks would reveal all as I pushed into territory that was higher than I had ever gone before.

In front of me was now the real tester. If I failed to cope with the altitude at camp three I would return to base camp and never go back up again.

Looking at the vast face ahead I tried to imagine being up there. I couldn't.

Thirty minutes after setting out we were still on the scree and ice moraine. It felt like we had hardly moved at all. But finally we reached the ice again and started heading up toward the start of the ice face that loomed some five thousand feet above us.

Beckoning. Silent, apart from a gentle breeze blowing across the ice.

The leap we were making in altitude—some three thousand, three hundred feet—was huge, considering the altitude we were at. Even on our trek into base camp we had only ever ascended around nine hundred feet a day.

We knew the risks in pushing through this invisible altitude boundary, but because of the severity of the gradient we were forced to take it. There were simply so few places where we could level out a small ice shelf to pitch a camp up there.

As soon as we could complete our trip to camp three we would return to base camp for one last time. From then on, it would all be weather-driven.

For the next five hours we continued up the sheer, blue ice. Crampon points in, calf muscles burning, lungs heaving—yet finding no relief.

The air was now very thin, and the exposure and drop increased with every faltering step we took up the ice.

Look only in front, never down.

The Sherpas had reached camp three the previous day and had spent the afternoon putting the two tents in. Their bodies still coped much better than ours up here. How grateful I was for their strength!

As we clawed our way up the final patch of glistening, sheer-blue ice, I could see the tents wedged under an overhanging serac above us.

Precarious, I thought.

But I knew that the serac would also offer some protection from avalanches above.

The tents were flapping in the now-stronger wind—alluring yet so elusive—and the cold had set in, ready for the coming night.

It was now also snowing hard and the light was fading fast.

The wind swept the snow across the dark ice and up into our bodies.

Mick was a little behind Neil and me, and as we both rolled over the ledge of camp three we looked down to see him stationary. Another weary step, then another rest.

Eventually he staggered onto the ledge.

A cold smile swept across his half-obscured face.

We were at camp three.

Alive and together.

CHAPTER 83

The headache that I had hoped I had left behind at camp two was with me again—but stronger now.

I swallowed an aspirin without letting anyone see. For the first time I didn't want the others to think I might be suffering. Not at this decision-point stage.

The tent we were in was better suited to one man with a minimum of kit, rather than three bodies, booted and spurred against the coldest, windiest place on earth.

Such close quarters require a huge degree of tolerance when you are tired and thirsty, with a splitting headache—either huddled over a stove melting ice, or cramped against the cold ice wall next to the tent.

It was at this sort of time that having good friends with you really mattered.

Good friends who you can rely on—the sort of people who smile when it is grim.

If ever friendships were to be tested and forged, it was now.

Quietly, we got on and did all the necessary chores that living at such extreme altitude entails.

Once your outer boots were off you didn't leave the tent.

Several lives had been lost because climbers had gone outside their tents wearing only their inner boots.

One small, altitude-induced slip on the blue ice had been their last conscious act before finding themselves hurtling down the five-thousand-foot glassy face to their deaths.

Instead, you peed in your pee bottle, which you then held tight against your chest for warmth.

And as for pooing—always a nightmare—that involved half an hour of getting everyone to move over so you could get redressed before putting your crampons and boots back on to venture outside.

Then you would squat, butt out from the face, hold on to a sling and ice screw, pull your trousers down, lean out, and aim.

Oh, and make sure there were no other climbers coming up from below.

⚜

When dawn finally arrived and I maneuvered myself from the tent, the fresh crisp air filled my nostrils. The heavy snow and driving wind of the previous day had been replaced by this beautiful stillness.

I just stared in awe as I waited for the others to get ready. I felt like I was looking down on half the world.

Those few minutes that I sat there, as Mick and Neil got ready, I experienced a stillness that I did not think existed.

Time seemed to stand still, and I did not want the moment to end.

The ice face dropped away before me to the vast valley of white beneath, and the whole range of Himalayan peaks stretched away in the distance to our west.

This really was a land apart.

We were now almost two vertical miles above base camp. Mountains that had once towered above us were now level or below. What a sight—what a privilege—to enjoy and soak in!

But today we would undo all that slog once more, as we descended back down to lower altitudes again.

As I looked back down the valley, I registered the severity of the face we had climbed up in the wind and snow only twelve hours earlier. I rechecked my harness as I sat there.

Soon we were ready and we started down.

The rope ran through my rappelling device and buzzed as I picked up speed. It was intoxicating bouncing down the ice face. My figure of eight rappelling device was warm to the touch as the rope raced through it.

This was the mountain at her best.

I tried not to think of the thousands of feet of sweat and toil that were flying through my hands. I did not want to remind myself that I would have to do it again on the way up to camp four and the summit.

The prospect hurt too much.

For now, I was content to have survived camp three; to have proved that my body could cope above twenty-four thousand feet, and to be on my way back to base in good weather.

Back at camp two the tension fell away. We were ecstatic.

The next day we left for base camp, crossing the crevasses with renewed confidence.

Our final acclimatization climb was over.

❧

We were now receiving daily very accurate weather reports from the Bracknell Weather Centre in the UK. These gave us the most advanced precision forecast available anywhere in the world. The meteorologists were able to determine wind strengths to within five knots accuracy at every thousand feet of altitude.

Our lives would depend on these forecasts back up the mountain.

Each morning, the entire team would crowd eagerly around the laptop to see what the skies were bringing—but it did not look good.

Those early signs of the monsoon arriving in the Himalayas, the time when the strong winds over Everest's summit begin to rise, didn't seem to be coming.

All we could do was wait.

Our tents were very much now home to us at base camp. We had all our letters and little reminders from our families.

I had a seashell I had taken from a beach on the Isle of Wight, in which Shara had written my favorite verse—one I had depended on so much through the military.

"Be sure of this, that I am with you always, even unto the end of the earth." Matthew 28:20.

I reread it every night at base camp before I went to sleep.

There was no shame in needing any help up here.

CHAPTER 84

I woke up very suddenly, feeling violently sick. I crawled to the door of my tent and threw up all over the ice and rock outside.

I felt like death and my head was throbbing.

Shit. This didn't bode well, and I knew it.

I lay curled in a ball in my tent throughout the heat of the day at base camp. I didn't know what to feel.

Andy, our team doctor, told me I was run down and had also got a chronic chest infection. He gave me a course of antibiotics and said I needed to rest.

I just needed some time to recover. Time that we didn't have.

Later that day, my greatest fear came to pass when Henry entered the mess tent with the latest forecast.

"Good news, the wind's beginning to rise. Looks as though we're going to get the break around the nineteenth. Right, that gives us five days to get up to camp four at the col and be ready in position for a summit bid. We need to start working toward this at once—and that means now."

The moment I had longed for was suddenly the moment I most dreaded.

Finally it had come, but at what a time—when I was sprawled out, unable to move.

I cursed myself as my body shivered and my joints ached with fever. There was no way I was going to be able to climb—and seventeen and a half thousand feet up is a nightmare of a place to recover.

✤

Mick, Neil, Karla, and Alan were to leave base camp at dawn the next morning. Michael, Graham, and Geoffrey would form a second wave, scheduled to leave a day later—weather permitting.

As for me, I kept throwing up all day. I was drained and pale. My Everest dream lay in a pool of vomit outside my tent.

I had given my everything for this chance at the top—and now all I could do was sit and watch it slipping away.

Please, God, help me get better—and fast.

That night was probably the longest and loneliest of the expedition.

I was dry, I was safe, I was near my friends—but I just felt desperate. And alone.

An opportunity lost.

In a matter of hours, Neil, Mick, Karla, and Alan would leave base camp for the first summit attempt on Everest's south side for more than six months—and I would not be part of it.

Graham and Michael were both also sick—coughing, spluttering, run down, and weak.

Henry had insisted that Geoffrey wait to be part of a second team. Four and four was safer than five and three. Nobly, he had agreed.

The four of us would form a pretty mediocre-looking reserve summit party—that's if there was going to be a chance for a second summit team.

I doubted there would.

At 5:00 A.M., I heard the first rustles from Mick's tent—but this morning things were different. There was no banter. Neil and Mick whispered to each other as they put on their harnesses in the cold air of dawn.

They didn't want to wake us. But I hadn't even come close to sleep.

The pair would want to get moving soon. They both crouched outside my tent to say good-bye. Mick shook my hand and held it.

"You've been such a backbone to this team, Bear. Just hang on in there and get strong again. Your chance will come, buddy."

I smiled. I so envied them—their timing, their opportunity— and their health.

At 5:35 A.M. the four of them, along with Pasang, left base camp. I could hear their boots crunching purposefully across the rocks toward the foot of the icefall.

My tent had never felt so quiet—and so bleak.

⚜

Two days later, as the guys started to head up toward camp three, I woke feeling much stronger. Against all the odds. Not 100 percent but definitely halfway there.

That was good enough for me. The antibiotics were kicking in.

That morning, though, the forecast that came in had changed— dramatically and very suddenly. Everest has a habit of doing this.

"Severe warning: Tropical cyclone forming south of Everest. Likely to turn into a typhoon as it approaches the mountain."

The typhoon was due in two days—that didn't give the guys much time up there.

It would not only bring gale-force winds, it could also potentially drop up to five feet of snow in a matter of hours. Anyone still up there in that would—in Henry's words—"become unreachable."

That afternoon, I went to Henry with a suggestion.

Michael and Graham were still ill. But I was feeling almost fit again.

"Why not let Geoffrey and me head up to camp two, so we can be in position just in case the typhoon heads away?"

It was a long shot—a very long shot—but as the golfer Jack Nicklaus once said: "Never up, never in."

Sure as hell, I wasn't going to stand any chance of the summit, sitting here at base camp twiddling my thumbs, waiting.

In addition, at camp two, I could be a radio go-between from base camp (where Henry was) and the team higher up.

That was the clincher.

Henry knew that Michael and Graham weren't likely to recover any time soon. He understood my hunger, and he recognized the same fire that he had possessed in his own younger days.

His own mountaineering maxim was: "Ninety-nine percent cautiousness; one percent recklessness."

But knowing *when* to use that 1 percent is the mountaineer's real skill.

I stifled a cough and left his tent grinning.

I was going up.

CHAPTER 85

Geoffrey and I were steadily approaching the lip at the top of the icefall. I clipped my karabiner into the last rope between us and camp one. It was 7:20 A.M.

We took most of the day to reach camp two in the distance, eventually arriving at 3:30 P.M.

I felt drained and dizzy.

Fifty percent fit is hard to climb on, especially at this altitude, but I wasn't going to share that feeling with anyone. There was too much at stake now.

Geoffrey and I sat and drank with our backpacks at our feet, our wind suits open to the waist to let the cool breeze dry our sweat. The two Sherpas up at camp two, Ang-Sering and my friend Thengba plied us with hot lemon.

It was good to have made it up here.

I knew that Mick and Neil and the others would be somewhere between camp three and camp four by now. They would be breaking into new territory, going higher than at any point so far on the expedition.

We had studied the route in detail.

It was a treacherous traverse across the Lhotse Face, and a long haul up what is known as the Geneva Spur—a steep band of jutted rock that pokes out from the blue ice. This spur then leads to the windswept, desolate saddle known as the South Col, the site of our high camp—camp four.

The Sherpas pointed out the climbers through binoculars. They were dots on a vast canvas of white far above us.

Go, Mick—go, buddy. I smiled to myself.

❦

It was 11:00 P.M. Mick and Neil would be leaving camp four any minute now. They would be going through the ritual of getting re-booted, checking gear, checking oxygen, and tightening crampons.

Not an easy task for four people in a tiny tent at twenty-six thousand feet—in the dark.

The full moon had been on May 11, the ideal summit time. By now, though, more than a week later, that moon was fading.

It meant they would need the light from their head lamps on all the time—but batteries don't last long in those subzero conditions. Extra batteries mean extra weight. And changing batteries in minus thirty-five degrees, with thick down mittens on, is harder than you think.

I had never wanted to be beside my best buddy Mick so much as I did right now.

The jet-stream winds were silent; the night was still, and they left camp in good time, ahead of the two other teams up there. It was a good decision.

Mick describes feeling unsure about his oxygen supply from early on after leaving the col. It was a hunch. It was almost prophetic.

Five hours later the trail of climbers was snaking its way unroped up the ice and deep snow toward what is nonchalantly known as the balcony—a ledge at twenty-seven and a half thousand feet.

The team was moving slower than expected. Mick's head lamp had failed. Changing batteries had proved too hard in the darkness and deep snow.

The weather that had looked so promising was now turning.

Mick and Neil still pushed on. Karla and Alan were behind them, moving slowly—but continuing.

Eventually, at 10:05 A.M., Neil and Pasang reached the South Summit. Neil could see the final ridge that led to the infamous snow and ice couloir called the Hillary Step—and above this the gentle slope that ran four hundred feet to the true summit.

In 1996 the disasters on the mountain had robbed Neil of the chance to go above camp four. Two years on he was here again—only this time the summit was within his reach.

He felt strong and waited anxiously for Mick to arrive. They would need to be together to manage the last ridge and the Hillary Step.

Something told Neil that things were not going right.

As the precious minutes slipped by, as he waited for Mick and the others to reach him, he sensed that the dream that had eluded him once was going to do so again.

Somewhere along the way, there had been a misunderstanding between the climbers over who had what rope. It happens at high altitude. It is a simple mistake.

But mistakes have consequences.

Suddenly, here, at four hundred feet beneath the summit of Mount Everest, it dawned on them all that they had run out of rope. They would have no choice now but to retreat. Continuing was not even an option.

Neil stared through his goggles at the summit: so close, yet so very far. All he felt was emptiness.

He turned and never looked back.

⚜

At 10:50 A.M., the radio flared into life. It was Mick's voice. He sounded weak and distant.

"Bear. This is Mick. Do you copy?"

The message then crackled with intermittent static. All I could make out was something about oxygen.

I knew it was bad news.

"Mick, say that again. What about your oxygen, over?"

There was a short pause.

"I've run out. I haven't got any."

The words hung in the quiet of the tent at camp two.

Through eyes squeezed shut, all I could think was that my best friend would soon be dying some six thousand feet above me—and I was powerless to help.

"Keep talking to me, Mick. Don't stop," I said firmly. "Who is with you?"

I knew if Mick stopped talking and didn't find help, he would never survive. First he would lose the strength to stand, and with it the ability to stave off the cold.

Immobile, hypothermic, and oxygen-starved, he would soon lose consciousness. Death would inevitably follow.

"Alan's here." He paused. "He's got no oxygen either. It's . . . it's not good, Bear."

I knew that we had to contact Neil, and fast. Their survival depended on there being someone else above them.

Mick came back on the net: "Bear, I reckon Alan only has ten minutes to live. I don't know what to do."

I tried to get him back on the radio but no reply came.

CHAPTER 86

Eventually, two Swedish climbers and a Sherpa called Babu Chiri found Mick. By chance—by God's grace—Babu was carrying a spare canister of oxygen.

Neil and Pasang had also now descended, and met up with Mick and the others. Neil then located an emergency cache of oxygen half-buried in the snow nearby. He gave one to Alan and forced both him and Mick to their feet.

Slow and tired, his mind wandering in and out of consciousness, Mick remembers little about the next few hours. It was just a haze of delirium, fatigue, and cold.

Descending blue sheet ice can be lethal. Much more so than ascending it. Mick staggered on down, the debilitating effects of thin air threatening to overwhelm him.

Somewhere beneath the Balcony Mick suddenly felt the ground surge beneath him. There was a rush of acceleration as the loose topping of snow—covering the blue ice—slid away under him.

He began to hurtle down the sheer face on his back, and then made the all-too-easy error of trying to dig in his crampons to slow the fall. The force catapulted him into a somersault, hurtling him ever faster down the steep ice and snow face.

He resigned himself to the fact that he would die.

He bounced and twisted, over and over, and then slid to a halt on a small ledge. Then he heard voices. They were muffled and strange.

Mick tried to shout to them but nothing came out. The climbers who were now at the col then surrounded him, clipped him in, and held him. He was shaking uncontrollably.

When Mick and Neil reached us at camp two, forty-eight hours later, they were utterly shattered. Different men. Mick just sat and held his head in his hands.

That said it all.

That evening, as we prepared to sleep, he prodded me. I sat up and saw a smile spread across his face.

"Bear, next time, let me choose where we go on holiday—all right?"

I began to laugh and cry at the same time. I needed to. So much had been kept inside.

The next morning, Mick, Neil, and Geoffrey left for base camp. Their attempt was over. Mick just wanted to be off this forsaken mountain—to be safe.

I watched them head out into the glacier and hoped I had made the right decision to stay up at camp two without them all.

⚜

The longer you stay at altitude, the weaker your body becomes. It is a fine balance between acclimatization and deterioration. I chose to risk the deterioration, and to wait—just in case. In case we got another shot at the summit.

Some called it brave. More called it foolish.

The typhoon was slowing and wouldn't be here for two days. But it was still coming. Two days wasn't long enough to reach the summit and return. So, by tomorrow, if it was still moving toward us, I promised Henry and Mick that I would come down.

My next few days revolved around the midday radio call from base camp, when they would give me the forecast. I desperately longed for news that the typhoon was moving away.

The first day it was reported to be stationary. The next was the same. So I agreed to wait even longer.

The next day's call would be vital.

Then at 12:02 P.M., the radio came to life.

"Bear at camp two, it's Neil. All okay?"

I heard the voice loud and clear.

"Hungry for news," I replied, smiling. He knew exactly what I meant.

"Now listen, I've got a forecast and an e-mail that's come through for you from your family. Do you want to hear the good news or the bad news first?"

"Go on, then, let's get the bad news over with," I replied.

"Well, the weather's still lousy. The typhoon is now on the move again, and heading this way. If it's still on course tomorrow you've got to get down, and fast. Sorry."

"And the good news?" I asked hopefully.

"Your mother sent a message via the weather guys. She says all the animals at home are well."

Click.

"Well, go on, that can't be it. What else?"

"Well, they think you're still at base camp. Probably best that way. I'll speak to you tomorrow."

"Thanks, buddy. Oh, and pray for change. It will be our last chance."

"Roger that, Bear. Don't start talking to yourself. Out."

I had another twenty-four hours to wait. It was hell. Knowingly feeling my body get weaker and weaker in the vain hope of a shot at the top.

I was beginning to doubt both myself and my decision to stay so high.

I crept outside long before dawn. It was 4:30 A.M. I sat huddled, waiting for the sun to rise while sitting in the porch of my tent.

My mind wandered to being up there—up higher on this unforgiving mountain of attrition.

Would I ever get a shot at climbing in that deathly land above camp three?

By 10:00 A.M. I was ready on the radio. This time, though, they called early.

"Bear, your God is shining on you. It's come!" Henry's voice was excited. "The cyclone has spun off to the east. We've got a break. A small break. They say the jet-stream winds are lifting again in two days. How do you think you feel? Do you have any strength left?"

"We're rocking, yeah, good, I mean fine. I can't believe it."

I leapt to my feet, tripped over the tent's guy ropes, and let out a squeal of sheer joy.

These last five days had been the longest of my life.

CHAPTER 87

I have always loved the quote from John F. Kennedy: "When written in Chinese, the word *crisis* is composed of two characters. One represents danger and the other represents opportunity."

Looking back on my life, I can see that I have never had a crisis that didn't make me stronger. And here was all that I loved before me: great risk, but also great opportunity.

I had never felt so excited.

Neil was already preparing to come back up. Mick, so fortunate to be alive, was staying firmly, and wisely, at base camp.

But for me, my time had come.

That evening, camp two was again full of friends. Neil and Geoffrey were there along with Michael and Graham, Karla and Alan. But the weariness of coming back up to camp two again oozed painfully from Karla's gaunt face.

She was utterly exhausted, and you could see it.

Who wouldn't be after three months on Everest, and having got within four hundred feet of the summit only days earlier?

Tomorrow the biggest battle of our lives would begin.

✤

That night, the tent that I had been alone in for so long was suddenly heaving with bodies, and piles of rope and kit—with Neil, Geoffrey, and Graham squeezed in beside me.

I tried to drink as much boiled water as I could get down. I knew that I would need to be as hydrated as I could possibly be to tackle what lay ahead. So I drank and I peed. But still my pee was dark brown.

It was almost impossible to hydrate at this altitude.

The ritual of peeing into a water bottle had become second nature to us all, even in the dark, and even with someone's head inches away from the bottle. We each had two bottles: one for pee, one for water. It was worth having a good system to remember which was which.

At 10:00 P.M. I needed to pee—again. I grabbed my bottle, crouched over and filled it. I screwed it shut—or so I thought— then settled back into my bag to try and find some elusive sleep.

Soon I felt the dampness creeping through my clothes.

You have got to be joking. I swore to myself as I scrambled to the crouch position again.

I looked down. The cap was hanging loosely off the pee bottle.

Dark, stinking brown pee had soaked through all my clothes and sleeping bag. I obviously hadn't done it up properly. Brute of a mistake. Maybe an omen for what lay ahead.

On that note I fell asleep.

At 5:45 A.M. we all sat huddled on the ice outside our camp, as we put on our crampons.

In silence we started up toward camp three. I hoped it wouldn't take as long as last time.

By 10:00 A.M. we were well into the climb. We were climbing methodically up the steep blue ice. I leaned back in my harness and swigged at the water bottle that hung around my neck. I was moving okay. Not fast, but I was moving.

And I was stronger than last time I'd gone up to camp three. That boded well.

Five and a half hours of climbing, and the tents were just a hundred feet away. It still took me twenty minutes to cover that minuscule distance.

Just keep patient and keep moving. Ignore the heaving lungs, the numb feet and toes, and the drop beneath you. Keep focused on the step in front of you. Nothing else matters.

The laws of physics dictate that if you keep moving up, however slowly that might be, you will eventually reach the top. It's just that on Everest the process hurts so much.

I had had no real idea beforehand how a mountain could so powerfully make you want to give up—to quit.

I had never been a quitter—but I would have given anything to make the pain and exhaustion go away. I tried to push the feeling aside.

So began the battle that would rage inside me for the next forty-eight hours, without respite.

We collapsed into the tent, now half-buried under the snow that had fallen over the previous week. We were four scared climbers in that one tent—perched on a small precarious ledge—cold, migrainous, thirsty, and cramped.

Many times I have been grateful for the simple, military skill of being able to live with people in confined spaces. It has helped me so much over the years on expeditions and beyond. And I was especially glad to be with Neil.

When we hang with good people, some of their goodness rubs off. I like that in life.

The other thing the army had taught me was how, and when, to go that extra mile. And the time to do it is when it is tough—when all around you are slowing and quitting and complaining.

It is about understanding that the moment to shine brightest is when all about you is dark.

It is a simple lesson, but it is one of the keys to doing well in life. I see it in friends often. On Everest that quality is everything.

Karla had given her word to Henry that she would only continue if the winds died down. Henry knew that in anything but perfect conditions Karla, in her exhausted state, would not survive.

At 6:00 P.M. the radio crackled with his voice from base camp.

"The winds are going to be rising, guys. I'm sorry, Karla, but you are going to have to come down. I can't risk you up there." There was a long pause.

Karla replied angrily, "No way. I'm going up. I don't care what you say, I'm going up."

Henry erupted down the radio. "Karla, listen, we had a deal. I didn't even want you up there, but you insisted—now the ride ends. I am doing this to save your life."

Henry was right.

It had taken Karla three hours longer than us to reach camp three. If she was slow like that higher up, she would probably die.

CHAPTER 88

At dawn, Karla started down.

We continued up—ever higher.

Only minutes out of camp three, I felt as if I were choking on my oxygen mask. I didn't seem to be getting any air from it. I ripped it from my face, gasping.

This is crazy, I thought.

I checked the air-bubble gauge that told me the oxygen was flowing. It read positive. I refitted the mask and carried on.

Five minutes later it hadn't got any easier and I was struggling. I felt stifled by the mask. I stopped again and tore it from my face, gulping in the outside air.

Geoffrey stooped behind me, leaning over his axe. He didn't even look up.

I replaced my mask, determined to trust it. It read that it was working. That meant it would be giving me a meager trickle of about two liters of oxygen a minute. A small, steady, regulated flow that would last some six hours.

But two liters a minute is a fraction of what we were gasping down every minute in the thin air—working hard with a heavy load up a sheer face.

Yet this steady trickle of oxygen was just enough to take the edge off the hypoxia, and therefore justified the extra weight. Just.

I told myself that a sore back and shoulders mattered less than low oxygen saturation and death.

⚜

The rope stretched above me, straight up the face.

Away to my right the ice soared away, up toward the summit of Lhotse. To my left the ice fell at an alarming angle straight down toward the Western Cwm, some four thousand feet below.

Any mistakes would be punished by death up here now.

I tried to stop myself from looking down, and instead to focus on the ice in front of me.

Slowly I began to cross the ice toward the band of steep rock that divided the face in two.

The Yellow Band, as it is known, is a stretch of sandstone rock that was once a seabed of the ancient Tethys Sea, before tectonic shifting over many millennia sent it vertically up into the sky.

Here it was, this yellow rock stretching above me into the mist.

I leaned against the cold rock, hyperventilating in my effort to get more oxygen into my lungs. I tried to recover some strength to start up the rock face.

I knew that once we were over this band, then camp four was only a few hours away.

My crampons grated eerily as they met the rock for the first time. They had no grip, and they skidded across the surface awkwardly. I dug my points into any small crevices I could find and carried on up.

As I cleared the steep yellow band of rock, the route leveled out into a gentle snow traverse across the face. At the end of this was the Geneva Spur, a steep, rocky outcrop that led up to camp four.

There was a mesmerizing simplicity to what we were doing. My mind was uncluttered, clear, entirely focused on every move. I love that feeling.

As I started up the Geneva Spur I could see Geoffrey some way below me—and behind him, the figures of Graham, Alan, Neil, and Michael.

I climbed steadily up the spur and an hour later found myself resting just beneath a small lip. The infamous South Col awaited me over the top.

I longed to see this place I had heard and read so much about. The highest camp in the world at twenty-six thousand feet—deep in Everest's Death Zone.

I had always winced at the term *Death Zone*. Mountaineers are renowned for playing things down, yet mountaineers had coined the phrase—I didn't like that.

I put the thought aside, pulled the last few steps over the spur, and the gradient eased. I turned around and swore that I could see halfway around the world

A thick blanket of cloud was moving in beneath me, obscuring the lower faces of the mountain. But above these, I could see a vast horizon of dark blue panned out before me.

Adrenaline filled my tired limbs, and I started to move once more.

I knew I was entering another world.

❧

The South Col is a vast, rocky area, maybe the size of four football pitches, strewn with the remnants of old expeditions.

It was here in 1996, in the fury of the storm, that men and women had struggled for their lives to find their tents. Few had managed it. Their bodies still lay here, as cold as marble, many now partially buried beneath snow and ice.

It was a somber place: a grave that their families could never visit.

There was an eeriness to it all—a place of utter isolation; a place unvisited by all but those strong enough to reach it. Helicopters can barely land at base camp, let alone up here.

No amount of money can put a man up here. Only a man's spirit can do that.

I liked that.

The wind now blew in strong gusts over the lip of the col and ruffled the torn material of the wrecked tents.

It felt as if the mountain were daring me to proceed.

PART 4

✦

FAITH

Both faith and fear may sail into your harbor, but allow only faith to drop anchor.

CHAPTER 89

The last four thousand feet on Everest is a deathly place, where humans are not meant to survive. Once inside the mountain's jaws, at this height, your body is now literally dying.

Every hour is borrowed time.

Two tents, one from the Singapore expedition and the other belonging to our Bolivian friend, Bernardo, stood in the middle of the col. Both teams had come up the day before us.

The tents now stood empty.

I wondered what those climbers were going through right now, somewhere above us. The whole of Singapore awaited news of their attempt.

I hoped they had succeeded.

We'd also agreed with Bernardo beforehand to share resources and use his camp as he made his own summit bid. So I crawled awkwardly inside his now vacant tent.

At this height the effect of thin air makes people move like spacemen. Slow, labored, and clumsy. On autopilot, I removed my oxygen tank and pack, and then slumped into the corner.

My head ached painfully. I just had to close my eyes—just for a second.

The next thing I heard was the sound of Bernardo, and I sat up wearily as he peered into his tent.

He smiled straight at me. His face looked tired, with dark bags under his panda eyes, from where he had been wearing goggles in the high-altitude sun for so many weeks.

Yet his face was radiant.

I didn't have to ask if he had reached the summit. His eyes said it all.

"It is beautiful, Bear. Truly beautiful."

Bernardo repeated the words again in a dreamy voice. He had done it. We huddled together in the tent, and I helped to get a stove going to melt some ice for him to drink.

It would have been many, many hours since his last swig of any liquid.

Yet, despite his fatigue, he seemed so alive. For him, all the pain was now gone.

The two Singapore climbers also returned. They, too, had been successful. All of Singapore would be celebrating.

Two hours later, Neil and Alan reached the col. They had over-taken Geoffrey and Michael. Neil shook my arm excitedly as he poked his head into Bernardo's tent.

We were here together, and that togetherness gave me strength.

It was time to leave Bernardo and help Neil get a tent up.

Now Geoffrey and Michael were also staggering slowly across the col. They told us that Graham, an Everest summiteer in his own right, had turned around some three hundred feet above camp three.

He had felt too weakened by the illness we had both had. He knew he would not survive any higher up.

What did he know about the next stage that I didn't?

I pushed the thought aside.

The weather was worsening—we needed shelter fast.

The wind ripped a corner of our tent from Neil's hands, and the material flapped wildly as we both fought to control it.

What should have taken us minutes actually took almost an hour. But finally we had it erected.

We huddled in the tent and waited. Waited for night to come.

CHAPTER 90

The thought of seventeen hours weighed down by those ruddy heavy oxygen tanks filled me with dread.

I could feel that slowly, methodically, my strength was deserting me.

I had no idea how I would lift the tanks onto my back—let alone carry them so far, and so high, through the waist-deep snow that lay ahead.

Instead, I tried to remind myself of all that lay on the other side.

Home, family, Shara. But they all felt so strangely distant.

I couldn't picture them in my head. Oxygen deprivation does that. It robs you of memory, of feeling, of power.

I tried to push negative thoughts from my mind.

To think of nothing but this mountain.

Just finish this, Bear, and finish strong.

⚜

The lethargy that you feel at this height is almost impossible to describe. You have nothing to drive you—and you just don't care. All you want is to curl up in a ball and be alone.

It is why death can seem so strangely attractive—as if it is the only way to find blessed relief from the cold and pain.

That is the danger of the place.

I tried to sit up from where I lay. The zip of our porch was slightly broken. It fluttered half-closed.

From where I sat, I could see across the desolate col toward the start of the deep-snow face ahead. The mountain looked cold and menacing as the wind licked across the ice, picking up loose fragments of powdered snow and chasing them away.

I could see the route where Mick had fallen. He had been so lucky.

Or had he been protected? My mind swirled.

I thought of all those mountaineers who had lost their lives in pursuit of their summit dreams.

Was it worth it?

I could find no answer.

What I did know was that they had almost all died above the col.

⚜

Seven P.M. Half an hour to go until we started the laborious task of getting kitted up again.

It would take us at least an hour.

By the end no part of our bodies or faces would be visible. We would be transformed into cocooned figures, huddled, awaiting our fate.

I reached into the top pouch of my backpack and pulled out a few crumpled pages wrapped in plastic. I had brought them just for this moment.

Even the youths shall faint and be weary, and the young men shall utterly fall. But those who wait upon the Lord shall renew their strength. They shall mount up with wings like eagles. They shall run and not be weary. They shall walk and not faint.

Isaiah 40:29–31.

I felt that this was all I really had up here. There's no one else with enough extra strength to keep you safe. It really is just you and your Maker. No pretense, no fluff—no plan B.

Over the next twenty-four hours, there would be a one in six chance of dying. That focuses the mind. And the bigger picture becomes important.

It was time to look death in the eye. Time to acknowledge that fear, hold the hand of the Almighty, and climb on.

And those simple Bible verses would ring round my head for the next night and day, as we pushed on ever higher.

CHAPTER 91

We had decided to leave camp at 9:00 P.M. It was much earlier than climbers ever normally left for their summit bid.

Our forecast had promised strong winds higher up, which would increase during the day. We wanted to do as much of the climbing at night before they got any worse.

Geoffrey, Alan, and Michael soon also emerged from their tent, like astronauts preparing for a space walk. The Sherpa tent was still closed up. Neil roused them. They told us to go on. They would follow behind.

There was something mystical about the five of us moving across the col. Like soldiers wearily moving forward to battle.

As we reached the ice, the gradient steepened dramatically.

We bent lower into the face, our head lamps darting around as they lit up the snow in front of our feet. Our world became that light: it showed us where to kick our crampons, where to place our ice axes.

The light was all we knew.

⚜

As time passed, the group naturally divided into two. Alan, Neil and I led the way—Geoffrey and Michael followed. They both soon fell way back.

After two hours, the three of us were perched on a small lip of ice. We looked down below.

"Are you scared?" Alan asked me quietly. They were the only words any of us had spoken so far.

"Yes," I replied. "But not as scared as I'd be if I could see the angle of this face we're on," I continued, with no trace of irony.

It was true. It was too dark to see the danger. All we could see was the intensity of the snow and ice, lit brightly by our head lamps.

At midnight we came across deep powdery drift snow. We hadn't expected this. It drained our reserves as we floundered about attempting to wade up through it.

Each step we took, our feet would slide back. It took three steps just to make the ground of one. Snow filled my mask and gloves, and my goggles began to steam up. I swore under my breath.

Where the hell is the Balcony? It's got to be soon.

All I could see above was more ice and rock, disappearing into darkness. I was tiring.

At 1:00 A.M. we clambered over one more ledge and collapsed in the snow.

We were at the Balcony. A sense of excitement filled my body. We were now twenty-seven and a half thousand feet above sea level.

As I removed my mask in a bid to conserve oxygen, the thin air seemed to burn my lungs like frozen fire. Hellfire.

I sat back in the snow and closed my eyes.

We had to wait for the Sherpas, who were bringing the spare oxygen canisters, which we would swap with our half-empty ones. These fresh tanks should then last to the summit and back to the

Balcony. It would give us around ten hours to complete the final ascent.

Time up here was all about oxygen—and oxygen at this height meant survival.

The temperature was minus forty degrees Fahrenheit.

At 2:00 A.M. there was still no sign of the Sherpas—and both Neil and I were beginning to get really, really cold. On such a small flow of oxygen, frostbite can creep up on you—silently and quickly.

Suddenly the entire sky lit up.

The mountains flashed as if in daylight and then disappeared again. Thunder then rippled through the valleys.

This shouldn't be here, I thought.

Seconds later the sky flashed again. It was an electrical storm moving up through the valleys.

If it reached us, though, it would be fatal. It would turn the mountain into a raging mass of snow and wind that would be impossible to endure.

Somewhere beneath us, Geoffrey and Michael were also fighting a battle.

And humans have a habit of losing any battles that they fight in Everest's Death Zone.

CHAPTER 92

Geoffrey was having problems with his oxygen set.

The flow wasn't running properly and was choking him. He struggled on but soon had to acknowledge that it was futile. He turned around. His attempt was over.

Michael also decided to turn back. He was utterly spent. The beckoning storm was the final clincher. He had climbed all his life and he knew both his body's limit and the mountain-weather rule. "If there is doubt, there is no doubt, you go down."

They both slowly started to descend back to the col—as we waited.

At 3:00 A.M., shivering incessantly and on the threshold of our ability to survive immobile much longer, we saw the lamps of the Sherpas below.

We then struggled with ice-cold fingers to change our tanks. At base camp we had got the process down to a fine art. But up here, in the dark and subzero cold, it was a different game altogether.

I just couldn't get the threads on the oxygen cylinder fittings lined up. Small, ice-choked screw threads, in the dark, in freezing subzero, make for a pig of a job.

I had no choice but to remove my outer mitts to be able to get a better grip on the regulator.

My shivering was now totally uncontrollable, and I screwed the regulator's screw threads on at an angle. It instantly jammed.

I swore out aloud.

Neil and Alan were ready by now. Neil knelt next to me, waiting. But Alan just got up and left, heading for the ridge.

I fumbled crazily.

Come on, you brute.

I felt the whole situation begin to slip away from me. We had come too far to fail now—too far.

"Come on, Bear, bloody get it working." Neil stammered through his mask.

I knew I was holding him up, but it was jammed, and there was little I could do, except keep trying.

By now, Neil had lost all feeling in his feet completely. This was bad. He was getting more and more frostbitten with every minute we waited. Then suddenly I managed to get the thread loose. I lined it up carefully, and this time it fitted snug.

We were on our way.

One of the three Sherpas then suddenly stopped. Silently, he pointed at the sky and shook his head. He turned around and headed down without a word.

Everyone makes their own choices up there. And you live by those decisions.

The storm lingered to the east and beneath us—still some way off.

Neil and I looked at each other, then turned and headed up on to the ridge.

It was just a relief to be moving again, and soon I found a renewed energy that I hadn't felt in a long time.

I guess that deep down I knew that this was my time.

I steadily moved past Neil to help blaze a trail through the snow. The pace was keeping me warm. Neil's head was low and his body seemed to ooze exhaustion—but I knew he wouldn't stop.

After an hour on the ridge, we hit even more of this deep drift snow—again. The energy that I had felt before began to trickle from my limbs with every labored breath and step.

I could see Alan up ahead, also floundering in the powder. He seemed to be making no progress. The face still soared away above—drift snow as far as I could see.

I hardly even noticed the views up here—of the entire Himalayas stretched below us, bathed in the predawn glow.

My mind and focus were entirely directed on what my legs and arms were doing. Summoning up the resolve to heave each thigh out of the deep powder and throw it another step forward was all that mattered.

Keep moving. Fight. Just one more step.

Yet the South Summit never seemed to arrive.

I could steadily feel every ounce of energy being sucked from my body.

It was like climbing a mountain of waist-deep molasses while giving someone a fireman's carry, who, for good measure, was also trying to force a pair of frozen socks into your mouth. Nice.

Each time I forced myself to stand, I felt weaker. I knew that my strength was finite. And was diminishing fast.

My body desperately needed more oxygen, but all it had was the meager two liters that trickled past my nostrils every minute.

It wasn't enough—and my tank was getting lower by the second.

CHAPTER 93

Why is it that the finish line always tends to appear just after the point at which we most want to give up? Is it the universe's way of reserving the best for those who can give the most?

What I do know, from nature, is that the dawn only appears after the darkest hour.

Finally, and still far above me, the South Summit was now discernible in the dawn light.

For the first time, I could almost taste the end.

Power began to build inside me: raw, irrefutable, and overflowing.

My old friend, a fierce, deep-rooted resolve, that I had only known a few times in my life—mainly from key moments on SAS Selection—was flooding back with each step that I took in the deep snow.

I would beat this damned snow and mountain.

My old friend overcame all pain and cold and fear—and persevered.

A few hundred feet beneath the South Summit we found the ropes that had been put in during the team's first summit attempt. They gave me a vague sense of comfort as I stooped and clipped in.

The South Summit is still some four hundred feet beneath the true summit, but it is a huge milestone in the pursuit of the top. I knew that if I could reach here, then for the first time, the roof of the world would be within my grasp.

Neil was soon close behind me again. Alan had already staggered over the lip and was hunched over, cowering from the wind, as he took a few minutes to regain some energy.

Ahead I could see the infamous final ridge stretching away toward the Hillary Step—the sheer ice wall that was the final gatekeeper to the true summit.

Sir Edmund Hillary, Everest's first conqueror, once said that the mountains gave him strength. I'd never really understood this until now. But it was intoxicating.

Something deep inside me knew that I could do this.

❦

The final ridge is only about four hundred feet along, but it snakes precariously along one of the most exposed stretches of mountain on this planet. On either side, down sheer faces, lies Tibet to the east, and Nepal to the west.

Shuffling along the knife-edge ridge, we moved ever onward, toward the Hillary Step.

This was all that then barred our way to the top.

The rope was being whipped out in a loop by the wind as I shuffled along.

I leaned on my ice axe, against the low bank of snow down to my right, to steady myself.

Suddenly my ice axe shot straight through the white veneer, as part of the snow bank gave way beneath me.

I stumbled to regain my balance and move away from the collapse.

We were effectively shuffling along a ledge with little but frozen water beneath us. I could see down through the hole where the snow had been, to the distant rocky plains of Tibet below.

We kept moving. A step at a time.

Steadily. Slowly.

Ever closer.

Ever farther away.

CHAPTER 94

Just under the South Summit I could make out the shape where Rob Hall lay. He had died up here some twenty-four months earlier.

His body, half covered in drift-snow, remained unchanged. Frozen in time. A stark reminder that those who survive the mountain do so because she allows you to.

But when she turns, she really turns.

And the further into her grasp you are, the greater the danger.

Right now, we were about as far into her grasp as it was possible to venture.

And I knew it.

Rob's last words to his wife, Jan, had been: "Please don't worry too much."

They are desperate words from a mountaineer who bravely understood he was going to die.

I tried to shake his memory from my oxygen-starved brain. But I couldn't.

Just get going, Bear. Get this done, then get down.

❦

At the end of the ridge we leaned on our ice axes and looked up.

Above us was the legendary Hillary Step, the forty-foot ice wall that formed one of the mountain's most formidable hurdles.

Cowering from the wind, I tried to make out a route up it.

This ice face was to be our final and hardest test. The outcome would determine whether we would join those few who have touched that hallowed ground above.

If so, I would become only the thirty-first British climber ever to have done this.

The ranks were small.

I started up cautiously. It was a long way to come to fall here.

Points in. Ice axe in. Test them. Then move.

It was slow progress, but it was progress. And steadily I moved up the ice.

I had climbed steep pitches like this so many times before, but never twenty-nine thousand feet up in the sky. At this height, in this rarefied thin air, and with 40 mph of wind trying to blow us off the ice, I was struggling. Again.

I stopped and tried to steady myself.

Then I made that old familiar mistake—I looked down.

Beneath me, either side of the ridge, the mountain dropped away into abysses.

Idiot, Bear.

I tried to refocus on only what was in front of me and above.

Up. Keep moving up.

So I kept climbing.

It was the climb of my life, and nothing was going to stop me.

CHAPTER 95

Breathe. Pause. Move. Pause. Breathe. Pause. Move. Pause.

It is unending.

I heave myself over the final lip and strain to pull myself clear of the edge.

I clear the deep powder snow from in front of my face. I lie there hyperventilating.

Then I clear my mask of the ice that my breath has formed in the freezing air.

I unclip off the rope while still crouching. The line is now clear for Neil to follow up.

I get to my feet and start staggering onward.

I can see this distant cluster of prayer flags semisubmerged in the snow. Gently flapping in the wind, I know that these flags mark the true summit—the place of dreams.

I feel this sudden surge of energy beginning to rise within me.

It is adrenaline coursing around my veins and muscles.

I have never felt so strong—and yet so weak—all at the same time.

Intermittent waves of adrenaline and fatigue come and go as my body struggles to sustain the intensity of these final moments.

I find it strangely ironic that the very last part of this immense climb is so gentle a slope.

A sweeping curve—curling along the crest of the ridge toward the summit.

Thank God.

It feels like the mountain is beckoning me up. For the first time, willing me to climb up onto the roof of the world.

I try to count the steps as I move, but my counting becomes confused.

I am now breathing and gasping like a wild animal in an attempt to devour the oxygen that seeps into my mask.

However many of these pathetically slow shuffles I take, this place never seems to get any closer.

But it is. Slowly the summit is looming a little nearer.

I can feel my eyes welling up with tears. I start to cry and cry inside my mask.

Emotions held in for so long. I can't hold them back any longer.

I stagger on.

CHAPTER 96

There had always been this part of me that had never really believed that I could make it.

Ever since that hospital bed and my broken back, a little part of me, deep down, had thought it was all sheer madness.

And that part of me hadn't always felt so little.

I guess too many people had told me it was foolish.

Too many had laughed and called it a pipe dream. And the more times I heard them say that, the more determined I had become.

But still their words had seeped in.

So we get busy, we do things. And the noise can drown out our doubts—for a while.

But what happens when the noise stops?

My doubts have an annoying habit of hanging around, long after I think they have been stilled.

And deep down, I guess I doubted myself more than I could admit—even to myself.

Until this moment.

You see, ever since that hospital bed, I had wanted to be fixed. Physically. Emotionally.

Heck. Ever since boarding school, age eight, all those years ago, I had wanted to be fixed.

And right here, at 29,030 feet, as I staggered those last few steps, I was mending.

The spiritual working through the physical.

Mending.

❧

Eventually, at 7:22 A.M. on the morning of May 26, 1998, with tears still pouring down my frozen cheeks, the summit of Mount Everest opened her arms and welcomed me in.

As if she now considered me somehow worthy of this place. My pulse raced, and in a haze I found myself suddenly standing on top of the world.

Alan embraced me, mumbling excitedly into his mask. Neil was still staggering toward us.

As he approached, the wind began to die away.

The sun was now rising over the hidden land of Tibet, and the mountains beneath us were bathed in a crimson red.

Neil knelt and crossed himself on the summit. Then, together, with our masks off, we hugged as brothers.

I got to my feet and began to look around. I swore that I could see halfway around the world.

The horizon seemed to bend at the edges. It was the curvature of our earth. Technology can put a man on the moon but not up here.

There truly was some magic to this place.

The radio suddenly crackled to my left. Neil spoke into it excitedly.

"Base camp. We've run out of earth."

The voice on the other end exploded with jubilation. Neil

passed the radio to me. For weeks I had planned what I would say if I reached the top, but all that just fell apart.

I strained into the radio and spoke without thinking.

"I just want to get home."

The memory of what went on then begins to fade. We took several photos with both the SAS and the DLE flags flying on the summit, as promised, and I scooped some snow into an empty Juice Plus vitamin bottle I had with me.*

It was all I would take with me from the summit.

I remember having some vague conversation on the radio—patched through from base camp via a satellite phone—with my family some three thousand miles away: the people who had given me the inspiration to climb.

But up there, the time flew by, and like all moments of magic, nothing can last forever.

We had to get down. It was already 7:48 A.M.

Neil checked my oxygen.

"Bear, you're right down. You better get going, buddy, and fast."

I had just under a fifth of a tank to get me back to the Balcony.

I heaved the pack and tank onto my shoulders, fitted my mask, and turned around. The summit was gone. I knew that I would never see it again.

Within moments of leaving the summit the real exhaustion set in. It is hard to describe how much energy is required just to go down.

Statistically the vast majority of accidents happen on the descent. It is because nothing matters any longer, the goal is attained; and the urge to make the pain go away becomes stronger.

*Years later, Shara and I christened our three boys with this snow water from Everest's summit. Life moments.

When the mind is reduced like this, it is so easy to stumble and fall.

Stay alert, Bear. Keep it together just a little longer. You're only going to make that cache of oxygen at the Balcony if you stay focused.

But then my oxygen ran out.

I was stumbling—going from my knees to my feet, then back to my knees. The world was a blur.

I can. I can. I can.

I kept repeating this to myself. Over and over. An old habit from when I had been dead-tired on SAS Selection. I was mumbling the words without knowing it.

They were coming from somewhere deep inside me.

Eventually, too tired even to feel any relief, I made it. I slumped on the ground next to the tanks we had cached at the Balcony on the way up.

I feasted on the fresh oxygen. I breathed it in gulps. Both warmth and clarity flooded back into my body.

I knew we could make it now. If we went steady, we would soon be back at the col.

The distant tents began to grow as we came carefully down the ice.

CHAPTER 97

At the col it was strange not to feel ice or snow beneath me any longer. The teeth of my crampons scraped and yawned as they slid over the stones.

I leaned on my axe to steady myself for those last few meters.

For eighteen hours we had neither drunk nor eaten anything. My body and mind both felt strangely distant. Both were aching for some relief.

In the porch of our tiny single-skinned tent, I reached out to hug Neil again. Then—unceremoniously—I collapsed.

"Bear, come on, buddy. You've got to get inside the tent properly. Bear, can you hear me?" Michael's voice brought me round. He had been waiting for us at the col—hoping.

I shuffled backward into the tent. My head was pounding. I needed to drink. I hadn't peed for more than twenty-four hours.

Neil and Alan were slowly shedding their harnesses. Neither had the energy to speak. Michael passed me a warm drink from the stove. I was so happy to see him and Geoffrey in one piece.

As the afternoon turned to evening we talked.

I hadn't really known fully why Michael and Geoffrey had retreated. They told their story. Of the impending storm and their growing fatigue, as they struggled in the deep snow and thin air. Their retreat had been a decision based on sound mountain judgment.

A good call. Hence they were alive.

We, though, had kept going. That decision had been based on an element of recklessness. But we got lucky, and that storm never came.

Daring had won out—this time.

It doesn't always.

Knowing when to be reckless and when to be safe is the great mountaineering game. I knew that.

Michael turned to me later as we were getting ready for our last night in the Death Zone. He told me something that I have never forgotten. It was the voice of twenty years' climbing experience in the wild Rockies of Canada.

"Bear, do you realize the risk you guys were taking up there? It was more recklessness than good judgment, in my opinion." He smiled and looked right at me.

"My advice: from now on in your life, rein it back a fraction—and you will go far. You've survived this time—now go use that good fortune."

I have never forgotten those words.

❧

The next day, coming down the Lhotse Face seemed to take as long as going up it.

But finally, after six long, slow hours, Neil and I shuffled those last few meters into camp two, on the glacier.

That night, I did not move an inch for twelve straight hours—until just before dawn, when Neil started shuffling around.

"Bear, let's just get going, eh? It's the last leg. I can't sleep when it's this close," Neil said excitedly in the chilly air, condensation pouring from his mouth.

My eyelids felt like they were sealed shut. I had to pry them open.

We didn't bother to eat before leaving, in anticipation of the fresh omelette we had been promised over the radio from base camp. Instead we just got ready hurriedly.

But I was still slow, and I kept the others waiting as I moved laboriously from rucksack to tent to crampon. All remnants of any strength had long since gone.

My backpack seemed to weigh a ton, now that I was bringing all my stuff off the mountain. We started moving, and together we shuffled steadily along the glacier.

An hour along the route, we were stopped suddenly in our tracks.

The mountain around us roared violently, and the sound of an echoing crack shook through the place. We crouched, looked up, and watched.

Five hundred yards in front of us, on the exact route we were going, the whole side of the Nuptse Face was collapsing.

White thunder poured down the thousands of feet of mountain. It then rolled like an all-enveloping cloud across the glacier. We stood in silence as the avalanche swept by in front of us.

If we had left a few minutes earlier, it would have devoured and buried us. Game over.

Sometimes, being slow is good.

We waited until the mountain had stopped moving before slowly beginning to cross the avalanche debris.

Strangely, it was then that I felt most terrified for my life. As if that small stroke of good fortune—missing the avalanche—had shaken me to my senses about the risks we were taking.

Above: Finally finishing our epic transatlantic Arctic voyage, flying the naval white ensign and so relieved.

Right: Dropping from our dining table under a hot-air balloon at twenty-five thousand feet. Record-breaking and in aid of the Duke of Edinburgh Awards.

Top left: Up to my neck in sand at the hands of the French Foreign Legion, going through simulated basic training in the Sahara.

Middle left: Being filmed for the two-minute tester of the *Man vs. Wild* concept. And we've never looked back.

Bottom left: My first-ever jump in the opening episode of *Man vs. Wild*. Six seasons on and it's still fun and wild.

Man vs. Wild has taken me to the edge many times, whether on volcanoes or in swamps and freezing-cold glacial lakes.

Doing what I do best—living my dream.

I've learned a healthy respect for both white water and the freezing cold.

It's Bear's world. Wanna play?

MAN VS.WILD
WITH BEAR GRYLLS

Discovery CHANNEL

Watch, but you'll only be encouraging him

FRIDAY 9PM E/P
discovery.com/**manvswild**

Left: One of the billboards the Discovery Channel used around the world.

Below: The northern territories and swamplands of Australia stretched me to the max. Don't mess with saltwater crocodiles!

Top left: Dave Pearce, ex-commando, one of the *Man vs. Wild* mountain guides. Keeping the crew safe.

Middle left: Dan Etheridge (cameraman) and Pete Lee (sound) working in minus twenty-five degrees and always smiling. Inspirations.

Bottom left: One of my favorite *Man vs. Wild* pictures. Paul Ritz, me, and Simon Reay at the end of a shoot. Drenched in sweat, beer in hand, and always laughing.

Right: Prince Charles and the royal family are always such great supporters of the Scouting movement.

Below: Everything I love about Scouting: fun, adventure, and togetherness.

Left: With so many inspirational Scouting stories, I feel so proud to be the Chief Scout.

Below: Handing out the Queen's Scout Award at Windsor Castle each year is always such a great honor.

I guess the closer to the end we got, the more I realized we had almost done the impossible. We had cheated death—so far. But we were still within the mountain's grasp, and we still had one last descent through the icefall to complete.

As we crossed each of the Western Cwm's deep crevasses in turn, the mountain slowly began to feel more distant. I hadn't descended below camp two now for more than ten days, and I knew that I was leaving something extraordinary behind me.

We moved in silence, lost in our own thoughts.

Two hours later, and we sat on the lip of the icefall. The tumbling cascade of frozen water below seemed to beckon us in one last time. We had no choice but to oblige.

Fresh, deep powder snow now covered the icefall, spectacularly. It had snowed almost continually here while we had climbed up high. The route through had also changed beyond all recognition. The ice was always on the move.

The new route snaked over these giant ice cubes, and led us under lethal overhanging blocks that would crush us like mice if they chose that moment to collapse.

With each mousetrap that we passed through, I felt a little bit more of the tension drain from me.

Each step was a step toward home.

We could see base camp below us, and my breathing was becoming more and more excited. I felt as though an entire lifetime had passed since I had last been here.

The tents shimmered in the sun as we hurried through the jumbled ice at the foot of the icefall.

At 12:05 P.M. we unclipped from the last rope for the final time. I looked back at the tumbling, broken glacier and shook my head in disbelief.

Quietly, and to myself, I thanked the mountain for letting us through. Waves of worry and tension flooded from me and I couldn't stop crying. Again.

All I could think of was Dad. I wished he could be here right now. Beside me.

But he was.

Just like he had been all the way.

CHAPTER 98

The sun was warm on my face. I knew we were safe at last.

The vast bottle of Champagne, that had sat like some Buddha at base camp for three months, was ceremoniously produced. It took four of us almost ten minutes, hacking away with ice axes, finally to get the cork out.

The party had begun.

I felt like drinking a gallon of this beautiful bubbly stuff, but my body just couldn't. Sipping slowly was all I could manage without sneezing, and even like that I was soon feeling decidedly wobbly.

I closed my eyes and flopped against the rock wall of the mess tent—a huge smile plastered across my face.

Later on in my tent, I put on the fresh socks and thermal underwear that I had kept especially for this moment.

First change in ninety days. Heaven.

I sealed the underpants in a plastic Ziploc bag and reminded myself to be very cautious when it came to opening the bag again back home.

⚜

Neil's feet were still numb from the frostbite. Long exposure up high, sat waiting in the snow for all those hours at the Balcony, had taken their toll. At base camp, we bandaged them up, kept them warm, and purposefully didn't discuss the very real prospect of him losing his toes.

He didn't need to be told that he was unlikely ever to feel them again properly.

Either way, we realized that the best option for them was to get him proper medical attention and soon.

There was no way he was going to be walking anywhere with his feet bandaged up like two white balloons. We needed an air-evacuation. Not the easiest of things in the thin air of Everest's base camp.

The insurance company said that at dawn the next day they would attempt to get him out of there. Weather permitting. But at 17,450 feet we really were on the outer limits of where helicopters could fly.

True to their word, at dawn we heard the distant rotors of a helicopter, far beneath us in the valley. A tiny speck against the vast rock walls on either side.

In a matter of sixty short minutes, that thing could whisk Neil away to civilization, I thought. *Hmm.*

My goodness, that was a beautiful prospect.

Somehow I had to get on that chopper with him.

I packed in thirty seconds flat, everything from the past three months. I taped a white cross onto my sleeve, and raced out to where Neil was sat waiting.

One chance.

What the heck.

Neil shook his head at me, smiling.

"God, you push it, Bear, don't you?" he shouted over the noise of the rotors.

"You're going to need a decent medic on the flight," I replied, with a smile. "And I'm your man." (There was at least some element of truth in this: I *was* a medic and I *was* his buddy—and yes, he did need help. But essentially I was trying to pull a bit of a fast one.)

The pilot shouted that two people would be too heavy.

"I have to accompany him at all times," I shouted back over the engine noise. "His feet might fall off at any moment," I added quietly.

The pilot looked at me, then at the white cross on my sleeve.

He agreed to drop Neil somewhere down at a lower altitude, and then come back for me.

"Perfect. Go. I'll be here." I shook his hand firmly.

Let's just get this done before anyone thinks too much about it, I mumbled to myself.

And with that the pilot took off and disappeared from view.

Mick and Henry were laughing.

"If you pull this one off, Bear, I will eat my socks. You just love to push it, don't you?" Mick said, smiling.

"Yep, good try, but you aren't going to see him again, I guarantee you," Henry added.

Thanks to the pilot's big balls, he was wrong.

The heli returned empty, I leapt aboard, and with the rotors whirring at full power to get some grip in the thin air, the bird slowly lifted into the air.

The stall warning light kept buzzing away as we fought against gravity, but then the nose dipped and soon we were skimming over the rocks, away from base camp and down the glacier.

I was out of there—and Mick was busy taking his socks off.

As we descended, I spotted, far beneath us, this lone figure sat on a rock in the middle of a giant boulder field. Neil's two white "beacons" shining bright.

I love it. I smiled.

We picked Neil up, and in an instant we were flying together through the huge Himalayan valleys like an eagle freed.

Neil and I sat back in the helicopter, faces pressed against the glass, and watched our life for the past three months become a shimmer in the distance.

The great mountain faded into a haze, hidden from sight. I leaned against Neil's shoulder and closed my eyes.

Everest was gone.

CHAPTER 99

Once back in Kathmandu, Neil and I kind of let it all go—and it felt great. We had worked hard for this, and sometimes it is good to let your hair down. Totally.

The next morning, slightly the worse for wear, I remember wandering lazily along the rickety balcony of our small, back-street Kathmandu hostel.

I found several members of the Russian Everest team, who had been on the north side of the mountain, sat on the corridor floor, talking in low voices. They glanced up at me wearily. To a man they looked mentally exhausted.

Then I noticed that they had been crying; big Russian, bearded men, crying.

Sergei and Francys Arsentiev were recently married. They had loved to climb. Everest had been their dream together. But it had gone horribly wrong.

Francys had been on her way down from the summit when she had collapsed. Nobody knew why: maybe cerebral edema, or the cold—maybe just that killer Everest exhaustion. She simply had not been able to find the energy to carry on. She had died where she sat.

Sergei, her husband, had stumbled down to find help for her. Dazed, fatigued, and desperate, he then fell to his death.

The Russians asked me if we had seen a body, or just . . . anything.

Their voices were weak. They knew that it was unlikely, but they had to try. Their eyes looked dead. I felt a numbness well up inside as I thought of Sergei and his wife both dead on the mountain—and us somehow strangely alive.

That fine line between survival and disaster can be so slender.

That afternoon, lying on my bed, I struggled to understand why we were alive, when others weren't. Sergei and Francys Arsentiev hadn't been the only ones to die in the past few weeks.

Roger Buick, a New Zealand climber, had collapsed and died from a heart attack. Mark Jennings, from Britain, had reached the top but, again, died on the descent.

They'd all been experienced, fit climbers.

What a waste, what an unnecessary waste.

As I lay there, I found no real answers. But the Russians, buried in deep despair, weren't interested in answers. They had simply lost their buddies.

Human nature hungers for adventure—and true adventure has its risks. Everyone knows Everest is dangerous, yet the reality of seeing this firsthand makes words like *adventure* seem so hollow.

These were real lives, with real families, and their loss still confuses me today.

I remain loyal, though, to the belief that those brave men and women who died during those months on Everest are the true heroes. They paid the ultimate sacrifice, in pursuit of their dreams.

This must be their families' only relief.

⚜

It is always strange looking back at a time that has had such a pro-found impact on one's life. And when it comes to Everest, I see two very clear things: friendships that were forged in a tough cru-cible, and a faith that sustained me through the good, the bad, and the ugly.

I survived and reached the top of that mountain because of the bonds I had with those beside me. Of that I am in no doubt. Without Mick and Neil, I would have been nothing.

Down that dark crevasse, I also learned that sometimes we really need one another. And that is okay. We are not designed to be islands. We are made to be connected.

So often life teaches us that we have to achieve everything on our own. But that would be lonely.

For me, it is only by thinking about our togetherness that I can begin to make some sense of what happened on that mountain: the highs, the lows, the fatalities, the fear.

Such things have to be shared.

Looking back, it is the small moments together that I value the most. Like Neil and myself on the South Summit, holding each other's hands so that we could both stand.

It was only because our friendships were honest that, time after time, when we were tired or cold or scared, we were able to pick ourselves up and keep moving.

You don't have to be strong all the time. That was a big lesson to learn.

When we show chinks it creates bonds, and where there are bonds there is strength.

This is really the heart of why I still climb and expedition today.

Simple ties are hard to break.

That is what Everest really taught me.

CHAPTER 100

It took me quite a while to begin to recover physically from Everest.

The thick, rich air of sea level, in comparison to the ultrathin air of Everest, was intoxicating—and at times it felt like too much.

Several times I fainted and had quite bad nosebleeds. As if from oxygen overload.

Above all, I slept like a baby.

For the first time in years, I had no fear, no doubts, no sense of foreboding. It felt amazing.

Everest had taken all my heart, soul, energy, and desire, and I was spent. The way I was after SAS Selection.

Funny that. Good things rarely come easy.

Maybe that is what makes them special.

I didn't feel too guilty about taking a little time off to enjoy the British summer and catch up with my friends. It just felt so great to be safe.

I also did my first-ever newspaper interview, which carried the headline: "What Makes a Scruffy 23-Year-Old Want to Risk It All for a View of Tibet?" Nice.

Before I left I would have had a far slicker reply than I did afterward. My reasons for climbing seemed somehow more obscure. Maybe less important. I don't know.

I just knew that it was good to be home.

The same journalist also finished up by congratulating me on having "conquered" Everest. But this instinctively felt so wrong. We never conquer any mountain. Everest allowed us to reach the summit by the skin of our teeth, and let us go with our lives.

Not everyone had been so lucky.

Everest never has been, and never will be, conquered. This is part of what makes the mountain so special.

One of the other questions I often got asked when we returned home was: "Did you find God on the mountain?" The real answer is you don't have to climb a big mountain to find faith.

It's simpler than that—thank God.

If you asked me did He help me up there, then the answer would be yes.

Every faltering step of the way.

⚜

My Everest story would be incomplete if I didn't give final credit to the Sherpas who had risked their lives alongside us every day.

Pasang and Ang-Sering still climb together as best friends, under the direction of their Sirdar boss—Kami. The Khumba Icefall specialist, Nima, still carries out his brave task in the jumbled ice maze at the foot of the mountain: repairing and fixing the route through.

Babu Chiri, who so bravely helped Mick when he ran out of oxygen under the South Summit, was tragically killed in a crevasse in the Western Cwm several years later. He was a Sherpa of many years' Everest experience, and was truly one of the mountain's greats. It was a huge loss to the mountaineering fraternity.

But if you play the odds long enough you will eventually lose. That is the harsh reality of high-altitude mountaineering.

You can't keep on top of the world forever.

Geoffrey returned to the army, and Neil to his business. His toes never regained their feeling, but he avoided having them amputated. But as they say, Everest always charges some sort of a price, and in his own words—he got lucky.

As for Mick, he describes his time on Everest well: "In the three months I was away, I was both happier than ever before, and more scared than I ever hope to be again."

Ha. That's also high-altitude mountaineering for you.

Thengba, my friend, with whom I spent so much time alone at camp two, was finally given a hearing aid by Henry. Now, for the first time, he can hear properly.

Despite our different worlds, we shared a common bond with these wonderful Sherpa men—a friendship that was forged by an extraordinary mountain.

Once, when the climber Julius Kugy was asked what sort of person a mountaineer should be, he replied: "Truthful, distinguished, and modest."

All these Sherpas epitomize this. I made the top with them, and because of their help, I owe them more than I can say.

The great Everest writer Walt Unsworth, in his book *Everest: The Mountaineering History*, gives a vivid description of the characters of the men and women who pit their all on the mountain.

I think it is bang on the money:

But there are men for whom the unattainable has a special attraction.

 Usually they are not experts: their ambitions and fantasies are strong enough to brush aside the doubts which more cautious men might have.

Determination and faith are their strongest weapons.

At best such men are regarded as eccentric; at worst, mad . . .

Three things they all had in common: faith in themselves, great determination, and endurance.

If I had to sum up what happened on that journey for me, from the hospital bed to the summit of the world, I tend to think of it as a stumbling journey.

Of losing my confidence and my strength—then refinding it. Of seeing my hope and my faith slip away—and then having them rekindled.

Ultimately, if I had to pass on one message to my children it would be this: Fortune favors the brave.

Most of the time.

CHAPTER 101

Shara met me at the airport in London, dressed in her old familiar blue woolen overcoat that I loved so much. She was bouncing
like a little girl with excitement.

Everest was nothing compared to seeing her.

I was skinny, long-haired, and wearing some very suspect flow-
ery Nepalese trousers. In short, I looked a mess, but I was so
happy.

I had been warned by Henry at base camp not to rush into anything "silly" when I saw Shara again. He had told me it was a
classic mountaineers' error to propose as soon as you get home.
High altitude apparently clouds people's good judgment, he had
said.

In the end, I waited twelve months. But during this time I knew
that this was the girl I wanted to marry.

We had so much fun together that year. I persuaded Shara,
almost daily, to skip off work early from her publishing job (she
needed little persuading, mind), and we would go on endless, fun
adventures.

I remember taking her roller-skating through a park in central
London and going too fast down a hill. I ended up headfirst in the
lake, fully clothed. She thought it funny.

Another time, I lost a wheel while roller-skating down a steep, busy London street. (Cursed skates!) I found myself screeching along at breakneck speed on only one skate. She thought that one scary.

We drank tea, had afternoon snoozes, and drove around in "Dolly," my old London black cab that I had bought for a song.

Shara was the only girl I knew who would be willing to sit with me for hours on the motorway—broken down—waiting for road-side recovery to tow me to yet another garage to fix Dolly. Again.

We were (are!) in love.

I put a wooden board and mattress in the backseat so I could sleep in the taxi, and Charlie Mackesy painted funny cartoons inside. (Ironically, these are now the most valuable part of Dolly, which sits majestically outside our home.)

Our boys love playing in Dolly nowadays. Shara says I should get rid of her, as the taxi is rusting away, but Dolly was the car that I will forever associate with our early days together. How could I send her to the scrapyard?

In fact, this spring, we are going to paint Dolly in the colors of the rainbow, put decent seat belts in the backseat, and go on a road trip as a family. Heaven. We must never stop doing these sorts of things. They are what brought us together, and what will keep us having fun.

Spontaneity has to be exercised every day, or we lose it.

Shara, lovingly, rolls her eyes.

⚜

The summer of 1999, we went on holiday to Spain to visit my cousin Penny, who runs a horse farm in Andalucia. It is a beautiful, wild part of the country.

Shara would ride out early each day in the hilly pine forests and along the miles of huge, deserted Atlantic beaches. I was told I was too tall for the small Andalucian ponies.

But I didn't want to be deterred.

Instead I ran alongside Shara and tried to keep up with the horse. (Good training, that one.)

Eventually, on the Monday morning we were to leave, I took her down to the beach and persuaded her to come skinny-dipping with me. She agreed. (With some more eye-rolling.)

As we started to get out after swimming for some time, I pulled her toward me, held her in my arms, and prepared to ask for her hand in marriage.

I took a deep breath, steadied myself, and as I was about to open my mouth, a huge Atlantic roller pounded in, picked us both up, and rolled us like rag dolls along the beach.

Laughing, I went for take two. She still had no idea what was coming.

Finally, I got the words out. She didn't believe me.

She made me kneel on the sand (naked) and ask her again.

She laughed—then burst into tears and said yes.

(Ironically, on our return, Brian, Shara's father, also burst into tears when I asked him for his blessing. For that one, though, I was dressed in a jacket, tie, and . . . board shorts.)

I was unsure whether his were tears of joy or despair.

What really mattered was that Shara and I were going to get married.

That same day we drove to Seville to celebrate. I asked someone for the name of the smartest hotel in Seville. Alfonso XIII, came the reply. It is where the King of Spain always stays.

We found the hotel and wandered in. It was amazing. Shara was a little embarrassed as I was dressed in shorts and an old holey jersey, but I sought out a friendly-looking receptionist and told her our story.

"Could you help us out? I have hardly any money."

She looked us up and down, paused—then smiled.

"Just don't tell my manager," she whispered.

So we stayed in a $1,000-a-night room for $100 and celebrated—like the King of Spain.

The next morning we went on a hunt for a ring.

I asked the concierge in my best university Spanish where I would find a good (aka well-priced) jeweler.

He looked a little surprised.

I tried speaking slower. Eventually I realized that I had actually been asking him where I might find a good mustache shop.

I apologized that my Spanish was a little rusty. Shara rolled her eyes again, smiling.

When we eventually found a small local jeweller, I had to do some nifty subcounter mathematics, swiftly converting Spanish pesetas into British pounds, to work out whether or not I could afford each ring Shara tried on.

We eventually settled on one that was simple, beautiful—and affordable. Just.

Love doesn't require expensive jewelery. And Shara has always been able to make the simple look exquisite.

Luckily.

CHAPTER 102

Pretty soon after returning from Everest, I was asked to give a lecture on the Everest expedition to my local sailing club in the Isle of Wight.

It would be the first of many lectures that I would eventually give, and would soon become my main source of income after returning from the mountain.

Those early talks were pretty ropey, though, by anyone's standards.

That first one went okay, mainly due to the heavy number of family members in the audience. Dad cried, Mum cried, Lara cried. Everyone was proud and happy.

The next talk was to a group of soldiers on a course with the SAS. I took one of my old buddies along with me for moral support.

Hugo Mackenzie-Smith always jokes to this day how, by the time I finished, the entire room had fallen asleep. (They had been up all night on an exercise, I hasten to add—but still—it wasn't my finest hour.)

We had to wake them—one by one.

I had a lot to learn about communicating a story if I was to earn any sort of a living by giving talks.

My worst ever speech was one I did for a pharmaceutical company in South Africa. They were paying me $1,000 and my airfare. It was a fortune to me at the time, and I couldn't believe my luck.

That would last Shara and me for months.

I soon found myself at a hotel in the Drakensberg Mountains, waiting for six hundred sales staff to arrive at the conference center.

Their bus journey up had been a long one and they had been supplied with beer, nonstop, for the previous five hours. By the time they rolled off the buses, many of them were tripping over their bags—laughing and roaring drunk.

Nightmare.

I had been asked to speak after dinner—and for a minimum of an hour. Even I knew that an hour after dinner was suicide. But they were insistent. They wanted their thousand's worth.

After a long, booze-filled dinner that never seemed to end, the delegates really were totally paralytic. I was holding my head in my hands backstage. *Sweet Jesus.*

Then, just as I walked out on stage, the lights went out and there was a power cut.

You have got to be joking.

The organizers found candles to light the room (which also meant no slides), and then I was on. It was well after midnight by now.

Oh, and did I mention that all the delegates were Afrikaans-speaking, so English was their second language, at best?

Sure enough, the heckling started before I even opened my mouth.

"We don't want an after-dinner speaker," one drunk man shouted, almost falling off his chair.

Listen, nor do I, big fella, I thought.

I suspect it was just as painful an hour for him as it was for me.

But I persevered and endeavored to learn how to tell a story well. After all, it was my only source of work, and my only way of trying to find new sponsors for any other expeditions that I hoped to lead.

The best advice came from the legendary actor the late Sir John Mills, who I sat next to backstage at a lecture we were doing together. He told me he considered the key to public speaking to be this: "Be sincere, be brief, be seated."

Inspired words. And it changed the way I spoke publicly from then on. Keep it short. Keep it from the heart.

Men tend to think that they have to be funny, witty, or incisive onstage. You don't. You just have to be honest. If you can be intimate and give the inside story—emotions, doubts, struggles, fears, the lot—then people will respond.

I went on to give talks all around the world to some of the biggest corporations in business—and I always tried to live by that. Make it personal, and people will stand beside you.

As I started to do bigger and bigger events for companies, I wrongly assumed that I should, in turn, start to look much smarter and speak more "corporately." I was dead wrong—and I learned that fast. When we pretend, people get bored.

But stay yourself, talk intimately, and keep the message simple, and it doesn't matter what the hell you wear.

It does, though, take courage, in front of five thousand people, to open yourself up and say you really struggle with self-doubt. Especially when you are meant to be there as a motivational speaker.

But if you keep it real, then you give people something real to take away.

"If he can, then so can I" is always going to be a powerful message. For kids, for businessmen—and for aspiring adventurers.

I really am pretty average. I promise you. Ask Shara . . . ask Hugo.

I am ordinary, but I am determined.

I did, though—as the corporations started to pay me more— begin to doubt whether I was really worth the money. It all seemed kind of weird to me. I mean, was my talk a hundred times better now than the one I gave in the Drakensberg Mountains?

No.

But, on the other hand, if you can help people feel stronger and more capable because of what you tell them, then it becomes worthwhile for companies in ways that are impossible to quantify.

If that wasn't true, then I wouldn't get asked to speak so often, still to this day.

And the story of Everest—a mountain, like life, and like business—is always going to work as a metaphor. You have got to work together, work hard, and go the extra mile. Look after each other, be ambitious, and take calculated, well-timed risks.

Give your heart to the goal, and it will repay you.

Now, are we talking business or climbing?

That's what I mean.

CHAPTER 103

During the year before Shara and I got married, I managed to persuade the owners of a small island, situated in Poole Harbor, to let me winter house-sit the place in return for free lodging.

It was a brilliant deal.

Chopping logs, keeping an eye on the place, doing a bit of maintenance, and living like a king on a beautiful twenty-acre island off the south coast of England.

Some months earlier, I had been walking along a riverbank outside of London when I had spotted a little putt-putt fishing boat with an old 15 hp engine on the back. She was covered in mold and looked on her last legs, but I noticed her name, painted carefully on the side.

She was called *Shara*. What were the chances of that?

I bought her on the spot, with what was pretty well my last £800.

Shara became my pride and joy. And I was the only person who could get the temperamental engine to start! I used the boat, though, primarily, as my way of going backward and forward to the small island.

I had some properly dicey crossings in *Shara* during the middle of that winter. Often done late at night, after an evening out, the three-mile crossing back to the island could be treacherous in bad weather. Freezing waves would crash over the bows, threatening to swamp the boat, and the old engine would often start cutting in and out.

I had no nav-lights, no waterproofs, no life jacket, and no radio. And that meant no backup plan—which is bad.

Totally irresponsible. But totally fun.

I held my stag weekend over there with my best buddies—Ed, Mick, Neil, Charlie, Nige (one of Shara's uni friends who has become such a brilliant buddy), Trucker, Watty, Stan, and Hugo—and it was a wild one.

Charlie ended up naked on a post in the middle of the harbor, we got rescued twice having broken down trying to water-ski behind the underpowered *Shara,* and we had a huge bonfire while playing touch-rugby by firelight.

Perfect.

At this stage, I was also living a pretty unhealthy lifestyle. I was eating too much, smoking, and drinking (which is always daft), and not training at all.

Predictably, I piled on the pounds and looked pretty rough.

But I just wanted to get away from fitness and training and being focused and all of that.

I wanted a life. Away from the military, away from the mountains, away from pressure.

All through university, while my friends had played, I had worked my guts out on SAS Selection, and then on Everest.

Now I just wanted a break.

Eventually, I remember doing one of my earliest TV interviews and watching myself in horror afterward. I looked bloated and pale. I realized that if I didn't get a hold of this and rein it all back, I would be in danger of never doing anything else of value with my life.

That wasn't in my game plan.

I didn't want to live in the past—just talking about Everest and looking like a has-been.

If I was to move on and make something of all that I had risked and built over the past few years, then I needed to start walking the talk.

It was time to get fit again.

Going through this phase, though, did confirm in my mind that at least Shara wasn't marrying me for either my looks or money.

I was both broke and bloated.

She, bless her, still loved me all the same.

CHAPTER 104

Our wedding took place on a blustery midwinter day. The fifteenth of January 2000. Yet the sun shone through the clouds brightly.

Shara's father, Brian, who so sadly was suffering with multiple sclerosis, gave her away from his wheelchair in the church.

Brian cried. Shara cried. Everyone cried.

We left the church to our friends singing a cappella versions of "Hey, Hey, We're the Monkees" and "I'm a Believer."

I was the happiest I had ever been.

Right decisions make you feel like that.

We then danced to a Peruvian street band that Trucker had come across, and ate bangers and mash at long tables. The day was above all, love-filled.

We were both among the first, and youngest, of our group of friends to be married, which made it feel even more special. (A wedding was novel for all of us in those days.) And Charlie and Trucker made everyone cry some more with their best-men speeches.

Several months earlier Shara and I had bought a home together. Well, to be more accurate it was a barge, moored on the Thames in central London.

Neil had spotted it for us, and we looked around it straight away. I instantly loved it.

We had previously been quite close to putting in an offer on a tiny, poky studio flat in London—but deep down I was concerned.

For a start, I couldn't really afford it. Dad had offered to help me secure a mortgage if I could make the repayments, but I knew it would be a stretch to make those every month.

The barge, on the other hand, was less than half the price—and way cooler.

It was pretty sparse, cold, and damp when we looked around it, and Shara and her family were definitely a little tentative at first.

But I got to work on the PR front.

"Hey, it will be fun. We can do it up together—it will be a challenge. We can then make it all cozy and a home."

Shara tilted her head at me in her way.

"I'm a little nervous about the 'challenge' bit. Can we focus on the homely and cozy part of the plan instead, sweetheart?" she replied, still looking concerned.

(Sure enough, she totally changed after we got to live on our barge for a while, and nowadays, wild horses couldn't force her to sell the boat. I love that in her. Shara always takes such a lot of convincing, and then once she makes something "hers," it is hers forever. Me included.)

We spent two months doing up the boat with our good friend Rob Cranham. He was amazing. He lived on board and worked tirelessly to help us make it a home. Rob converted it to just how we had envisaged. This included an old bathtub mounted on the deck and a captain's cabinet bed in the "dungeon"!*

We lowered Shara's granny's old sofa and chest of drawers in

---

*Rob suffered from narcolepsy and sadly died in 2010 from a heart attack. Now safely settled in heaven, he was truly one of life's heroes, and such a friend to us.

through the roof, and painted and varnished furiously. By the time of the wedding, all was done.

The marital bed was neatly made, Shara's nightie was carefully laid out on the pillow, and all was set for when we would return from honeymoon, ready to spend our first night together there.

I couldn't wait.

The day after our wedding, we flew off on honeymoon. I had recklessly waited until two days before our wedding to book the holiday, in the hope that I would get some great last-minute deal somewhere.

Always a dangerous tactic.

I pretended to Shara that it was a surprise.

But, predictably, those "great deals" were a bit thin on the ground that week. The best I could find was a one-star package holiday, at a resort near Cancun in Mexico.

It was bliss being together, but there was no hiding the fact that the hotel sucked. We got put in a room right next to the sewer outlet—which gave us a cracking smell to enjoy every evening as we sat looking out at the . . . maintenance shed opposite.

As lunch wasn't included in the one-star package, we started stockpiling the breakfasts. A couple of rolls down the jersey sleeve, and a yogurt and banana in Shara's handbag. Then back to the hammock for books, kissing, and another whiff of sewage.

When we returned to the UK it was a freezing cold January day. Shara was tired, but we were both excited to get onto our nice, warm, centrally heated barge.

It was to be our first night in our own home.

I had asked Annabel, Shara's sister, to put the heating on before we arrived, and some food in the fridge. She had done so perfectly.

What she didn't know, though, was that the boiler packed in soon after she left.

By the time Shara and I made it to the quayside on the Thames, it was dark. Our breath was coming out as clouds of vapor in the freezing air. I picked Shara up and carried her up the steps onto the boat.

We opened the door and looked at each other. Surprised.

It was literally like stepping into a deep freeze. Old iron boats are like that in winter. The cold water around them means that, without heating, they are Baltically cold. We fumbled our way, still all wrapped up, into the bowels of the boat and the boiler room.

Shara looked at me, then at the silent, cold boiler.

No doubt she questioned how smart both choices had really been.

⚜

So there we were.

No money, and freezing cold—but happy and together.

That night, all wrapped up in blankets, I made a simple promise to Shara: I would love her and look after her, every day of our life together—and along the way we would have one hell of an adventure.

Little did either of us realize, but this was really just the beginning.

PART 5

✦

THE BEGINNING

When the ball rolls your way grab it. We so rarely get a second chance. (Although miraculously this does sometimes happen, too.) And remember that life is what you make of it—and that is what makes the possibilities so exciting.

—My granny Patsie Fisher

CHAPTER 105

So Shara and I started our married life fairly hard up, but much in love.

The latter has never changed.

Shara was never the ambitious one for my work, and I am so grateful for that in many ways. I can think of few things as exhausting or disempowering as a pushy wife, desperate for her husband to better himself.

Instead, I have always applied my own pressure, and have been just quietly grateful for such a cozy, fun, loyal, family-centered best friend in Shara.

Within a year of being married, though, both Shara and I lost our fathers. It was the ultimate trial for us at such a young age, just starting out on our journey together.

Brian had fought the bravest of fights against multiple sclerosis for more than fifteen years—but finally, and quietly, he passed over to the other side.

He was one of the most unique, self-motivated, and brave men I would ever meet.

He had come to the UK from South Africa with only a small brown suitcase and a determination to succeed. He went on to build the most wonderful life and family.

Above all, he and Vinnie, his wife, gave me Shara.

Brian suffered the agony of this cruelest of diseases, which systematically began to reduce him.

First it forced him into a wheelchair, then it robbed him of his power of speech, and eventually the ability to clothe, feed, or look after himself. But he never, ever lost his sparkle, and he fought so hard not to let himself be totally bed-bound—despite his severe disability.

One can only admire such courage.

I just wish I could have known him when he was fit and healthy. We would have had a blast together, I know.

His death, though, totally broke Shara's heart. And all I could do was hold her as she grieved, night after night.

Then, out of the blue, and totally unexpectedly, my own father died—only ten weeks after Brian. Like some sick joke.

He was due to have a pacemaker fitted and had asked if I could be with him during the operation. I used my old SAS medic card to blag my way in to watch the surgeons at work.

Something, though, didn't feel quite right as Dad squeezed my hand and fell asleep.

Several days after the op, he died—just like that. He had been sat up in bed at home. Alive one minute. Dead the next.

My dad.

Nobody ever knew what had happened. It was kind of academic at that point. He was gone.

The world felt like it had been pulled out from beneath Shara and me.

But we found solace and strength in each other.

I am sure both Brian and my father would have wanted it that way.

Since then, though, we have been blessed to have had three gorgeous children of our own. Together.

Funny that, isn't it?

New life from old.

CHAPTER 106

Unsurprisingly—maybe—all three of our children are boys.

Jesse is now seven, Marmaduke is four, and little Huckleberry is just two. They are truly a taste of heaven, and nothing, and I mean nothing, beats being all snuggled up in our bed, or having a picnic together in the grass on our little Welsh island that we now own.

I really hunger for nothing else.

All three boys are showing a worrying tendency toward adventure: endlessly climbing trees, making camps, and trying to catch worms and bugs. Along with possessing a magnetic pull toward mud, they make me the proudest father on the planet.

Daily, they remind me that everything of true value in life can't be bought.

And how both our dads would have adored them!

So much happened, though, in our early, prechildren days, that served to turn our life around irretrievably.

Much of it came from small, serendipitous, unlikely turns of events—like driving for many hours to do a small Everest talk for a charity and finding out afterward that the young son of the head of Channel 4 (the large UK TV network) was there.

He then told his dad that I should do a TV show for the network.

Kids, eh?

Or getting spotted by the Discovery Channel, after having been chosen out of many climbers to be the subject of a big worldwide "Sure for Men" deodorant TV campaign. (Ironically, this one came just days after Dad died—which always felt like his little spark of a parting gift to me. And, wow, there were so many little gifts from him throughout his life.)

But would I ever have done the bigger TV shows without mini-breaks like those?

I doubt it.

But from small acorns grow big oaks.

Along the way, though, I was always careful not to get greedy or to go for the quick buck—despite the temptations in the early days.

Financially, it was hard saying no to big appearance fees from TV shows like *I'm a Celebrity . . . Get Me Out of Here* or *Survivor*—but I always had the long goal in mind and tried to keep the main thing the main thing.

And not get distracted by fluff.

Instead, know your strengths.

I also tended instinctively to shy away from both TV and the whole concept of fame—partly, I am sure, because I didn't have the self-belief to feel I deserved either fame or money. (Time and experience have since taught me that fame and money very rarely go to the worthy, by the way—hence we shouldn't ever be too impressed by either of those impostors. Value folk for who they are, how they live, and what they give—that's a much better benchmark.)

So I resisted TV quite heavily—even ironically spurning the

offers of the original *Man vs. Wild* producer, Rob MacIver, some three times, before finally agreeing to do a pilot show.

But what a dope I was.

Bear, didn't you listen to your grandma when she wrote: "When the ball rolls your way grab it. We so rarely get a second chance. (Although miraculously, this does sometimes happen, too.)"?

But I just didn't want to be pushed into TV, I wanted to keep focused on my strengths, and trust those skills.

My father always used to say that if you focus on doing your job well, then money will often follow. But chase the money and it has a habit of slipping through your fingers.

I always liked that.

But learning that I could do both things—TV, as well as my core skills—was a big lesson.

Maybe it *would* be possible to do programs without having to be a smiley media person.

I wondered.

Grandma?

"Indeed—when the ball rolls your way—grab it."

CHAPTER 107

Sometimes, in the quiet moments, it is quite surreal to look back on all the madness and think: how on earth did all this happen?

I mean, the TV show *Man vs. Wild* has now become among the most-watched shows on the planet—reaching a global audience of almost 1.2 billion people in a hundred and eighty different countries. (I've read that BBC's *Top Gear* reaches some three hundred and fifty million, to give you a perspective on this.)

The program was nominated for an Emmy, has done three seasons for Channel 4 in the UK, and six seasons in the USA and around the world.

It has also become the number one cable show in all of North America.

The success of the show in the US has been reflected internationally, with some of the highest TV ratings in Australia, New Zealand, India, China, Russia, Mexico, Brazil, Argentina, Italy, Germany, Spain, and beyond.

It messes with your head a little.

I do, though, like the fact that the country I am least well known in is the UK—it gives me breathing space and a degree of normality where it matters.

It means that my family can just get on with the business of living without too much hassle at home.

What it is like for us abroad is almost my family's little secret.

❧

It is because of the program's global reach that I do, though, experience so many weird, disconcerting moments.

Like being in some far-flung small village in the tip end of the Borneo jungle, and finding that the little barefoot kids running around from wooden shack to wooden shack know exactly who I am.

Hardly a TV in sight.

Dan, one of our cameramen, says it never fails to make him smile as I wander on blissfully unaware. But I remind myself that this monster is not of my doing—it is purely the power of television.

And there is so much of it that I struggle to understand.

One thing I am clear on, though, is why the show *Man vs. Wild* has been so successful.

I consider it is down to the magic three: good fortune, an amazing team, and a willingness to risk it all.

My magic trio.

There is no doubt that good fortune and blessed timing have been at the heart of why the program has worked.

All too often I meet extraordinarily talented people: whether they are world-class climbers, champion skydivers, or survival-bushcraft gurus.

Invariably, they are more skilled than me—and, annoyingly, often better-looking and more muscled to boot!

And, if the truth be told, they could all probably do my job better than me, as well.

So how come I get to do it?

I got lucky.

I got given a privileged platform to express myself, make my mistakes, learn, and improve.

In turn, as the seasons of the show have progressed, so has my confidence in what I do. That counts for a lot.

Along the way, though, the show has come close to being axed on multiple occasions. New execs; new directives; new demands.

Any of these could have resulted in an axing. But it hung in there, ratings grew, and before I knew it we were part of people's vocabulary and consciousness. That takes time—but when, and if, it happens, it all then becomes simpler.

Let me explain.

When a TV show starts out, it is incredibly competitive: maybe one in a hundred TV ideas goes on to get made into pilot (tester) episodes. Maybe one in twenty of those pilots will go on to have a first series commissioned. And maybe one in ten of those will be asked back for a second season.

It takes a sprinkling of fairy dust and a lot of goodwill.

But do two seasons and you will quite probably go on to do five—or more.

So we got lucky. No doubt. And I never even asked for it. Let alone expected it.

I was simply, and blissfully, unaware.

But on this journey, *Man vs. Wild* has had to endure a lot of flak from critics and the press. Anything successful inevitably does. (Funny how the praise tends just to bounce off, but small amounts of criticism sting so much. Self-doubt can be a brute, I guess.)

The program has been accused of being set up, staged, faked, and manipulated. One critic even suggested it was all shot in a studio with CGI. If only.

Another recurring negative was that following my advice would be dangerous to the viewer. In fact, more likely, lethal.

But the format has always been what to do if you are faced with the ultimate wilderness disaster.

I work within my own skill levels to show what I would do—from all my training—in order to survive.

Watch. Enjoy. It just might save your life one day.

Of course, such situations don't happen often. It is why the crew have a pretty clear idea that I am going to come across certain obstacles—whether they are rapids, cliffs, snakes, or sinkholes. That is the show.

The team do the recces. Then we get briefed by local rangers, indigenous people, and Search and Rescue. It is all part of our preparation. Including grab bags, satellite phones, ropes, med kits, even antivenoms.

If you are going to tackle the wild—then be prepared.

It would have been much easier just to have gone out there and made a safe, predictable survival show—showing you how to sit tight and wait for rescue. And it would have bombed.

If you want that, then there are a multitude of bushcraft DVDs on offer.

As for me—I just wanted to go wild and have fun with my buddies.

CHAPTER 108

On one occasion, after a particularly long spell away from home, I got Shara to fly into the mountains we were filming in.

"Bring the boys, my love, I miss you."

That night, I hitched a lift with the crew, jumped into the helicopter that was extracting them back to base, and went to the lodge they were staying in.

Shara was there, waiting.

I spent the night in my family's arms and went back to film the next day. Reckless, I know.

But the press got wind of it, as they do, and they went for the jugular. It made for a killer headline. I totally understood. But who hasn't made the odd mistake?

In hindsight, it was more than reckless—it was an error, and it opened a can of worms for the papers to feed on.

But, for the record, it had been total heaven to see Shara and the boys.

So which do I value more—being a hero or being a father?

There's a third option, Bear. It is called patience.

I know. It is never my strong point.

So this was another moment that could have sunk the show,

but Channel 4 and Discovery backed me. They knew all too well how hard I work and the risks I take every day.

And the best response to the critics was the show's subsequent runaway success.

✤

The second element to why the show has worked is undoubtedly my team.

And guess what? I am not alone out there.

I work with a truly brilliant, small, tight-knit crew. Four or five guys. Heroes to a man.

They work their nuts off. Unsung. Up to their necks in the dirt. Alongside me in more hellholes than you could ever imagine.

They are mainly made up of ex–Special Forces buddies and top adventure cameramen—as tough as they come, and best friends.

It's no surprise that all the behind-the-scenes episodes we do are so popular—people like to hear the inside stories about what it is really like when things go a little "wild." As they often do.

My crew are incredible—truly—and they provide me with so much of my motivation to do this show. Without them I am nothing.

Simon Reay brilliantly told me on episode one: "Don't present this, Bear, just do it—and tell me along the way what the hell you are doing and why. It looks amazing. Just tell me."

That became the show.

And there is the heroic Danny Cane, who reckoned I should just: "Suck an earthworm up between your teeth, and chomp it down raw. They'll love it, Bear. Trust me!"

Inspired.

Producers, directors, the office team and the field crew. My buddies. Steve Rankin, Scott Tankard, Steve Shearman, Dave Pearce,

Ian Dray, Nick Parks, Woody, Stani, Ross, Duncan Gaudin, Rob Llewellyn, Pete Lee, Paul Ritz, and Dan Etheridge—plus so many others, helping behind the scenes back in the UK.

Multiple teams. One goal.

Keeping one another alive.

Oh, and do the field team share their food with me, help collect firewood, and join in tying knots on my rafts?

All the time. We are a team.

⚜

The final magic ingredient has been a willingness to risk it all. All in. No questions asked.

The program started, and grew, from a determination to push the boundaries. Do the impossible. Climb the impassable—eat the inedible.

Of course, there was often a safer, easier way down the water-fall or cliff face. But I rarely took it. That wasn't my aim. I wanted to show you how to survive when you have no safe options.

And I loved it.

I had learned a while back that whenever I had succeeded, it had always come about because of total commitment. Heart and soul. No holds barred.

I realized, early on, that this would also be the key to this show.

It's not rocket science. It's a lesson as old as the hills: Hold back from the tackle and that's when you get nailed.

This commitment built the show. But I nearly paid for it with my life. Many times.

There have been a multitude of near-death moments. None of which I am proud of. The list, though, is long. For old times' sake, I used to write them down.

Then I gave up when I passed the fiftieth.

Anyway, I don't like to think about those—they are in the past. Part of the learning process.

Part of what made me stronger.

Nowadays, the show is still crazy, but I manage the risk way better. I use ropes much more, off-camera. I think twice, not once, before I leap. I never did that before. It is called being aware.

Aware of being a husband. Aware of being a dad.

I am proud that I am learning; you only ever get it wrong once.

CHAPTER 109

There has been one further element to *Man vs. Wild*'s success, and that is its underlying message. I believe it is actually the biggest factor.

If you think about it, at heart, there is such a strong link between survival and life. I mean, we are all in a battle of some sort, aren't we?

Surviving.

It feels like day by day sometimes.

But talent, skill, and luck are only a part of what carries people through.

A small part.

There is a bigger element that separates the real survivors. It is heart, hope, and doggedness. Those are the qualities that really matter.

Ditto in life.

A young kid came up to me in the street a few days ago. He looked me square in the eye and asked me: "If you could tell me one survival message, what would it be?"

I thought about it for a moment. I wanted to give him a decent answer.

Then I saw it very clearly.

"Smile when it's raining, and when you're going through hell—keep going."

The boy thought for a moment.

Then he looked up at me and said: "It rains a lot where I live."

We all know the feeling.

Maybe he'll remember the message one day—when he really needs it.

✠

So suddenly here we are.

Six years on.

I genuinely never believed we would film more than six episodes of *Man vs. Wild,* let alone six seasons.

I mean, where has the time gone?

I also really had no idea quite how many hellholes, remote jungles, stinking swamps, searing deserts, and forbidding, unexplored mountain ranges we have on this small planet of ours.

People forget. Me included.

Along the way, we have filmed almost seventy one-hour-long episodes, as well as twelve episodes of *Worst-Case Scenario,* and a whole series on what it is like to go through basic training inside the French Foreign Legion. (Remind me not to repeat that one.)

It has spawned a mini-industry.

I have authored eleven books, including two bestsellers (mainly written on airplanes); we have launched *Man vs. Wild* games on Xbox, PlayStation, and Wii. I own a worldwide adventure clothing range and have fronted worldwide advertising campaigns for the likes of Rexona, Degree, Sure for Men, Nissan, and Dos Equis beer, among many others.

I was so proud to have been made a lieutenant-commander in the Royal Navy in 2005 (Dad would have approved!), and through the expeditions that I have led in Antarctica, the Himalayas, and the Arctic, we have now raised more than $2.5 million for children's charities around the world.

Those things really matter to me. Especially when you can actually see lives saved. There's not much tough-guy nonsense going on when I hear those young kids' stories.

It is called perspective.

In addition, and somewhat worryingly, I was voted the thirtieth most influential man in America. Hmm. And back home in the UK, I read one morning that I was considered the seventh coolest British man, as well as the most admired person by the middle classes, second only to the Queen. Double hmm.

All are very flattering, but they are not very accurate. Ask Shara how cool I am not!

They have, though, led to one great thing: becoming Chief Scout and figurehead to twenty-eight million Scouts around the globe.

And that has been a really fun journey.

CHAPTER 110

One of the greatest privileges in my life was to be appointed the youngest ever Chief Scout to the Scouting Association. (And the best bit, for me, was that the young people themselves had such a hand in the appointment.)

The Scouts stand for so much that I value in life—friendships, family, faith, and adventure.

I am learning every day that young people around the world don't lack ambition, they just lack opportunities, and the Scouts are a shining light that brings camaraderie, adventure, and a sense of belonging to those who might never normally get the chance to experience any of these magical things.

We tour around the UK, visiting hundreds of different troops and leaders, and I always try and set up meetings with local Scout groups after we finish filming, in whatever country we find ourselves in.

One movement. Many nations. One set of values. It is so infectious because it works so darned well. Just meet some of the kids and you'll see.

I love the days I spend with them.

Each summer, Shara and I host an island survival camp for the most improved young Scouts; I get to host special awards ceremonies for those who have reached the highest rank and achievement in Scouting; and we celebrate both the newest of Scouts and the oldest of leaders.

Their stories are always incredible.

Members of the Royal family invariably attend these ceremonies. Like me, moved by Scout tales of courage and hope. Often against impossible odds.

It is about everyday people, serving as leaders in their communities, giving kids a confidence, sense of purpose, life values, and outdoor skills that are hard to find anywhere else.

To be their Chief Scout is a source of great pride for me, and I hope I can do all those young lives justice.

And make no mistake, the more time I spend with Scouts the more I feel that it is them who inspire me, rather than the other way around.

⚜

So, with all of these elements, including the Scouts, life keeps running at a hell of a pace.

Sometimes too fast, and I find it hard to keep up. That part I don't like.

It is why I take such pride in having assembled such an amazing team to help me.

Based in LA and London, they are both crazy fun and frighteningly efficient. Where I bring the ideas, they bring the sense and clarity. We pray together, we laugh together, we try and do the things that really make a difference.

Money is some way down the list of priorities—but weirdly I am sure that is one of the reasons the whole thing works so well. Profit is such a boring goal in comparison to time and fun together—both as a family and as friends.

Dave Segel, Del, Todd, Michael, Jen, George, and the others. My goodness we go through a lot of juice, sushi, air miles, and conference calls. And it is, above all, a blast.

Nowadays, I tend to be more the front man for this extraordinary team of people, who are not only the best at what they do—whether as adventure cameramen, clothing designers, lawyers, or producers—they are also my buddies.

Much of the success of the business side of things, though, is simply the product of great people, great ideas, tidy execution, and a sprinkling of good luck. (Although I guess I have always fought hard to make the most of any luck that has come my way.)

There is no doubt, though, that I feel quite detached from that official persona of Bear Grylls. The man looking back at me in the mirror each morning, a bit bleary-eyed, with annoying scars and persistent aches, is a different person.

I consider the Bear Grylls from the TV to be just my work and a brand. The team call him simply BG.

The man in the mirror, though, is the husband to Shara, father to our boys, and just a regular guy with all the usual struggles, self-doubts, and flaws that tend to go with life.

And of those there are plenty. Trust me.

I'll let you in on two secrets: sometimes I get so anxious in front of large groups of people that I get a little nervous twitch. The twitch makes me feel embarrassed and ashamed inside. It becomes all I can think about. It makes me hate the fact that people are looking at me.

It is called fear. And I am scared.

Just a regular guy.

Then there are heights. Sometimes when I am climbing or hanging from a helicopter, I get struck by this all-consuming fear. But no one ever sees. I hold it inside. One minute I am fine, the next I am shaking like a leaf.

For no reason.
I know I am safe.
But am I?
It is called fear. And I am scared.
Just a regular guy.

Relieved?
 I am.

EPILOGUE

I am going to wrap up this book somewhere around this point, as in many ways it was these pivotal, early experiences—from childhood to the SAS, from Shara to Everest—that shaped so much of my character.

These are also the elements that helped to open the doors to many of the adventures that I have been lucky enough to have been a part of since.

These include tales such as leading one of the first teams ever to cross the frozen North Atlantic Arctic Ocean in a small open boat. This was in aid of the Prince's Trust, a charity that helps young, disadvantaged people have the chance to follow their own dreams.

The mission nearly turned ugly when we were caught five hundred miles offshore, in an arctic, force 9 gale—with crashing waves, and driving wind and hail. All our electronics and tracker systems went down, and the navy had to notify Shara that we had vanished off the radar, potentially lost in the eye of this ferocious storm.

In the nick of time, with Search and Rescue on the verge of launching, we emerged off the coast of Iceland, scared, near hypothermic, but alive. Just. And running, literally, on vapor fuel.

The whole expedition of some three thousand miles was an awfully long time to be utterly cold, wet, and afraid.

Then there was the crazy TV idea of signing up to go to North Africa to endure the simulated basic training that the French Foreign Legion was notorious for. Gritty, exhausting, and as hot as hell in the Western Saharan summer.

Twelve of us recruits got whittled down to four at the hands of some of the most brutal and draining military training techniques imaginable. Marching, crawling, fighting from dawn to dusk; shifting hillsides of rocks, being buried alive, and running everywhere twenty-four/seven. Blister-ridden and sleep-deprived. We ate camel skin stew and stale bread, and day after day, week after week, we dragged our sorry carcasses through the desert until we dropped under the weight of our packs, which were full of sand.

I have been so lucky to lead amazing teams to incredible places: the remote Venezuelan jungles of the "Lost World" in search of Jimmy Angel's lost gold; or the remote white desert that is Antarctica to climb unclimbed peaks. (I managed to break my shoulder in a fall on that trip, but you can't win them all!)

Then we returned to the Himalayas, where my buddy Gilo and I flew powered paragliders to above the height of Everest. Once again, we were raising funds for the charity Global Angels, an extraordinary charity that champions the most needy kids around the world. But the flight itself was a mission that so nearly had fatal consequences.

All the aviation and cold-weather experts predicted almost certain disaster; from frozen parachutes to uncontrollable hurricane-force winds, from impossible takeoffs to bone-breaking landings—and that was before they even contemplated whether a small one-man machine could even be designed to be powerful enough to fly that high.

And if we could, it certainly then would not be possible to lift it on to our backs. But we pulled it off: Gilo designed and built the most powerful, supercharged, fuel-injected, one-man powered paraglider engine in history, and by the grace of God we somehow got airborne with these monsters on our backs.

Some blessed weather and some ball-twitching flying, and we proved the skeptics wrong—even, at the end, landing effortlessly at the foot of the Everest range, nimbly on two feet, like twinkle-toes. Mission complete.

Then, recently, I got to lead the first expedition to travel through the Arctic's infamous Northwest Passage in a rigid inflatable boat—a mission that showed me, without doubt, some of the most remote landscapes I have ever witnessed, as well as some truly monstrous waves through the Beaufort Sea and beyond. It's a wild, inaccessible place with little chance of rescue if things turn nasty.

Yet, by chance, on one of the thousands of tiny, unexplored islands, surrounded by fragmenting pack ice, we discovered European-style makeshift graves, a human skull and myriad bones. The finds pointed toward the potential discovery of what happened to the fated members of Captain Franklin's Victorian expedition, who died in the ice after enduring the worst sort of frozen, starving, lingering death imaginable—all in pursuit of a route through the Northwest Passage.

Adventures such as these, and many more beyond.

Among these have been an unhealthy number of near-death moments, many of which I look back on now and wince. But I guess our training in life never really ends—and experience is always the best tutor of all.

Then there are the more bizarre: like jet-skiing around Britain in aid of the UK lifeboats. Day after day, hour after hour, pounding the seas like little ants battling around the wild coast of Scotland and Irish Sea. (I developed a weird bulging muscle in my forearm that popped out and has stayed with me ever since after that one!)

Or hosting the highest open-air dinner party, suspended under a high-altitude hot-air balloon, in support of the Duke of Edinburgh's kids awards scheme.

That mission also became a little hairy, rappelling down to this tiny metal table suspended fifty feet underneath the basket in minus forty degrees, some twenty-five thousand feet over the UK.

Dressed in full naval mess kit, as required by the Guinness Book of World Records—along with having to eat three courses and toast the Queen, and breathing from small supplementary oxygen canisters—we almost tipped the table over in the early dawn, stratosphere dark. Everything froze, of course, but finally we achieved the mission and skydived off to earth—followed by plates of potatoes and duck à l'orange falling at terminal velocity.

Or the time Charlie Mackesy and I rowed the Thames naked in a bathtub to raise funds for a friend's new prosthetic legs. The list goes on and on, and I am proud to say, it continues. But I will tell all those stories properly some other place, some other time.

They vary from the tough to the ridiculous, the dangerous to the embarrassing. But in this book I wanted to show my roots: the early, bigger missions that shaped me, and the even earlier, smaller moments that steered me.

Along the way, I have since had the struggle of coming to terms with recognition and the press; the tightrope of balancing the inherent risks of my work with having a beautiful young family.

Both are still unresolved.

There have been so many mistakes, failures, and losses. Too many to mention.

But I do possess an acute awareness that, through it all, someone has been blessing me greatly.

Make no mistake—luck has played a huge part in all that has

happened, and there is not a day that goes by without me being aware of that.

The by-product of being aware of being blessed is learning—against so many of the values of our society—to try to walk modestly, give generously, and help those who need a little leg up.

Simple lessons, but they have shaped the way that Shara and I try to live our lives together.

And, I am the first to admit, we often get it wrong.

Life continues to be an adventure, and in many ways more so than ever.

I am still away from home more than I would like. (Although much less than I think people often believe.) And I have learned that when I am at home, I am at home—not away doing press or meetings. Both of which are so boring!

Instead, I have had to learn to prioritize clearly in my life: to be safe, get home fast, and keep it fun—the rest is detail.

I still do have more risk in my life than feels comfortable—and you can't depend on luck too often. Be grateful for the lucky escapes but don't bank on them.

But there is no getting away from the fact that risk is with me every day when I am away filming or on expeditions.

I mean, in the last few months alone, I've been pinned in a big set of white-water rapids, been bitten by an angry snake in a jungle, had a close escape with a big mountain rockfall, narrowly avoided being eaten by a huge croc in the Australian swamps, and had to cut away from my main parachute and come down on my reserve, some five thousand feet above the Arctic plateau.

When did all this craziness become my world?

It's as if—almost accidentally—this madness has become my life. And don't get me wrong—I love it all.

The game, though, now, is to hang on to that life.

Every day is the most wonderful of blessings, and a gift that I never, ever take for granted.

Oh, and as for the scars, broken bones, aching limbs, and sore back?

I consider them just gentle reminders that life is precious—and that maybe, just maybe, I am more fragile than I dare to admit.

INDEX

INDEX

INDEX